COOKING
with MONA

This book is dedicated to good cooks everywhere, male and female, and especially to all those who contributed to this group of my favorite recipes:

To the many viewers in British Columbia, Alberta and Washington who shared with me their treasured recipes; to the B.C. Marketing Branch of the B.C. Ministry of Agriculture; to Joan Smith and the Bea Wright Kitchen of Woodward's Stores; to Jean Cannem, the gracious television hostess; to the Canadian Salmon Association of B.C.; to my daughter Maureen, who tested, assembled and proofread a large percentage of the recipes; and lastly, to my French Mother-in-law, Mère, who taught me to consider cooking an art; and to a very special lady named Mary.

Mona Brun

CONTENTS

Mona says . . .

Appetizers are intended to whet not satisfy the appetite. Plan appetizers to suit the type of meal planned — casual appetizers for casual dinners or elegant appetizers for a formal dinner. All appetizers whether delicate or hearty should be tart so that they hone rather than kill the appetite. Do not use ingredients in appetizers that will be served at dinner.

For Cocktail Hour Appetizers
Usually more appetizers will be eaten at these parties as they tend to take the place of a light supper.

Plan to serve not only more appetizers but also more substantial appetizers.

Always serve hot appetizers piping hot and cold appetizers icy cold. It is preferable to have fewer, very delicious appetizers, being careful not to duplicate flavours. Whenever possible use edible garnishes. Use plenty of attractively cut vegetables to set hors d'oeuvres off. Provide small plates with forks if food cannot easily be eaten with the fingers. It is easier to replenish several smaller dishes than one large platter.

TRY ONE OF THESE IDEAS:
Vegetable Tray

Pick a selection of vegetables such as — cauliflower flowerets, green pepper strips, onion rings, carrot sticks, whole raw mushrooms, tomato wedges, celery sticks, green onion sticks or cucumber chunks. Arrange on platter around bowl containing your favourite dip.

Prickly Cabbage
Select a good-sized head of cabbage and stud with toothpicks. Place cabbage on platter on bed of parsley. A few suggestions of what to place on the toothpicks are the following: cubed cheeses (several varieties); cubed meats such as salami, summer sausage, beer sausage or garlic sausage; whole cherry tomatoes; black olives or pimiento stuffed olives; chunks of dill pickle; tinned water chestnuts. Do not use food that would dry out very quickly or that have juices that would drip. This also makes an attractive centre-piece for a large platter of appetizers.

Cold Shish Kabob Sticks
Pick a selection from the following (or use your own ideas) and skewer on small toothpicks. These should be served well chilled.
— pieces of ham or bacon with gherkins
— squares of cheese with green onions
— cubes of turkey with radish slices and green pepper squares
— sour onions with cocktail sausages and gherkins
— dill pickle chunks with corned beef cubes
— cubes of tongue or ham with thin carrot slices
— cucumber slices with shrimp and cherry tomato halves
— drained, tinned smoked oysters with water chestnuts and green onion pieces.
— pieces of kippered salmon or herring and onions.
The list is endless and the results are most attractive.

APPETIZERS
HORS D'OEUVRES
SNACKS
DIPS

Barbecups

Brown ¾ lb. ground beef and drain. Add ½ c. barbecue sauce, 1 tbsp. minced (instant) onion, 2 tbsp. brown sugar. Add salt and pepper to taste. Take 1 pkg. of refrigerated tenderflake biscuits (Pillsbury). Press each biscuit into an ungreased muffin tin making sure the dough goes up to the edge of cup. Spoon meat mixture into cups and sprinkle with ¾ c. shredded sharp cheese. Bake in a 375 F. oven 10 to 12 minutes, or until done. Check often.

Cheese Onion Broil

2 tbsp. butter
1/4 tsp. salt
dash pepper
2 medium onions,
 thinly sliced
6 slices white bread,
 toasted and buttered

6 tbsp. chili sauce
6 thick slices Swiss cheese
3 slices bacon, cooked,
 drained and crumbled
6 thinly sliced
 green pepper rings

Melt butter; add salt and pepper. Saute onions until tender but not browned. Spread each slice of hot buttered toast with 1 tbsp. chili sauce. Top with onions and slice of cheese. Broil until cheese melts. Garnish with crumbled bacon and green pepper rings. *Makes 6 sandwiches* - A great lunch dish or late night snack.

Quick Quiche Lorraine

1 - 9-inch unbaked pastry shell; 8 slices diced bacon; 1/2 lb. Swiss cheese, shredded; 1 tbsp. flour; 1/2 tsp. salt; dash nutmeg; 3 eggs, beaten; 1-1/3 cups milk.

Bake pastry shell at 450 degrees F. for 7 minutes or until lightly browned. Remove from oven and reduce heat to 325 degrees. Fry bacon until crisp. Drain and crumble. Reserve 2 tbsp. for trim. Place remaining bacon in pie shell; add cheese. Combine remaining ingredients (flour, salt, nutmeg, beaten eggs, and milk); pour in pie shell over cheese and bacon. Sprinkle remaining 2 tbsp. bacon on top in circle. Bake at 325 degrees for 35 - 40 minutes; or until almost set in centre. Cool 15 - 30 minutes before serving. *Serves 6.*

Crab Asparagus Roll-Ups

* Excellent for a special dish for bridge parties, luncheons, showers, etc.

6 to 8 ozs. crabmeat, fresh or canned; 1 tbsp. lemon juice; 1/2 cup diced celery; 2 green onions finely chopped; 1/4 tsp. salt; 1/8 tsp. pepper; 1/8 tsp. tarragon; 1/4 tsp. Worcestershire sauce; 1/2 cup sharp cheddar cheese, grated; 2 tbsp. mayonnaise; 24 stalks asparagus (frozen, canned or fresh); 1½ packages refrigerated crescent dinner rolls.

Break up crabmeat. Drain if canned. Combine crab, lemon juice, celery, green onions, salt, pepper, tarragon, Worcestershire sauce, cheese and mayonnaise. If frozen or fresh asparagus is used, cook until just tender. Drain well if canned asparagus is used. Place a spoonful of crab mixture and 2 stalks of asparagus on each individual triangle of dough. Roll from shortest side of triangle into crescent shape and place with point down on ungreased cookie sheet. Bake 375 degrees F. 10 - 12 minutes or until golden brown.

Bacon Cheese Rollups

3/4 cup processed cheese spread; 1 tablespoon mayonnaise; 2 tablespoons Imperial Cheese; 8 to 10 rashes of bacon (cut in half); 1 unsliced loaf of bread.

Mix cheeses and mayonnaise together. Remove crusts from loaf of bread. Cut bread into lengthwise slices, 1/3 inch thick. Spread with cheese and roll up each slice jelly roll fashion. Cut each roll into three pieces and wrap each with a piece of bacon secured with a toothpick. Toast under broiler turning frequently.

Appetizer Meatballs

2 lb. lean ground pork, 1 egg, well beaten, 1/4 cup tomato paste, 2 cups dry bread crumbs, 1 tsp. salt, 1/2 tsp. pepper, 1/2 tsp. oregano, 1 tsp. basil, 1 recipe B.C. Barbecue Sauce (below).

Combine pork, egg, tomato paste, bread crumbs and seasonings. Shape into bite-size balls. Brown in hot skillet. Pour off drippings and add barbecue sauce to skillet. Simmer until thickened, about 1 hour. Makes 50 appetizers.

B.C. Barbecue Sauce

1 tbsp. salad oil, 3/4 cup finely minced onion, 1 beef bouillon cube, 1 cup boiling water, 2/3 cup catsup, 2/3 cup vinegar, 1/2 cup brown sugar, 2 tbsp. cornstarch, 2 tsp. dry mustard, 1/2 tsp. garlic salt.

In skillet, heat oil and saute onion. Dissolve bouillon cube in boiling water; stir into skillet. Add remaining ingredients. Cover and simmer 20 minutes. Yields 2 1/2 cups.

Recipe from B.C. Swine Breeders Association.

Salmon Pancake Appetizers

Curried Salmon - Mushroom Filling

1 tin (7-3/4 oz.) salmon	2 tbsp. butter
4 tsp. butter	1/2 lb. fresh
4 tsp. flour	mushrooms, chopped
1/4 tsp. curry powder	1 large onion,
or to taste	chopped
1/4 tsp. salt	salt and pepper to taste
1/2 cup milk	

Drain and mash salmon (reserving juice for later use in fish stock, soups, etc). Melt the 4 tsp. butter; add flour, curry powder and salt. Blend. Add milk gradually. Cook and stir until sauce becomes bubbly. Remove from heat; set aside. In skillet, melt the 2 tbsp. butter. Add mushrooms and onion; cook until onions are tender and the mushroom juices evaporated. Add sauce and salmon. Cook 2 to 3 minutes longer. Season to taste with salt and pepper.

Pancake Wrappers

1 cup packaged	1/2 cup milk (extra)
pancake mix	2 tbsp. butter

Prepare pancakes according to package directions for 1 cup mix, using 1/2 cup extra milk. Cook over medium high heat in lightly oiled skillet, on both sides, using 1 tbsp. of batter for each tiny pancake. Place approximately 1 tsp. of salmon filling in middle of each cooked pancake; roll up and place seam side down in a buttered casserole dish. Melt 2 tbsp. butter and drizzle over top of pancake roll. Bake uncovered at 350 degrees F. for 15 minutes. Makes approximately 40 tiny pancakes.

Note: Pancakes may be prepared and filled ahead and refrigerated. Increase baking time to 25 minutes.

Salmon Cheese Pate

1 tin (7-3/4 oz.) salmon,	1-1/2 tbsp. finely
well drained	chopped celery
1 package (8 oz.)	1 tbsp. lemon juice
cream cheese, softened	1 tsp. Worcestershire sauce
1/4 cup blue cheese,	1/2 small clove garlic,
crumbled	crushed (optional)
2 tbsp. grated Parmesan cheese	dash freshly ground
2 tbsp. grated onion	black pepper
1 tbsp. chopped parsley	parsley sprigs

Drain salmon thoroughly. Set aside. Blend cream cheese, blue cheese and Parmesan cheese together until smooth. Stir in drained salmon, onion, parsley, celery, lemon juice and Worcestershire sauce. Add garlic, if desired and sprinkle with freshly ground black pepper. Stir until all ingredients are well combined. Mold in small bowl lined with plastic wrap. Chill several hours. Unmold. To serve, garnish with parsley sprigs. Serve with melba toast, crackers, toast rounds or thin slices of rye bread.

Note: Salmon Cheese Pate is also delicious to stuff celery sticks, or hollowed cherry tomatoes. Try it to stuff mushrooms and broil until bubbly.

Salted Pumpkin Seeds

Separate seeds from the fibres. Spread 2 cups seeds in flat shallow pan. For each 2 cups, measure 1 1/2 tbsp. melted butter or salad oil and 1 1/4 tsp. salt. Bake in slow oven 250 degrees F until seeds are dried out and crispy brown. stir occasionally so that seeds toast evenly.

Note: Squash seeds may be prepared this way also.

Olive Cheese Balls

1 cup finely grated
   cheddar cheese
1/4 cup softened butter
   or margarine

1/2 cup flour
pinch salt
1/2 tsp. paprika
24 pimiento stuffed green olives

Blend cheese with butter. Add flour, salt and paprika. Mix well. Mold about 1 teaspoon of dough around each olive, covering it completely. Bake in 400 degree F. oven for approximately 10 minutes or until golden brown. Either serve immediately or allow to cool. To serve, reheat Olive Cheese Balls in 300 degree F. oven for 7 to 8 minutes.

Zippy Tomato-Cucumber Juice

2 cups tomato juice, 1 cucumber, peeled, seeded and grated, 1 tbsp. vinegar, 2 tbsp. salad oil, 1/2 tsp. salt, dash paprika, 1/4 tsp. basil, dash Worcestershire sauce, dash freshly ground black pepper, 1/2 cup cracked ice, chopped parsley and lemon slices for garnish, if desired.

In shaker, combine tomato juice, cucumber, vinegar, salad oil, salt, paprika, basil and Worcestershire sauce. Sprinkle with freshly ground black pepper. Shake well. Allow to chill. Just before serving add cracked ice. Pour into glasses and garnish with chopped parsley and lemon slices if desired. *Makes 4 servings.*

Note: This recipe can easily be doubled.

Rosy Pickled Eggs

1 cup juice from
   canned pickled beets
1 cup vinegar
4 cups water
1 clove garlic
1 medium bay leaf
2 tsp. mixed pickling
   spice

1/2 tsp. salt
12 hard-cooked eggs
   [shelled]
1 small onion, sliced
   and separated
   into rings

Combine beet juice, vinegar, water, garlic, bay leaf, pickling spices and salt in a large bowl or jar. Mix well. Add eggs and onion rings. Cover and refrigerate for several days.

Danish Camembert Layer

A great hors d'oeuvre!

1 round Danish
   Camembert cheese
4 oz. cream cheese

1 tbsp. dry sherry
2 tbsp. sliced almonds
2 tbsp. pitted sliced grapes

With a sharp knife, cut camembert in half lengthwise, forming 2 round layers. In small bowl, blend cream cheese with sherry to soften; add almonds and grapes. Reserve 1 tbsp. cream cheese mixture for garnish and spread remainder on bottom layer of cheese. Carefully place top layer on filling. Garnish with reserved cream cheese mixture in centre on top. Add a few more almond and grape slices, if desired, as garnish.

Samsoe Cheese Fingers

1 cup sifted all-purpose flour, 1/2 teaspoon salt, pinch cayenne pepper, 1/2 teaspoon dry mustard, 1/2 teaspoon ground ginger, 1/2 teaspoon sugar, 2 ounces Danish Samsoe Cheese, grated, 5 tablespoons sesame seeds, 1 egg yolk, lightly beaten, 6 tablespoons butter, melted, 1 tablespoon water.

Place sesame seeds in a shallow baking pan and toast in a 350 degree F. oven for 20 to 22 minutes, stirring 2 or 3 times to obtain uniform toasting. Sift dry ingredients together. Stir in the cheese and sesame seeds. Combine egg yolk, melted butter and water. Add to cheese mixture and stir to combine. Shape into a ball, wrap in wax paper and chill. Roll dough out on a lightly floured surface to 1/8 inch thickness. Cut in 1 inch x 2 inch strips and place on an ungreased baking sheet. Bake in a 350 degree F. oven for 15 minutes or until done. These tasty little finger biscuits make an excellent appetiser cold or still warm.

Smoked Oyster Spread

1 [3 2/3 oz.] tin
   smoked oysters, drained
   and finely chopped
1 tsp. lemon juice
1 green onion, finely
   chopped
1 tbsp. mayonnaise
2 tsp. chili sauce

1 tbsp. chopped parsley
1/4 tsp. dry mustard
   dash pepper
   dash Worchestershire
   sauce
   chopped parsley [or
   halved stuffed olives]
   optional

Prepare oysters; sprinkle with lemon juice. In small bowl, combine thoroughly oysters, lemon juice, green onion, mayonnaise, chili sauce, parsley, dry mustard, pepper and Worcestershire sauce. Cover; chill for several hours. Spread over crackers. Garnish with parsley or olive halves, if desired.

Cheese Porcupine

A delicious eye catching addition to any party.

4 oz. blue cheese
1 package [8 oz.] cream
   cheese
1 lb. sharp cheddar
   cheese, shredded
1 tbsp. minced onion
1 tsp. Worchestershire
   sauce

1/2 cup finely chopped
   walnuts
1 tbsp. finely chopped
   parsley
   pepper to taste
   paprika
   pimiento stuffed olives

Have cheeses softened at room temperature. Cream well. Add onion, Worcestershire sauce, walnuts, parsley and pepper. Combine thoroughly. On waxed paper form mixture into oval shape. Refrigerate several hours. Roll "porcupine" in paprika. Allow to stand at room temperature 1/2 hour before serving. To garnish use olives studded with toothpicks for "quills." Serve with variety of crisp crackers. Makes 1 "porcupine."

Cheese Fondue

3 cups medium
  cheddar cheese, shredded
1 tbsp. all-purpose flour
1 clove garlic, halved
  French bread or hard rolls,
  torn in bite-sized pieces,
  each with 1 crust

1 1/4 cups dry white wine
  dash freshly ground
  pepper
  dash nutmeg
3 tbsp. dry sherry

Toss cheese with flour to coat. Rub inside of fondue pot with cut surface of garlic. Pour in white wine; warm until small air bubbles start to rise. DO NOT BOIL OR COVER. Stirring constantly, add a handful of flour-coated cheese at a time. When melted, toss in another handful. When cheese is blended and bubbling, GENTLY stir in pepper and nutmeg, also sherry. Sprear bread cube on long-handled fondue fork; dip into cheese.

Note: If fondue becomes too thick to handle, add a little WARMED white wine.
Serve with steaming mugs of hot apple juice or coffee.

Curry Dip

1 1/2 cups salad dressing
2 teaspoons curry
1 tablespoon green onion

1/2 tsp. hot dry mustard
1/2 tsp. salt
  pepper
  dash Tabasco

Combine all ingredients. Mix thoroughly. Cover and place in refrigerator to marinate for one hour or more.

Beer-Cheddar Fondue

1 lb. shredded sharp cheddar cheese (4 cups)
1/2 cup beer
1 garlic clove, crushed
2 tsp. Worcestershire sauce
1/2 tsp. dry mustard
dash tabasco
1 tbsp. cornstarch
2 tbsp. water
French bread, cubed

Have cheese at room temperature. With electric mixer, beat cheese at low speed until blended; gradually add beer, mixing at medium speed until mixture is light and fluffy. Add garlic, Worcestershire sauce, dry mustard and tabasco. Beat thoroughly to distribute seasonings. Place mixture in fondue pot. Place pot on range and melt. Blend together cornstarch and water; add to fondue. Cook, stirring constantly until mixture is thickened and bubbly. Transfer fondue pot from stove to fondue burner. To eat, spear a bread cube with fondue fork and dip.

Cheddar Puffs

1/2 cup butter
1 cup grated sharp
  cheddar cheese
1 1/4 cups sifted
  all-purpose flour
1/4 tsp. salt

Cream butter with cheese, in medium-sized bowl, until smooth. Blend in flour and salt. Knead lightly with hands to form soft dough. Roll 1 teaspoon at a time into small balls. Place on greased cookie sheet. Bake 400 degrees F. — 12 minutes or until golden. Serve hot. Makes approx. 3 dozen.

Crispy French Fried Onion Rings

4 to 5 large onions
  ice water
1 1/2 to 1 3/4 cups flour
1 tsp. salt
3/4 tsp. soda

2 eggs
1 1/2 to 2 cups buttermilk
  oil for deep frying,
  heated to 375 degrees F.

Slice onions 1/4 inch thick. Soak in ice water for 1 hour. (**Note:** Soaking in ice water is essential for crisp results.) Sift together flour, salt, and soda. Combine with eggs and buttermilk to make batter. Dry onions thoroughly; dip in batter. Deep fry several at a time in preheated oil until crisp and brown. Drain on absorbent paper. Keep onions hot by placing in 275 degrees F oven while cooking remaining onions. Serve hot and crisp. Makes 4 servings.

Note: Batter is excellent for cheese or poultry fondues.

Broiled Oysters on the Half Shell

Shuck and drain 36 oysters; place on deep half of shells. Sprinkle with ½ Tsp. salt, 1/8 Tsp. pepper and buttered bread crumbs (½ c. bread crumbs and 2 Tbsp. melted butter). *PLACE on broiler pan about 3 inches from heat and broil 5 minutes or until brown.*

Crepes with Creamed Seafood

Batter
1/2 cup cold water; 3 eggs; 1/2 tsp salt; 1½ cups sifted flour; 3 tbsp melted butter or margarine.

Filling
2 cups hot medium cream sauce; 2 tbsp dry sherry or sauterne; 1/2 cup grated Swiss cheese; 2 cup fresh or canned shellfish meat; 3 tbsp chopped scallions; salt and pepper.

Combine all batter ingredients in blender container; whirl for about 1 minute. Refrigerate for at least 1 hour. Coat a 7-8-inch skillet with oil. Heat over moderately high heat just until jt begins to smoke. Pour 3 tbsp of batter into pan.

Quickly tilt pan to cover bottom with a thin film. Bake crepe about 1 minute, until brown; turn over and bake other side about 1/2 minute. Remove to plate. Continue same method for remaining crepes; stack crepes with sheet of wax paper between. *Makes about 12 crepes.*

Filling: Combine dry sherry and cheese with cream sauce. Blend half of the sauce with seafood and scallions; season to taste. Spoon a large spoonful over top of each crepe. Roll up and place in baking dish. Pour remaining sauce over top. Sprinkle with additional cheese. Bake in 425°F oven about 15 minutes, until hot and browned. *Makes 6 servings.*

For more Crepes see Quick Breads page 106

Guacamole

2 medium-size ripe avocados	1 cup finely chopped onion
1 tbsp. lemon juice	1-1/2 tsp. seasoned salt
2 medium tomatoes, peeled and finely chopped	1/2 tsp. seasoned pepper

Peel avocados; mash well with a fork or place in blender with lemon juice. Add remaining ingredients. Combine thoroughly. Serve with warm broken Taco shells or corn chips. *Makes about 3 cups.*

If a creamier consistency is desired, add mayonnaise.

Curry of Shrimp

1/3 c. butter
½ c. chopped green pepper
2 c. sour cream
2 Tsp. curry powder
½ Tsp. ginger
Dash pepper
½ c. onions, chopped
2 cloves garlic minced
2 Tsp. lemon juice
¾ Tsp. salt
Dash chili powder
3 c. cleaned cooked or canned shrimp

Melt butter; add onions, green pepper, garlic. Cook till tender but not brown. Stir in sour cream, lemon juice, and seasonings; add shrimp. Cook over LOW heat, stirring constantly, just until hot through. (Sauce is traditionally thin). Serve over hot rice.

Antipasto Salad

A tasty, colourful dish for holiday entertaining.

1 head romaine lettuce,	1 green pepper, seeded, sliced into rings and halved,
1 tin (14 oz.) garbanzo beans,	
Zippy Parmesan Dressing **see page 23**	1 red pepper, seeded, sliced in rings and halved,
1 small cantalope,	½ cup fresh sliced mushrooms,
¼ cup pitted ripe olives, halved,	Parmesan cheese, if desired.

Several hours before serving, wash romaine; dry well; tear into bite-size pieces. Store in plastic bag. Drain garbanzo beans; place in small bowl and marinate with ⅓ cup Zippy Parmesan Dressing. Cover and refrigerate for at least 1 hour. Just before serving, line a long, shallow platter that has curved sides, with romaine lettuce. Halve, seed and peel cantalope; cut into thin slices; halve slices. Arrange beans, cantalope, olives, green pepper, red pepper and mushrooms attractively over romaine. Sprinkle with Parmesan cheese, if desired. Serve remaining dressing separately. *Makes 12 servings.*

Note: For a smaller group, this recipe can easily be halved.

Scandinavian Stuffed Eggs

A great smorgasbord dish.

6 hard-cooked eggs	2 tsp. chopped parsley
4 oz. smoked salmon, finely chopped (1/2 cup)	1/4 tsp. salt or to taste
	dash pepper
1/4 cup mayonnaise	drained, pitted black olives
2 tsp. prepared mustard	1 pimiento, cut in thin strips

Halve eggs lengthwise with a sharp knife. Carefully remove yolks. Place yolks in small bowl. Set egg whites aside. Mash yolks. Add salmon, mayonnaise, mustard, parsley, salt and pepper. Combine well. Fill whites with yolk mixture, mounding it high, (or use a decorator bag). Garnish with pieces of olive and pimiento strips. Refrigerate, covered, for at least 2 hours before serving. *Makes 12 stuffed eggs.*

Mona says . . .

- *Purchase mushrooms that are firm and feel dry. Small brown spots or opened caps merely indicate the mushrooms are more mature — their flavour is still delicate and delicious.*

- *Store fresh mushrooms in refrigerator on rack or shallow tray. Place a dampened paper towel over mushrooms — redampen towel each day.*

- *Store cooked mushroom in dish, covered, in refrigerator (add a dash of lemon juice when cooking to help retain colour). Use as soon as possible.*

- *To prepare mushrooms — wash gently; do not soak; dry thoroughly (otherwise mushrooms to be sauteed in butter or oil will steam rather than brown nicely). This also helps to prevent shrivelling and loss of juices.*

- *Sprinkle mushrooms lightly with lemon juice to prevent darkening.*

- *Unless otherwise specified in recipe, cook mushrooms only until tender-crisp, for best results.*

- *Seasonings: garlic, lemon, onion, nutmeg, tarragon, thyme, rosemary, or dill seed.*

- *Use raw in salads or as dippers. Use cooked with meat, poultry, seafood, and vegetable. Casseroles or omelet dishes.*

Tomato - Mushroom Bake

2 large tomatoes, quartered, Italian salad dressing, salt and pepper to taste, chopped parsley, dash basil, 12 medium size mushrooms, 1 tbsp. melted butter, salt and pepper to taste, dash MSG, 1 tbsp. grated Parmesan cheese.

On foil pie plate, place tomato quarters cut side up. Brush cut surfaces with Italian dressing. Season with salt and pepper. Sprinkle parsley and basil on top. Dip whole mushrooms in melted butter; place on foil plate beside tomatoes. Season with salt and pepper, MSG. Sprinkle mushrooms with Parmesan cheese. Place uncovered on grill and cook approximately 10 minutes or until piping hot. Do not turn. *Makes 4 servings.*

Celery - Mushroom Bake

4 cups 1-inch slices celery	*1 tin (10 oz.) condensed*
boiling, salted water	*cream-of-mushroom soup,*
1 cup sliced mushrooms	*undiluted*
2 tbsp. butter	*1 tbsp. butter*
1-1/2 cups shredded	*1/3 cup toasted*
process cheese	*slivered almonds*

In saucepan, cook celery in boiling salted water until tender. Drain well. In skillet, cook mushrooms in 2 tbsp. butter until tender but not browned. In casserole dish, alternate layers of celery, cheese, mushrooms and soup ending with soup. Dot with 1 tbsp. butter. Sprinkle almonds over top. Bake in 350 degree F. oven for 25 minutes or until piping hot. *Makes 4 servings.*

Mushrooms and Oysters

1 to 1½ lbs. mushrooms, 6 tbsp. fresh white bread-
crumbs, 2 tbsp. melted butter, 2 egg yolks, 3 tbsp.
cream, 1 tbsp. chopped parsley, 1 tbsp. snipped
chives, 1 clove garlic, crushed with ½ tsp. salt,
oysters (1 to 2 per shell, as desired)

Mornay Sauce

4 tbsp. butter, 3 tbsp. flour, 2 cups milk, ¾ cup grated
cheese.

Melt butter. Blend in flour. Gradually add milk. Cook, stirring all
the time until mixture thickens. Do not overcook. Fold in grated
cheese.

Topping

2 tbsp. grated cheese, 1 tbsp. browned crumbs, 2 tbsp.
melted butter.

Wash mushrooms, cutting the stalks even with the
caps and set aside 2 to 3 for each person. Chop the
stalks and peelings and remaining mushrooms. Add
crumbs and then butter, egg yolks and cream. Mix in
parsley, chives, garlic and seasoning. Fill the mushroom caps with herb mixture; arrange in buttered
shells with the oysters. Coat with Mornay Sauce;
sprinkle with cheese-crumb topping. Bake in 425 F.
oven for 12 to 15 minutes.

Blender Mushroom Butter

1/2 lb. mushrooms	1/4 tsp. salt [or to taste]
1 tbsp. finely chopped onion	dash black pepper
1/4 cup butter	3 tbsp. dry sherry [or brandy]
1/2 cup softened butter	

Wash mushrooms; dry thoroughly. Slice. Saute mushrooms and
onion, until just golden, in 1/4 cup butter (do not overcook). Remove from heat; allow to cool. Place mixture in blender; add 1/2
cup softened butter, salt, pepper, and sherry. Blend until smooth.
Place in dish; cover; refrigerate. Before using, allow to soften to
easy spreading consistency. Use in making canapes and fancy
sandwiches.

Blue Cheese Stuffed Mushrooms

12 to 15 large fresh mushrooms, stems retained
1/4 cup butter or margarine
1/4 cup chopped green onions
2 tbsp. crumbled blue cheese

4 tbsp. fine dry bread crumbs
dash MSG
salt and pepper to taste

Wash mushrooms; dry well. Remove stems and chop stems. Melt butter in skillet and gently saute chopped stems
and green onions till tender. Add cheese, 3 tbsp. bread crumbs MSG, salt and pepper. Combine well. Fill
mushroom crowns with mixture; sprinkle with remaining 1 tbsp. bread crumbs. Place on baking sheet and bake at
350 degrees F. for 12 minutes or until piping hot. Makes 4 to 6 servings.

Italian Style Stuffed Mushrooms

15 medium-size fresh mushrooms	3 tbsp. grated Parmesan cheese
3 tsp. olive oil or salad oil	1 tbsp. chili sauce
1 tbsp. finely chopped onion	2 tsp. butter, melted
1/4 cup finely chopped salami	2 tbsp. fine soft bread crumbs
	1/2 tsp. finely chopped parsley

Wash mushrooms; dry thoroughly. Remove stems; finely chop
enough stems to yield 1/3 cup. Brush mushroom caps lightly
with 2 tsp. of the oil. In small skillet, heat remaining 1 tsp. oil;
add chopped mushroom stems and onion. Cook gently until
golden but not browned. Stir in salami, Parmesan cheese and
chili sauce. Spoon stuffing mixture into mushroom caps. In small
bowl, combine melted butter, bread crumbs and parsley.
Sprinkle mixture over stuffed mushrooms. Arrange prepared
mushrooms in shallow baking pan. Bake in a 425 degree F. oven
for 6 to 8 minutes or until piping hot. Serve immediately. Makes
15 stuffed mushrooms.

Mushroom Logs

2 tbsp. butter	1/2 tsp. salt
1 cup fresh mushrooms, finely chopped	1/4 cup cream
1 whole green onion, minced	1/4 cup dry sherry
1/4 tsp. dried tarragon	16 slices thinly sliced bread, lightly buttered
1 tsp. cornstarch	

In saucepan, melt butter; add mushrooms, green onions and
tarragon. Cook over medium heat for 3 minutes, stirring frequently. Remove pan from heat; add cornstarch and salt; stir until
well mixed. Add cream and sherry; cook, stirring constantly until
thick and creamy. Remove crusts from bread slices; butter slices
lightly. Spread with the mushroom mixture. Roll bread slices, as
tightly as possible, in jelly roll fashion. Hold with a toothpick and
place logs side by side in a cake pan. Bake in a 400 degree F.
oven for 15 to 20 minutes or until golden brown. These freeze
very well uncooked. To serve, bake frozen as above (will take
longer than for fresh).

Petit Cream Puffs Danablue Filling

3/4 cup water
1/3 cup butter
3/4 cup sifted all-purpose flour

1/4 tsp. salt
3 large eggs

In saucepan, bring water and butter to boiling. Turn heat on low and immediately stir in flour and salt beating vigorously until mixture forms a ball and leaves side of pan. Remove from heat; beat in eggs, one at a time, beating hard after each addition. Drop mixture by small tsp. onto a greased cookie sheet. Bake in 400 degree F. oven for 30 minutes. Turn off heat, open door, and leave for about 3 to 4 minutes. Cool on wire rack. Split puffs almost all the way through and fill with Danablue filling. *Makes approximately 30 puffs.*

Danablue Filling

2 cup blue cheese
1/4 cup whipping cream

3 tbsp. cognac or brandy
1/2 cup whipping cream

In bowl, crumble blue cheese and mix with 1/4 cup whipping cream and cognac or brandy until light and creamy. Whip 1/2 cup whipping cream and gently fold into the blue cheese mixture.

Mushrooms Romanoff

1/2 lb. fresh mushrooms
2 tbsp. butter or margarine
1 cup sour cream
1 tsp. dill seed
1/4 tsp. salt or to taste

dash freshly ground pepper
dash nutmeg
paprika
hot toast points

Wash mushrooms, dry well. Slice larger mushrooms through cap and stem. In skillet, melt butter; add mushrooms and cover. Cook stirring occasionally, over medium heat for approximately 6 to 8 minutes or until lightly browned. Stir in sour cream, dill seed, salt, pepper and nutmeg. Reduce heat; cook and stir over low heat just until heated through. Do not boil. Sprinkle with papika. Serve over hot toast points. *Makes 3 to 4 servings.*

Turkey Mushroom Salad

2 cups cooked, cubed turkey
1 cup fresh sliced mushrooms
3/4 cup chopped celery
1/4 cup diced green pepper
1/4 cup thinly sliced radishes
2 tbsp. sliced pimiento stuffed green olives

1/3 cup mayonnaise [or salad dressing]
1 tbsp. lemon juice
2 tsp. very finely chopped onion
Romaine lettuce leaves
freshly cracked black pepper
chopped parsley
1 medium tomato, cut in thin wedges

In bowl, lightly combine turkey, mushrooms, celery, green pepper, radishes and sliced olives. In small bowl, combine well, mayonnaise, lemon juice and onion. Add to turkey mixture. Toss lightly to coat evenly. Cover. Chill thoroughly. To serve, line bottom and sides of salad bowl with lettuce leaves. Spoon turkey mixture on leaves. Sprinkle pepper and parsley over top. Garnish around sides of salad with tomato wedges. Serve with crusty rolls. Makes 4 to 6 servings.

Mushrooms a la Grecque

1½ lb. small fresh mushrooms; 1/3 cup olive oil; 2 tbsp. wine vinegar; 1 clove garlic, finely chopped; 1/2 tsp. salt; 1/2 tsp. pepper; 2 sprigs parsley; pinch of thyme or oregano.

Quickly wash mushrooms in cold water, or wipe with damp cloth. Trim off tips of stems. In a saucepan, blend together oil, vinegar, garlic, remaining seasonings and 1 cup water. Cook to boiling point. Reduce heat and cook gently for 5 minutes. Add mushrooms and continue cooking over low heat another 5 minutes. Chill mushrooms in the seasoned liquid. Drain just before serving. Serve as a relish with meat or as an hors d'oeuvre.

Fluffy Danish Blue Dip

2 cups Danish Blue Cheese, crumbled and firmly packed

3/4 cup whipping cream
3 tbsp. cream sherry

In mixing bowl, blend together blue cheese, 1/4 cup whipping cream and sherry. Beat until light and creamy. Whip remaining 1/2 cup whipping cream until soft peaks form; gently fold into blue cheese mixture. Chill at least 1 hour to let flavours blend. Delicious served with favourite fruits for dipping. Serve also with chips. *Yields approximately 3 cups sauce.*

Seasoned Avacado-Tomato Dip

2 cups sour cream
1 envelope dehydrated onion soup mix
1/2 tsp. ground cumin (optional)

1 avocado, peeled, pitted and finely chopped
1 tomato, peeled, finely chopped and drained

In bowl, combine all ingredients. Cover and chill thoroughly. Serve with corn chips, potato chips or raw vegetable dippers. *Yields approximately 3 cups.*

Note: To vary this dip, the chopped tomato can be omitted, if desired.

Whipped Cheese Dip

1/2 cup shredded sharp cheddar cheese
1/2 cup crumbled blue cheese
2 tbsp. grated Parmesan cheese

1/2 cup cottage cheese
1/4 cup sour cream
2 tsp. grated onion
1/2 to 1 tsp. Worcestershire sauce

Combine prepared cheddar cheese, blue cheese, Parmesan cheese and cottage cheese. Allow to come to room temperature. Beat with electric mixer until mixture is smooth and creamy. Add sour cream, grated onion and Worcestershire sauce. Beat until fluffy. Chill thoroughly. Serve with crackers, chips or raw fresh vegetables. *Makes about 1-1/3 cups dip.*

Mona says . . .

All ingredients should be fresh, clean, dry and well chilled ahead of time; chill salad plates and bowl as well.

Aim for variety in greens. Try combinations of different lettuce varieties such as Romaine, Boston, Bibb, Leaf or Endive in addition to Iceberg.

Tear lettuce — do not cut it.

Choose a good salad oil or olive oil to use in making of dressing.

Prepare salad ingredients in generous size portions, with attention to variety in colour, shape and texture.

A chef's flavour trick is to lightly sprinkle salt into a wooden salad bowl. Place a toothpick in a clove of garlic and rub the bowl thoroughly.

Toss ingredients gently — never stir.

Before storing salad greens, remove any wilted or discoloured leaves; shower with cold water but don't soak. Drain well; dry very carefully. Store in crisper in refrigerator.

Add cut-up tomatoes just before serving to prevent dressing from becoming diluted.

Use Butter Lettuce when making Danish style open-face sandwiches.

Chop, dice and mince are similar terms, yet there is a distinction. To chop is to cut food into pieces about the size of peas. Diced food is cut in small cubes of uniform size and shape. Minced means very finely chopped.

To peel cooked potatoes for a hot salad score raw potatoes around centre with point of knife. Cook covered in boiling, salted water until tender. Spear potato with fork tines in the score mark and peel.

SALADS and SALAD DRESSINGS

Jellied Salads

When adding ingredients (vegetables, fruits, meat, etc.) always chill dissolved gelatin until partially set (consistency of unbeaten egg white) to have food evenly distributed throughout.

If gelatin becomes too set during chilling, place bowl containing gelatin in pan of hot water (don't let any water in gelatin mixture) and stir until gelatin is liquid again; replace in refrigerator and chill again until partially set.

When preparing layered salads, chill first gelatin layer until it is almost firm (appears set but is sticky to the touch). Pour next layer over; chill until it is almost firm. Repeat layering as desired.

When wanting a pattern of fruit or vegetables on the bottom of the mold (the top when unmolded), spoon a thin layer of dissolved gelatin in bottom of mold. Arrange fruit or vegetable. Chill until almost firm. Then add the remaining dissolved gelatin.

When adding carbonated beverages to gelatin salads, cool dissolved gelatin to room temperature; then pour beverage slowly down side of bowl. Gently stir up and down. Chill immediately until firm.

To unmold gelatin salads, carefully loosen gelatin around edges of mold with spatula. Dip mold in warm water for a *few seconds*. Tilt mold slightly easing gelatin away from one side to let air in. Tilt and rotate mold so air can loosen gelatin all the way around. Place serving platter upside down over mold. Hold platter and mold together; invert and shake gently to release. Carefully lift off mold. If gelatin does not release, tilt mold again or quickly redip in warm water.

To prepare mold for easy removal of your gelatin salads, either run under cold water to chill completely (dry well) or rub with oil (very lightly) before filling with gelatin mixture.

Molded Salmon Salad

1 tbsp. gelatin
1/2 cup cold water
1/2 cup boiling water
2 cups fresh or tinned Sockeye Salmon
1/2 cup finely chopped celery
2 tbsp. sweet pickle, finely chopped

1/3 cup vinegar
1/2 cup mayonnaise
1/2 cup tomato ketchup

Soften gelatin in cold water; add boiling water and stir till gelatin is dissolved. Add the other ingredients; season to taste and mix well. Turn into individual molds or large mold that has been rinsed with cold water. Chill till firm. Unmold on bed of crisp lettuce and garnish with ripe olives, devilled eggs and tomato slices if desired. *Makes 4 to 6 servings.*

Mandarin Mold

2 (10-ounce) cans mandarin orange segments, 1/2 cup water, 1 tablespoon sugar, 1 tablespoon lemon juice, 1 tablespoon un-flavoured gelatin, 1/2 pint whipping cream, 2 tablespoons sugar.

Drain mandarin orange segments and reserve 1 cup syrup. Combine syrup, water, 1 tablespoon sugar, lemon juice and gelatin in a heavy saucepan. Cook over medium heat until mixture boils and gelatin is dissolved. Pour into a 4 cup mold and chill until partially set. Whip cream until soft peaks form, then add 2 tablespoons of sugar and beat until stiff. When gelatin mixture is partially set fold in mandarin segments and whipping cream. Chill until firm.

Golden Glow Salad

1 pkg. (3 oz.) lemon jelly powder	2 tsp. lemon juice
1 pkg. (3 oz.) orange jelly powder	1-1/2 cups grated carrots
4 cups hot liquid	1 tin (19 oz.) crushed pineapple
(water and pineapple juice)	(drain juice and use with
dash salt	water as directed above)

Dissolve jelly powders in hot liquid; add salt and lemon juice. Let chill until syrupy. Fold in carrots and pineapple. Place in a 12-cup mold that has been brushed lightly with salad oil. Chill until firm. To serve, unmold salad onto platter (on a bed of lettuce, if desired). Garnish with parsley. *Makes 12 servings.*

Cabbage-Carrot Mold

2 packages (3 oz. each)	1 cup shredded cabbage
lemon flavoured gelatin	1/2 cup shredded carrots
2 cups boiling water	1/4 cup diced green pepper
1-1/2 cups cold water	1/4 cup diced celery
1/4 tsp. salt	1/4 cup sweet pickle relish
1/4 cup lemon juice	

Dissolve gelatin in boiling water; stir in cold water, salt and lemon juice. Stir well. Chill until partially set. Fold in cabbage, carrots, green pepper, celery and relish. Pour mixture into 5-1/2 cup mold. Chill until firm. This recipe goes beautifully with ham. *Makes 8 to 10 servings.*

Perfection Jellied Salad with Marinated Carrots

2 envelopes	2 cups shredded
unflavoured gelatin	cabbage
1 tsp. salt	3 tbsp. finely chopped
1/2 cup sugar	pimiento
1 1/2 cups boiling water	1 cup finely chopped
1 1/2 cups cold water	celery
2 tbsp. lemon juice	1/2 cup chopped
1/2 cup vinegar	green pepper
pimiento stuffed	Bibb lettuce
olives, halved	marinated carrots
	[recipe below]

Combine gelatin, salt, and sugar. Add boiling water; stir to dissolve gelatin. Stir in cold water, lemon juice, and vinegar. Chill until mixture is partially set. Pour approx. 1/2 cup gelatin mixture into a 6 1/2 cup ring mold. Arrange olive halves in petal patterns in mold; chill until firm. Meanwhile, combine remaining partially set gelatin, cabbage, pimiento, celery, and green pepper. Carefully spoon over firm gelatin and olives in mold. Chill until set. To serve: Unmold over bed of Bibb lettuce. Fill centre of ring mold with marinated carrots; decorate around outside of salad with remainder of carrots.

Marinated Carrots

1 1/2 cups sliced
carrots, cut on bias
boiling, salted water
1/2 cup Italian-style
dressing
1 tbsp. chopped parsley

Cook carrots in boiling, salted water until tender. Drain well. Place in shallow dish. Cover with Italian dressing and chopped parsley. Cover; refrigerate. Allow to marinate several hours or overnight.

Winter Molded Garden Loaf

2 pkts. (3 oz. each) lemon flavoured gelatin jelly powder	3/4 cup cooked cauliflower flowerettes
3-1/2 cups hot water	1/2 cup cooked sliced carrots
2 tbsp. vinegar	1/4 cup chopped green pepper
1 tbsp. lemon juice	1/4 cup chopped celery
1/2 tsp. salt	1/4 cup chopped green onions
12 **whole** green beans OR asparagus spears,	1/4 cup thinly sliced radishes
very well drained (or use whole frozen beans	lettuce leaves
or asparagus spears, cooked and well drained)	tomato wedges and parsley sprigs
4 long thin strips pimiento	for garnish, if desired

In bowl, place gelatin. Add hot water and stir to dissolve; add vinegar, lemon juice and salt. Pour about 1/2-inch of gelatin mixture into 8-1/2 x 4-1/2 x 2-1/2 inch loaf pan (or similar size). Chill until set. Divide beans or asparagus into 4 bundles; wrap each with pimiento strip around centre. Arrange on gelatin in pan. Chill remaining gelatin until partially set; pour enough gelatin over bean or asparagus bundles to cover; chill until firm. Meanwhile combine remaining gelatin with cauliflower flowerettes, carrots, green pepper, celery, green onions and radishes (do not chill). Pour over firm gelatin in pan - then chill until set. To serve, unmold salad loaf on bed of lettuce and garnish with tomato wedges and parsley sprigs, if desired. *Makes 8 servings.*

Tangy Tomato Aspic

2 envelopes unflavoured gelatin; 1/2 cup cold beef stock; 2 tablespoons butter; 1 small onion, finely chopped; 3 tablespoons tomato paste; 4½ cups canned tomatoes with liquid; 1 teaspoon salt; dash of pepper; 1 teaspoon sugar; 1 teaspoon Worcestershire sauce; 1 teaspoon lemon juice; 1/2 teaspoon dried tarragon; 1 teaspoon vegetable oil.

Soften gelatin in cold beef stock for 5 minutes. In heavy large saucepan melt butter and saute onion until transparent. Stir in tomato paste, canned tomatoes and the softened gelatin. Mix until well blended. Add salt, pepper, sugar, Worcestershire sauce, lemon juice and dried tarragon. Bring mixture to a boil stirring constantly. Reduce heat to simmer and cook gently with saucepan partially covered for approximately 30 minutes. Watch carefully and stir frequently to prevent scorching. Force tomato mixture through sieve into large mixing bowl.

Use a 1 quart mold. Rub well with 1 teaspoon vegetable oil. Pour mixture into mold and allow to set several hours in refrigerator. Unmold on bed of crisp greens.

Cottage Cheese Jellied Salad

1 tin (14 oz.) crushed pineapple, drained, juice retained, 1/2 pint whipping cream, whipped, 2 tbsp. lemon juice, 1 package (16 oz.) large curd cottage cheese, water as needed, 1/2 cup grated carrot, pinch salt, 1 green pepper, finely chopped, 1 package (3 oz.) lemon jelly powder, 1/2 cup chopped walnuts, 10 marshmallows.

Combine retained pineapple juice and lemon juice; add water to increase liquid to 1 3/4 cup. Add salt. Heat mixture to boiling. Remove from heat; add lemon jelly powder and marshmallows. Stir until marshmallows are melted. Cool mixture till partially thickened. Whip whipping cream until stiff. Into this fold cottage cheese, grated carrot, green pepper and walnuts. Add cottage cheese mixture to partially thickened jelly mixture. Mix until well combined. Pour into large mold and allow to chill until firm.

Tangy Cole Slaw

1 cup wine vinegar
1 cup mild
  flavoured honey
1 small onion,
  finely chopped
1 tsp. celery seed

1 tsp. salt
  or to taste
4 cups shredded cabbage
1 cup chopped celery
1 cup chopped
  green pepper

In small saucepan, combine vinegar, honey, onion, celery seed and salt. Bring mixture to boiling; reduce heat; simmer 5 minutes. Cool completely. In large bowl, place cabbage, celery and green pepper. Toss vegetables with enough of prepared dressing to coat lightly and evenly. Cover; chill several hours or overnight to blend flavours. Great with ham or chicken. Makes 10 to 12 servings.

Tomato-Onion Salad

1 clove garlic, minced
1 tsp. salt
1 tsp. sugar
1/4 tsp. pepper
2 tsp. prepared mustard
1/4 cup olive oil or salad oil

2 tbsp. tarragon vinegar
6 firm tomatoes, sliced
1 large onion, thinly sliced
1 head lettuce, broken in pieces

chopped parsley, for garnish

In small bowl, combine garlic and salt. Stir in sugar, pepper, mustard, oil and vinegar. Mix well. Pour over sliced tomatoes and onions. Toss lightly with pieces of lettuce. Sprinkle with chopped parsley. Chill well. Makes 6 to 8 servings.

Jellied Chicken Salad

1 can[14 oz.] sliced
  peaches, drained
  [reserve juice]
1/2 cup reserved
  peach juice
2 envelopes
  unflavoured gelatin
3 cups hot chicken
  broth
1/4 cup lemon juice

1/2 tsp. salt
1 1/2 cups diced cooked
  chicken
1/2 cup chopped celery
1/3 cup chopped
  green pepper
1/4 cup chopped walnuts
4 stuffed green olives,
  thinly sliced
mayonnaise

Drain peaches thoroughly, reserving juice. Chop peaches coarsely; set aside. Measure juice (add water if necessary to make 1/2 cup). Soften gelatin in juice. Dissolve in hot broth. Add lemon juice and salt. Chill until partially set. Stir in remaining ingredients, except mayonnaise. Pour mixture into 8 to 12 individual molds or a 5-1/2 cup ring mold. Chill until firm. Unmold. Garnish with mayonnaise. Makes 8 to 12 servings.

Spring Jellied Chicken Salad

2 envelopes unflavoured
  gelatin
1/2 cup cold water
3 cups hot
  chicken broth
1/2 tsp. salt
1/4 cup lemon juice
1 tin (14 oz.) pineapple
  tidbits, well drained

2 cups diced
  cooked chicken
1/3 cup chopped
  green pepper
1/3 cup celery, thinly
  sliced on bias
2 tbsp. sliced
  pitted ripe olives
mayonnaise

Soften gelatin in 1/2 cup cold water; dissolve mixture in hot broth. Stir in salt and lemon juice. Chill in refrigerator until partially set. Fold in remaining ingredients except mayonnaise. Pour into a 5 1/2 cup ring mold (or similar size). Chill until firm. Serve with mayonnaise or salad dressing. Makes 10 servings.

Apple-Lemon Molded Salad

1 package (3 oz.)
  lemon jelly powder
1-1/2 cups boiling water

1/2 cup sour cream
1 medium apple, quartered,
  cored and grated

Dissolve jelly powder in boiling water. Add sour cream; stir until well blended. Chill until partially set. Fold in grated apple. Pour mixture into 3-cup ring mold. Chill until set. Makes 4 to 5 servings.

Salad Tray with a Twist

Cucumber, scored, unpeeled and sliced
Radishes, sliced
Iceberg lettuce wedges
Green onion sticks
Cauliflower, raw, sliced
Green pepper, large strips
Mushrooms, halved
Tomato wedges
Onion rings

Prepare vegetables. Arrange "spokes" of vegetables on large, round platter, with several different dressings in bowls. Each guest selects preferred vegetables then either dips vegetables or spoons dressing onto salad.

Hot Potato Salad

1/2 lb. bacon; 1/3 cup bacon drippings; 1/3 cup vinegar; 2½ tbsp. water; 1 egg, slightly beaten; 1 tsp. sugar; 1 tsp. salt; dash pepper; 2 tsp. chopped parsley; 5 cups, diced, cooked potatoes; 1/3 cup chopped onion; 1/3 cup finely chopped celery.

Cook bacon until crisp; crumble. Reserve 1/3 cup of bacon drippings; combine drippings, vinegar, water, egg, sugar, salt, pepper and parsley. Stir and heat until thickened. Add potatoes, onion, celery and bacon; toss and heat through. *Makes 6 servings.*

Molded Potato Salad

10 medium potatoes, cooked, peeled and diced, 5 radishes, diced, 3 green onions, chopped, 3 stalks celery, finely chopped, 1/2 green pepper, chopped, 2 tablespoons chopped parsley, 3 hard cooked eggs, chopped, 1 cup mayonnaise, 1/4 cup vinegar, 1/8 teaspoon pepper, 1 teaspoon dry mustard, 1/2 teaspoon basil, crushed, 1 1/2 teaspoons salt, 1/8 teaspoon paprika.

Toss potatoes with radishes, green onions, green pepper, celery, parsley and eggs. Mix mayonnaise with vinegar, pepper, mustard, basil and salt. Pour mayonnaise mixture over potato mixture and mix well. Lightly oil an angel cake pan and spoon in potato salad. Press down lightly to pack and make top even. Cover and chill for at least 2 hours. When thoroughly chilled, place a plate over top of pan and invert. Sprinkle with paprika.

Creamy Waldorf Cole Slaw

2 cups red cabbage, grated or finely chopped
4 cups green cabbage, grated or finely chopped
1/4 cup green pepper, chopped
1/2 cup chopped walnuts
2 medium apples, unpeeled, diced
2 tsp. lemon juice
1/2 cup mayonnaise
1/4 cup sour cream
1 tbsp. lemon juice freshly ground black pepper
2 tsp. sugar parsley, chopped

Prepare cabbages. In large bowl combine red cabbage, green cabbage, green pepper and walnuts. In small bowl toss prepared apples with lemon juice. Add to cabbage mixture. Combine mayonnaise, sour cream, lemon juice, pepper and sugar. Toss with cabbage and apple mixture until all indredients are evenly coated. Garnish with chopped parsley. Serves 8.

Cottage Cheese Dressing

1 cup salad oil; 1/4 cup vinegar; 1/2 tsp. salt; 3 tbsp. cottage cheese; few grains cayenne pepper; 1/4 tsp. white pepper; 2 tbsp. chopped parsley; 1 tbsp. chopped chives.

Combine all ingredients and shake thoroughly. Serve with crisp, tossed greens.

Oil-Vinegar-Garlic Dressing

Rub 1/4 tsp. salt over 1 clove garlic; rub clove of garlic over salad bowl.

Mix together: —
1/8 tsp. dry mustard; 1/2 tsp. salt; 1/4 tsp. pepper; 1/2 tsp. sugar; 1 tbsp. white vinegar; 3 tbsp. salad oil.

Blend well. A quick tangy dressing for a tossed green salad.

Cobb Salad with French Dressing

1 head romaine lettuce, torn in fine pieces
1 head iceberg lettuce, torn in fine pieces
6 strips bacon, crisp-cooked, drained and crumbled
1/4 lb. Roquefort cheese, crumbled
3 hard cooked eggs, finely chopped
2 tomatoes, peeled, seeded and chopped
2 avocados, peeled, pitted and chopped
1/4 lb. gruyere cheese, chopped
1/2 cup chopped parsley

Arrange romaine and iceberg lettuce in bottom of salad bowl. Arrange remaining ingredients, except parsley, in rows across the top of the greens. Sprinkle parsley over all. At the table just before serving, add approximately 1/2 cup French dressing and toss. *Makes 8 servings.*

French Dressing

1/2 cup wine vinegar
1 tbsp. water
1 tsp. salt
1 tsp. Worcestershire sauce
1/2 tsp. cracked pepper
1/4 tsp. dry mustard
2/3 cup olive oil

To prepare dressing, combine all ingredients except oil in screw-top jar. Add oil and shake well. Prepare dressing several hours before serving to blend flavours. *Makes approximately 1-1/2 cups.*

Buffet Salad

1 small pkg. sea shells pasta, cooked, drained, chilled; 1/2 cup green pepper, finely diced; 1 cup finely chopped celery; 3 green onions, finely snipped (using green portion too); 1 cup canned shrimp, drained; 3/4 cup mayonnaise; 1/2 cup chili sauce.

Mix together shells, pepper, celery, onion and shrimp. In a bowl, combine mayonnaise and chili sauce. Add in vegetable-shrimp mixture; toss lightly. Correct seasoning to taste.

Celery Salad

3 cups thinly sliced celery; 1/2 cup grated carrot; 1/3 cup salad oil; 2 tbsp. red wine vinegar; 1 tbsp. sugar; 1 tsp. salt; dash pepper; dash paprika; 1/2 cup sour cream.

Place prepared celery and carrot in salad bowl. In small bowl beat together salad oil, vinegar, sugar, salt, pepper and paprika; beat in sour cream a little at a time. Pour over vegetables and toss lightly. *Makes 6 servings.*

Chef's Salad with Russian Dressing

1 clove garlic
1 large head romaine
  OR 1 bunch leaf lettuce
2 cups cooked ham strips
1/2 lb. sharp cheddar
  cheese, cut in strips
1 large tomato,
  cut in thin wedges
3 hard-cooked eggs,
  quartered lengthwise

1 bunch radishes,
  thinly sliced
1 bunch green onions
salt and pepper to taste
chopped chives
  or chopped parsley
  or sliced ripe olives
  for garnish, if desired
Russian Dressing (below)

Rub salad bowl with cut clove of garlic. Separate leaves, romaine or leaf lettuce. Arrange in bowl, lining sides and bottom. Arrange attractively ham, cheese, tomato, eggs, radishes and green onions. Sprinkle with salt and pepper. Serve with Russian Dressing. Garnish with chopped chives, chopped parsley or sliced ripe olives, if desired.

Russian Dressing

1/4 cup sugar
3 tbsp. water
1 1/2 tsp. celery seed
1/2 tsp. salt
1/2 tsp. paprika
2 1/2 tbsp. lemon juice

1 tbsp. Worcestershire sauce
1 tbsp. vinegar
1 cup salad oil
1/2 cup catsup
1/4 cup grated onion

Cook sugar and water until mixture spins a thread (232 degrees). Cool. Mix remaining ingredients, beat in syrup. Chill. *Makes 2 cups.*

Cucumber - Orange Salad

1 large cucumber, peeled
  and thinly sliced
3/4 tsp. salt or to taste
dash pepper
2 oranges, peeled, thinly
  sliced - then halved
2/3 cup coarsley chopped
  green pepper

1 tbsp. chopped parsley
1 cup unflavoured yogurt
  OR sour cream
1/2 tsp. crushed
  thyme, optional
walnuts for garnish,
  if desired

Place prepared cucumbers in large bowl; sprinkle with salt and pepper. Add prepared oranges, green pepper, parsley. Add yogurt or sour cream mixed with thyme if desired. Toss gently to mix dressing evenly. Refrigerate, covered for 1 hour to blend flavours. Serve on a bed of crisp lettuce leaves and garnish with walnuts, if desired.

This is a refreshing addition to a rich dinner or as a buffet salad.

Maxine's Buffet Salad

4 cucumbers,
  cut in 1/2 inch thick slices
  then quartered
4 green peppers,
  cut in 1/2 inch thick slices
  then quartered
  (remove all seeds and
  membrane)
3 tomatoes, cut in wedges

1 onion, sliced
  and separated into rings
1/4 to 1/3 cup black olives,
  halved
1/3 to 1/2 cup oil
salt and pepper to taste
dash oregano
3/4 lb. Feta cheese

Prepare cucumbers, green peppers, tomatoes and onion. Season oil with salt and pepper to taste. Add a dash of oregano. Pour oil over vegetables (amount for personal preference); Toss gently; allow to sit 2 hours, covered, in refrigerator. To serve, toss vegetables; sprinkle olives and Feta cheese over all. *Makes 8 large servings.*

Oriental Salad

Dressing

1 cup salad oil
1/2 cup sugar
1/4 cup vinegar
1 tbsp. Worcestershire sauce

2 tsp. salt
1 medium onion, finely chopped
1/3 cup catsup

In screw-top jar, combine all ingredients. Shake vigorously. Make dressing up well ahead of time. Chill. Shake well before using.

Salad

2 bunches spinach,
  well washed, dried
  and torn in bite-size pieces
1/2 lb. bacon,
  cut in small pieces -
  fry until crisp; drain well

1 lb. fresh bean sprouts
  (or use tinned equivalent,
  well drained)
1 bunch green onions, chopped
4 hard cooked eggs, sliced
1 - tin 8-1/2 oz. water chestnuts,
  drained

Combine all salad ingredients except eggs in large salad bowl. Just before serving, toss with enough dressing to coat salad lightly and evenly. Slice eggs on top. *Makes 6 to 8 large servings.*

Oriental Celery

2 or 3 small celery hearts, 1 medium-size sliced onion, 2½ cups water, 1/4 cup soy sauce, 1/2 cup salad oil, 1/4 cup rice wine vinegar, 1 clove garlic, crushed, 1/2 tsp. sugar, 1/2 tsp. salt, 1/2 tsp. dill weed, crushed.

Thoroughly wash celery hearts. Trim root ends and remove all but smallest leaves. Place onion and celery hearts in shallow saucepan or frying pan with cover. Add water and soy sauce. Cover pan. Bring sauce to boil, reduce heat and simmer about 15 minutes or until celery is tender. Remove from heat and cool celery in sauce. Meanwhile, blend together oil, vinegar, garlic, sugar, salt and dill weed. Remove hearts from sauce, cut in half lengthwise and place in shallow dish. Pour vinegar dressing over celery. Cover and chill for several hours. To serve, drain off most of dressing and place celery on shredded lettuce. Makes 4 to 6 servings.

Japanese Cucumber Salad

2 medium cucumbers, peeled and seeded, 2 tsp. salt, 1/3 cup seasoned gourmet vinegar, 1 tsp. soy sauce, 1/4 tsp. grated fresh ginger root, OR 1/8 tsp. ground ginger.

Cut cucumbers into thin slices; sprinkle with salt. Let stand at room temperature 1 to 2 hours. Drain and squeeze out excess liquid. Combine vinegar, soy sauce and ginger in bowl; stir in cucumbers and mix well. Chill thoroughly before serving. Makes 4 servings.

Variation: Marinate well-drained canned shrimp, canned B.C. salmon (flaked), mushrooms (whole or sliced), thinly sliced abalone or clams in 2 or 3 tbsp. seasoned gourmet vinegar about 2 hours. Drain and add to cucumber mixture.

Nicoise Salad

4 large potatoes, cooked, drained, and cooled
1 lb. green beans, cooked, drained, and cooled
2/3 cup olive oil [or other salad oil]
1/3 cup tarragon vinegar [or wine vinegar]
2 cloves garlic, crushed
2 to 3 tsp. Dijon mustard
salt and freshly ground black pepper [to taste]
1 small head Boston lettuce
1 medium head Romaine lettuce

1 red onion, coarsely chopped
1 green pepper, halved, seeded and cut into thin strips
4 hard-cooked eggs, shelled and quartered lengthwise
8 pitted ripe olives
1 tbsp. chopped parsley
2 large tomatoes, cut in wedges
2 cans (7 oz.) chunk tuna, drained and broken into chunks
2 tsp. lemon juice
1 can (2 oz.) rolled anchovy fillets,* drained (optional)

* Soak in milk to counteract excessive saltiness.

Prepare potatoes and beans; peel potatoes; cut into slices. Place in shallow dish. Place beans in separate shallow dish. In screw-top jar combine oil, vinegar, garlic, mustard, salt, and pepper. Shake vigorously. Drizzle 1/2 cup over potatoes and 2 tbsp. over beans. Allow to marinate for 1 hour. Line a large salad bowl with Boston and romaine lettuce. Layer in a mound, potatoes, beans, onion, and green pepper. Arrange quartered eggs and olives around edge of mound. Sprinkle over top with chopped parsley. Place tomato wedges in petal pattern around centre of mound. Sprinkle drained tuna with lemon juice. Mound tuna on top in centre of salad. Garnish with anchovy fillets, if desired. Pass remaining dressing separately. Do not toss. Makes 8 meal-sized servings.

Harvest Apple - Zucchini Toss

3 tbsp. salad oil
2 tbsp. vinegar
1-1/2 tsp. sugar
1/2 tsp. salt or to taste
pepper to taste
6 cups torn leaf lettuce

2 cups unpeeled diced red apple
1 cup unpeeled thinly sliced zucchini
1 small green pepper cut in thin julienne strips
2 tbsp. chopped walnuts (optional)

In screw-top jar, combine oil, vinegar, sugar, salt and pepper. Shake vigorously. Chill. Have all vegetables washed, dried and well chilled. In bowl, place prepared lettuce, apple, zucchini and green pepper. Shake prepared dressing just before using. Toss salad with just enough dressing to coat vegetables lightly. Sprinkle chopped walnuts over top, if desired. Serve immediately. *Makes 6 servings.*

Tomatoes a la Francaise

4 medium-ripe firm tomatoes, cut in slices
1 cup salad oil
1/2 cup vinegar
1 clove garlic, crushed
2 tbsp. sugar
1 tsp. salt
1 tsp. paprika

1 tsp. dry mustard
3/4 tsp. celery salt
1 tsp. minced onion
1/4 tsp. ground pepper
lettuce cups
bottled French dressing

Place tomato slices in bowl. In screw-top jar place salad oil, vinegar, garlic, sugar, salt, paprika, dry mustard, celery salt, minced onion, and ground pepper. Shake well. Pour over tomatoes. Allow to marinate several hours. Serve drained tomatoes on lettuce cups and sprinkle each with 1 tbsp. bottled French dressing. *Makes 4 to 6 servings.*

French Spinach Salad

Dressing
2 tbsp. lemon juice
2 tbsp. white wine vinegar
1/2 cup salad oil
1 tsp. salt

1 tsp. sugar
dash pepper
1 clove garlic
1/4 tsp. dry mustard

Salad
3/4 lb. tender young spinach leaves
1/3 cup sliced radishes
1/3 cup thinly sliced green onions

1 small cucumber, peeled and thinly sliced
1/2 cup halved cherry tomatoes

In screw-top jar, combine all dressing ingredients. Shake vigorously. Refrigerate several hours. Remove garlic clove just before using dressing.

Have all vegetables for salad washed; well dried; thoroughly chilled. Remove spinach stems; tear into bite-size pieces and place in salad bowl. Add radishes, green onions and cucumbers. Cover and refrigerate until just before serving. To serve, add halved cherry tomatoes to salad. Toss with dressing, as needed, until spinach is well coated. Serve immediately. *Makes 4 to 6 servings.*

Cold Bean Salad

1 can yellow wax beans
1 can green string beans
1 can kidney beans

1 can garbanzo beans
1 thinly sliced onion
1 chopped green pepper

Drain liquid from yellow and green beans. Rinse and drain kidney beans and garbanzo beans. Combine. Add sliced onion and chopped green pepper.

Dressing

1/2 cup salad oil
1/2 cup vinegar

1/2 cup honey or white sugar

Combine and pour over bean salad mix. Cover and refrigerate two hours or more before serving.

Creamy Waldorf Salad

2 cups diced tart
   red-skinned apples,
   unpeeled
1 tsp. lemon juice
1 tbsp. sugar or to taste
dash salt
1/2 cup chopped walnuts
1 cup sliced celery,
   cut on bias

1/2 cup whole seedless
   green grapes or Tokay grapes,
   halved and seeded
1/4 cup mayonnaise
1/2 cup whipping
   cream, whipped
lettuce leaves

Prepare apples; place in bowl; sprinkle with lemon juice, sugar and salt. Add walnuts, celery and grapes. In separate bowl, fold mayonnaise into whipping cream; fold dressing into apple-mixture. Chill thoroughly. To serve - line a salad bowl with lettuce leaves. Pile salad in centre. *Makes 6 servings.*

Summer Fruit Salad

2 large bananas,
   peeled and cut on bias
1 red-skinned apple, unpeeled,
   cored, and thinly sliced
3 medium oranges, peeled
   thinly sliced then cut in half

1 cup strawberries,
   washed, hulled, then
   sliced in half lengthwise
2/3 cup seedless green
   grapes, halved lengthwise
Honey - Sour Cream
   Dressing (below)

Slice bananas and apple into bowl. Cover completely with oranges, strawberries and grapes. Cover bowl and chill. Just before serving, pour dressing over fruit; toss gently until fruit is well coated. Serve immediately. *Makes 8 servings.*

Honey - Sour Cream Dressing

1/2 cup sour cream
1 tbsp. orange juice
1 tbsp. honey

In bowl, blend all ingredients. Pour over prepared fruits.

Winter Orange Salad Bowl

1 small head lettuce
1/2 head endive
2 oranges, peeled and sliced
bottled Italian dressing

1/2 mild white onion, sliced
   and separated into rings
Walnut Croutons (below)

Have all vegetables well chilled. Tear lettuce and endive into bite-size pieces. Place in salad bowl. Add prepared orange slices, onion rings and hot Walnut Croutons. Toss with enough Italian dressing to coat greens. *Makes 6 to 8 servings.*

Walnut Croutons

Melt 1 1/2 tsp. butter or margarine in skillet; add 1/4 tsp. salt. Add 1/3 cup walnut halves; brown mixture over medium heat, stirring constantly. Place Walnut Croutons over salad when hot.

Blender Mayonnaise

1 egg, 1 tsp. salt, 1 tsp. sugar, 1 tsp. mustard, ½ tsp. paprika, 3 tbsp. vinegar or lemon juice, 1½ cups salad oil.

Add egg, salt, sugar, mustard, paprika and vinegar or lemon juice into blender. Cover and blend for a few seconds; then uncover and gradually add salad oil with the motor running. Blend until very thick and smooth. Makes approximately one pint.

Uncooked Mayonnaise

2 eggyolks [save egg
   whites for use in
   another recipe]
1 tsp. dry mustard
1/2 tsp. salt

1 tsp. sugar
1/8 tsp. cayenne
4 tbsp. white vinegar
   or lemon juice
2 cups salad oil

In bowl, using electric mixer, beat egg yolks until thick and lemon-coloured. *This is important — do not underbeat. Have combined in small bowl, dry mustard, salt, sugar, cayenne and 2 tbsp. vinegar or lemon juice. Add dry mixture to beaten eggs; mix well. Continue beating while adding oil, 1 drop at a time, at first (do not rush this step), then gradually increase the amount of oil as mixture thickens until all is used. Slowly add remaining 2 tbsp. vinegar or lemon juice; beat well. Cover. Chill thoroughly before using.
Yields approximately 2 1/2 cups

Note: Do not halve this recipe or prepare in blender.

Dressing Variations

Cucumber Mayonnaise
Into 1 cup mayonnaise, fold 1/2 cup peeled, chopped and drained cucumber (good with fish).

Thousand Island Dressing
Into 2/3 cup mayonnaise, blend 1/3 cup chili sauce, 1 1/2 tbsp. chopped green pepper, 2 tbsp. chopped pimento, 1 tbsp. chopped chives and 2 tsp. chopped parsley.

Fruit Dressing
Into 1 cup mayonnaise, blend 2 tbsp. pineapple juice, 2 tbsp. orange juice and 2 tbsp. honey.

Russian Dressing
Into 2/3 cup mayonnaise, fold 3 tbsp. chopped olives, 2 tbsp. chopped sweet pickles, 1/3 cup chili sauce, 1 hard-cooked egg, finely chopped and 2 tsp. finely chopped parsley.

Cheesy Mayonnaise
In bowl, stir together 1/2 cup mayonnaise and 1/2 cup cream. Add 3 oz. softened and creamed cream cheese, 1/4 to 1/2 cup crumbled blue cheese and 1 tbsp. lemon juice. Blend thoroughly. Serve with vegetables, salad greens or fruits.

Whipped Cream Dressing
Whip 1/2 cup whipping cream; fold into 1 cup mayonnaise.

Berry Whipped Cream Dressing
Into Whipped Cream Dressing (above), fold 1 cup crushed strawberries or raspberries and sweeten with 1 to 2 tbsp. icing sugar.

Zippy Parmesan Dressing
⅔ cup salad oil,
½ cup vinegar,
1 tsp. salt,
1 tsp. mixed Italian
   herbs, crumbled,
pepper to taste,
2 tbsp. grated parmesan
   cheese.

Combine all ingredients in screw-top jar. Shake well. Chill. Serve with Antipasto Salad.

(see page 11)

Mona says . . .

To Clarify Stock:

Crush eggshell, mix with white of 1 egg; add ¼ cup water. Stir into hot stock. Bring to boil. Let stand 5 minutes; strain through fine wire strainer.

To Freeze Stock

Divide stock into desired quantities. Chill. Place into airtight containers. Freeze.

If a mistake in seasoning a recipe has been made, try one of these ideas:

Flavour is Too Bland

In a meat dish, add a dash of Worcestershire sauce, or hot pepper sauce, or bottled meat sauce or perhaps fried onions.

In a cream soup, try extra salt.

In almost anything, add salt and/or pepper.

Flavour is Too Salty

When food is too salty or too spicy, the ideal solution is to make a second batch, omitting the offensive seasoning. Combine the two batches and freeze half for later use.

For a stew or a soup, you can add cut raw potato to the pot, discarding the potato once it's boiled.

Flavour is Too Sharp

The second-batch trick works with food that tastes too sharp or too acid, but you can also soften the taste if you add a teaspoonful or two of sugar.

Flavour is Too Sweet

If the dish is a main dish or vegetable, add a teaspoon or two of vinegar.

White Stock

3 to 4 lbs. veal knuckle, cut in several pieces; 2-1/2 qts. cold water; 2 stalks celery and leaves; 1 onion, sliced; 1 carrot, sliced; 2 sprigs parsley; 2 cloves garlic; 1/2 bay leaf; 8 whole black peppers; 1 tbsp. salt.

Combine all ingredients in soup kettle. Simmer uncovered, not boiling, 5 hours. Strain. Clarify if desired. 1-1/2 qts. stock.

White stock is more delicate than Brown stock. Use in cream soups, substituting stock for part or all of the milk.

Brown Stock

6 lbs. beef soup bones (pieces); 1 cup sliced onions; 1/2 cup chopped celery with leaves; 1 large bay leaf; 4 sprigs parsley; 8 whole black peppers; 2 tsp. salt.

Remove meat from bones; cut up. Put meat, bones and 2 quarts cold water in kettle. Simmer, uncovered, not boiling, for 3 hours. Add remaining ingredients; cook uncovered 2 hours. Strain. Clarify, if desired. Remove any marrow in bones, add to stock. Skim off excess fat; or chill stock, lift off fat layer. *Makes approximately 6 cups.*

SOUPS and CHOWDERS

No finer compliment can be paid a cook than to eat freely and with relish of his cooking — *Ralph Connor,* THE PROSPECTOR, 1904

Hale and Hearty Hamburger Soup

1 tbsp. butter or margarine
1 lb. ground beef
4 small onions, sliced and separated into rings
1 clove garlic, crushed
1 tin (19 oz.) tomatoes
3 tbsp. lemon juice
3 tbsp. Worcestershire sauce
salt and pepper to taste
5 cups water
3 large carrots, thinly sliced on bias
3 celery stalks, thinly sliced on bias

3 medium potatoes, diced
1 tin (10 oz.) corn niblets, undrained
3/4 cup elbow macaroni

In large Dutch oven, melt butter; add beef and cook slightly, stirring with fork. Add onions and garlic. Cook until tender. Add tomatoes, lemon juice, Worcestershire sauce, salt, pepper and water. Bring to a boil; cover and simmer 1 hour. Add carrots, celery, potatoes and corn (undrained). Simmer, covered 1 hour longer or until vegetables are tender. Stir in macaroni during last 20 minutes of cooking. Serve hot with crusty rolls. *Makes 6 hearty servings.*

Clam and Corn Chowder

4 slices bacon, diced
1 large onion, chopped
1/3 cup chopped green pepper
2 tbsp. butter or margarine
2 tbsp. flour
3 tins (5 oz.) clams
  (or equivalent amount)
1 tin (12 oz.) whole kernel corn
1 medium tomato,
  peeled and chopped
2 cups diced peeled potato
1 tsp. salt or to taste
1/8 tsp. pepper
  or to taste
water

In Dutch oven, cook bacon until it is limp. Add onion, green pepper and butter. Continue cooking until bacon is crisp and onion is tender. Remove from heat. Add flour and stir until smooth. Drain clams and corn, reserving liquid. Add clams, corn, tomato, potato, salt and pepper to mixture in Dutch oven. Combine reserved clam and corn liquid. Add water to measure 4 cups. Add to mixture in Dutch oven. Bring to boiling; reduce heat and cover. Simmer for 25 to 30 minutes or until potatoes are tender, stirring occasionally. *Makes 6 to 8 servings.*

Westcoast Clam Chowder

6 medium peeled sliced
  raw potatoes
1 medium peeled
  sliced onion
3-1/2 cups water
2 tsp. salt or to taste
1 tsp. pepper or to taste
1/2 tsp. garlic powder
  or to taste
3 tbsp. butter
1 tin (16 oz.)
  evaporated milk
1 tin (16 oz.) clams
  (and their liquid)
2 tbsp. chopped parsley

Put potatoes and onion in 3 qt. heavy duty saucepan. Add 2-1/2 cups of water, salt, pepper, garlic. Cover tightly. Heat mixture to boiling; then simmer 10 minutes or until potatoes are tender. Mash potatoes and onions in their liquid (use rotary beater). Add butter, milk, remaining 1 cup water and clams (with their liquid). Heat to serving temperature. Garnish with chopped parsley. *Makes 4 to 6 servings.*

Note: If you desire a thicker soup, mix 1/4 cup flour with 1/2 cup water. Add to soup mixture. Simmer 3 to 4 minutes, stirring gently.

Bermuda Salmon Chowder

1/4 cup butter
2 large onions, chopped
2 tbsp. flour
1 tin (10 oz.) condensed
  beef consomme
2 cups clam juice
1 large green pepper,
  chopped
1 cup thinly sliced celery
  cut on bias
3 cups medium white sauce
  (below)
2 cups tinned salmon,
  undrained and broken
  into chunks
1 cup diced cooked potato
1/2 tsp. dried crumbled thyme
chopped chives and sliced
  hard-cooked eggs,
  for garnish if desired

In large saucepan, melt 2 tbsp. butter; cook onions slowly until tender but not browned. Add flour and allow it to brown. Add consomme and clam juice; cook and stir constantly until thickened. In small saucepan, melt remaining 2 tbsp. butter. Cook green pepper and celery until soft. Add to onion mixture. Make up white sauce (below). To white sauce, add salmon and salmon liquid, potatoes and thyme; heat salmon mixture to serving temperature; add hot clam juice mixture. Serve immediately. Garnish with chopped chives and sliced hard-cooked eggs, if desired. *Makes 8 servings.*

To make up white sauce, use 3 tbsp. butter, 6 tbsp. flour and 3 cups milk. Prepare using standard method.

Celery Chowder

1 tablespoon butter or margerine, 1 medium onion, chopped, 3 cups celery (stalks and leaves), chopped, 2 medium potatoes, peeled and diced, 2 eggs, hard cooked, sliced, 3 tablespoons flour, 2 1/2 cups milk, 1 1/2 teaspoons salt, 1/8 teaspoon pepper.

In a 10 inch skillet: saute onion in butter. Add celery and potatoes, cover with water and cook till tender. Combine flour with 1/2 cup milk; mix well. Add flour mixture to skillet with vegetables (a little water should still be in the pan, about 1/4 to 1/2 inch). Blend well. Add remaining milk gradually, stirring constantly. Add eggs, salt and pepper. Heat through, bring to a slow boil and simmer for 5 to 10 minutes. Serve.

Egg Drop Soup

4 chicken bouillon cubes; 4 cups hot water; 1 cup fresh tomato, diced; 1 egg, slightly beaten.

In a pan, dissolve bouillon cubes in hot water. Add in diced tomato; simmer for 5 minutes. Add slightly beaten egg to soup, then stir constantly 1 or 2 minutes, or until egg separates in shreds. Serve immediately. *Makes 4 to 6 servings.*

Broccoli Cream Soup

2 (10 oz) pkg. frozen chopped broccoli, thawed; 1/4 cup chopped onion; 2 cups chicken stock; 2 tbsp butter; 1 tbsp flour; 2 tsp salt; 1/8 tsp mace; dash pepper; 2 cups half-'n'-half (half milk, half cream).

In medium saucepan, combine broccoli, onion and chicken stock; bring to boil. Simmer about 10 minutes, or until broccoli is tender. Whirl broccoli mixture in blender until very smooth, or press through wire strainer. Melt butter in pan; add flour, salt, mace and pepper, stirring until smooth. Slowly stir in half-'n'-half, then add broccoli puree. Cook over medium heat, stirring frequently, until soup bubbles. Serve hot. *Makes 10 to 12 servings.*

Hungarian Potato Soup

3 tbsp. butter or margarine
1 medium onion, chopped
4 medium potatoes,
  peeled and diced
1-1/2 tsp. salt or to taste
1 cup water
1 cup sour cream
1/4 cup all-purpose flour
  (use 1 tbsp. less flour
  for a thinner soup)
1 tsp. paprika
2-1/2 cups milk
chopped chives

In saucepan, melt butter. Cook onion until tender but not browned. Add potatoes, salt and water. Cover and cook until potatoes are tender, approximately 15 minutes. In bowl, blend sour cream, flour and paprika until smooth. Stir into potato mixture. Add milk. Heat, stirring constantly, until mixture is piping hot but **not** boiling. Cook 1 minute. Season. Serve immediately. Sprinkle chopped chives over top. *Makes 6 servings.*

Pressure Cooked Vegetable Soup

3 tbsp. margarine
1/4 cup diced carrots
1/2 cup diced onions
1/2 cup sliced celery
1 tin (10 oz.) consomme
1 1/2 cups tomato juice
1 tin (19 oz.) tomatoes
1 tbsp. chopped parsley
salt and pepper to taste
1/2 cup chopped cabbage
  OR 1/2 cup diced turnip

Place margarine in pressure cooker. Saute carrots, onions and celery until tender. Add all other ingredients. Cook under pressure 3 minutes. Let stand 5 minutes then release pressure. *Makes 4 healthy servings.*

Hot Tomato Consomme

2 cups tomato juice   1/2 tsp. Lawry's Seasoned Salt
1 tbsp. Lawry's Garlic Spread

Pour tomato juice into a 1-quart saucepan. Add Garlic Spread and Seasoned Salt. Simmer for 10 minutes. *Makes 4 servings.*

Note: For larger quantity, double the recipe.

*Recipe courtesy of Lawry's Kitchens.

Super Gazpacho

1 cup finely chopped peeled tomato, 1/2 cup finely chopped cucumber, 1/2 finely chopped, green pepper, 1 stalk celery, finely chopped, 1 small onion, finely chopped, 1 tbsp. chopped parsley, 1 clove garlic, crushed, 2 tsp. chopped chives, 2 tbsp. vinegar, 2 tbsp. salad oil, salt and pepper to taste, 1 tsp. Worcestershire sauce, 1 tbsp. lemon juice, 2 1/2 cups tomato juice.

Prepare vegetables. Combine all ingredients in large bowl. Cover and chill several hours. Serve in chilled cups. Top with croutons, if desired. *Makes 6 delicious servings.*

Vichyssoise

4 leeks (white part) thinly sliced, 1 medium onion, thinly sliced, ¼ c. butter, 5 medium potatoes, thinly sliced (about 4 c.), 4 c. chicken broth *, 1 tbsp. salt, 2 c. milk, 2 c. cream, 1 c. whipping cream.

(* 4 chicken bouillon cubes to 4 c. boiling water)
Cook leeks and onion in butter until tender but not brown; add potatoes, broth and salt. Cook 35 to 40 minutes. Rub through fine sieve, return to heat; add milk and light cream. Season to taste. Bring to boil. Cool; rub through very fine sieve. When cold, add whipping cream before serving. Garnish with finely chopped chives. Makes 8 servings.

Frosty Gazpacho

2-1/2 cups
   tomato juice
1 tin (10 oz.) condensed
   beef broth or consomme
2 to 3 tbsp.
   finely chopped onion
3 tbsp. lemon juice
1/2 tsp. salt
   or to taste
tabasco to taste
1 small clove
   garlic, crushed

dash freshly
   ground black pepper
1 cup finely
   chopped cucumber
1 cup finely
   chopped tomato
2/3 cup finely
   chopped green pepper
1/3 cup finely
   chopped celery
Seasoned Croutons (below)

In large screw-top jar, combine tomato juice, beef broth, onion, lemon juice, salt, tabasco, garlic and pepper. Replace lid; shake vigorously. Refrigerate at least 4 hours to blend flavours. Prepare cucumber, tomato, green pepper and celery. Cover and chill thoroughly. Approximately 30 minutes before serving, place tomato juice mixture into freezer. Do NOT freeze. Have soup dishes well chilled. To serve divide prepared chilled vegetables among soup dishes. Pour soup over vegetables. Serve immediately with seasoned croutons. *Makes 8 servings.*

Seasoned Croutons

Cut slightly dry bread into 1/2-inch cubes. Melt a little butter in skillet. Add 1 small crushed garlic clove or 1/8 tsp. garlic powder. Add bread cubes. Toss lightly. Heat and stir well until croutons are golden brown. Remove from heat. Toss with enough chopped parsley and grated Parmesan cheese to coat lightly.

Blender Cucumber Soup

2 tins (10 oz.) condensed cream of celery soup, 1 small cucumber, peeled and chopped, 2 tbsp. finely chopped green onions, 1 tbsp. chopped parsley, pepper to taste, 2 sprigs watercress, chopped (optional), 2 cups milk, 1/2 cup sour cream, chopped chives for garnish, if desired.

In electric blender, whirl 1 can of soup at a time. Add cucumber, green onions, parsley, pepper and watercress. Blend until mixture turns pale green. Stir in milk; chill in refrigerator until serving time. Serve in mugs or soup bowls. Top each with a spoon of sour cream and sprinkle of chopped chives. *Makes 6 servings.*

Note: This recipe can be made with electric mixer. Ensure all vegetables are finely chopped before adding to condensed soup. Proceed as directed for blender.

Cream of Mushroom Soup

1 1/4 cups sliced mushrooms
1/4 cup chopped onion
2 tbsp. butter or margarine
2 tbsp. all-purpose flour
2 cups chicken broth, brown stock or beef broth

1/2 cup light cream
1/2 tsp. salt or to taste
dash pepper
1/4 tsp. nutmeg
chopped chives or snipped parsley for garnish, if desired

Slice mushrooms through cap and stem. In large saucepan, gently saute mushrooms and onion in butter until tender but not browned. Add flour and blend; add stock. Cook and stir until slightly thickened. Cool slightly; add cream, salt, pepper and nutmeg. Heat through. **Do Not Boil.** Serve immediately. Garnish with chopped chives or snipped parsley, if desired. *Makes 4 to 6 servings.*

Mona says . . .

Meat is an important part of the Canadian diet but compared with other foods it is expensive. Shop for it with care and make use of all the meat you buy. Save bones for soups and stocks, melt down fat trimmings for drippings, simmer lean trimmings for soup stock or gravy.

Buy meat in terms of meals. Leftovers that are not enough for a second meal become expensive. Leftovers can provide delicious meals with no leftover look or taste. A few suggestions are:

Use cooked ham, chicken or beef, mixed with rice or bread crumbs, herbs, onions and 1 egg for every 2 cups of the mixture to stuff a cabbage. The cabbage is steamed or cooked in stock. Serve with tomato sauce.

Leftover beef, pork, lamb or turkey makes a delicious meatloaf. Grind up meat; add onions and as a binder use bread crumbs that have been soaked in bouillon or bread crumbs mixed with a small amount of milk — squeeze crumbs dry, add 1 egg for every 2 cups of mixture. Add leftover vegetables such as cooked and chopped broccoli or spinach. For spices choose sage, thyme or garlic powder. Parmesan cheese makes a delicious addition. Cook meatloaf in loaf pan in 350 degree F. oven approximately 1 hour or until done.

Curry is an exotic way to transform leftover lamb, beef, veal or chicken.

For budget steaks, buy chuck or bottom round. marinate or tenderize; then broil medium rare for maximum tenderness.

Calculate costs on price per cooked serving rather than price per pound. As a general rule 1 lb. of bony meat (spareribs, etc.) equals 1 serving. 1 lb. of small-bone meat (roasts, etc.) equals 2 servings. 1 lb. of boneless meat equals 3 to 4 servings.

Less tender cuts of meat are usually cheaper than the more tender cuts, yet provide the same high-quality protein and when cooked properly can be very juicy and tender.

MEATS

Cooking Canada's Beef

Cooking Canada's Veal

Cooking Canada's Pork

Cooking Canada's Lamb

Cooking Canada's Ham and Bacon

Beef Chart

For most accurate results, use a meat thermometer when cooking roast beef. Insert thermometer so that the tip reaches into the centre of the thickest muscle. Here is an approximate guide to cooking times:

Beef Cut	Oven Temp.	Approximate Weight (in pounds)	Approximate Cooking Time (Total Time)
Rib Roast	325°F.	(rare) 4 to 6 (medium) (well done)	2¼ to 2¾ hours 2¾ to 3¼ hours 3¼ to 3½ hours
Rib Roast	325° F.	(rare) 6 to 8 (medium) (well done)	2½ to 3 hours 3 to 3½ hours 3¾ to 4 hours
Boneless Rib Roast (rolled)	325° F.	(rare) 5 to 7 (medium) (well done)	3¼ to 3½ hours 3¾ to 4 hours 4½ to 4¾ hours
Rib Eye Roast (Delmonico)	350° F.	(rare) 4 to 6 (medium) (well done)	1½ to 1¾ hours 1¾ hours 2 hours

Meat Thermometer readings are:
RARE — 140° F.   MEDIUM — 160° F.   WELL DONE — 170° F.

Mona says . . .

There are two basic methods of cooking BEEF:
1. *in dry heat*
2. *in moist heat*

Cook in dry heat (roast, broil, or pan-fry) for the more tender cuts of meat. Cook in moist heat (braising, stewing or cooking in water) for the less tender cuts of meat.

Roasting — *Place roast, fat side up, in shallow roasting pan (for accurate results, use a meat thermometer). Cook in a slow oven (325° F.) unless otherwise directed. This method is good for top quality roasts — Standing Rib, Sirloin Tip, Top quality Round Steak Roasts (also used for cooking tenderloin).*

Broiling — *Place steak on rack of broiler pan approximately 3 inches from source of heat. When top surface is browned, turn steak and season. Cook to desired degree of doneness. Good for steaks such as Sirloin, Porterhouse, Club, Rib, T-bone (and marinated or tenderized Flank or Top Round Steak; beef patties may also be broiled).*

Pan-Broiling — *Place steaks or patties (same types as listed for broiling) in a hot heavy skillet. Add a small amount of oil or butter if meat is very lean. Turn steaks with tongs to avoid piercing meat. Turn steaks only once for best results.*

Braising — *When braising use a deep pan (such as a Dutch oven) with a lid. Season meat with salt and pepper (follow recipe directions); brown either in its own fat or if meat is very lean, brown in a small amount of salad oil or butter (or combination of both); add a small amount of liquid. Cover and allow to simmer. Pot roasts, Swiss steak and Short Ribs are commonly cooked by this method.*

Stewing — *Usually when stewing meat (usually for stews). Meat is seasoned — sometimes browned, then covered with liquid and simmered gently until tender.*

Thick Gravy

If gravy is too thick, stir in a little more liquid.

Thin Gravy

If gravy is too thin, mix some water and flour, cornstarch or arrowroot to a smooth paste. Stir into the gravy and bring to a boil, stirring constantly.

If a gravy thickened with cornstarch or arrowroot becomes too thin, it has probably been overcooked. Rethicken with more cornstarch or arrowroot; cook just until thickened again; remove from heat.

Yorkshire Pudding

1 cup flour; 1/3 tsp. salt; 1 cup milk; 2 eggs, slightly beaten.

Sift flour with salt in mixing bowl. Make a well in center; gradually add milk to form smooth heavy batter; add slightly beaten eggs. Beat steadily for 2 minutes with beater.

In a baking pan containing 1/4 to 1/2-inch of hot roast beef fat, pour in batter. Bake in 400°F oven for 20 to 25 minutes, decreasing the heat to moderate as the baking nears completion and bake 5 to 8 minutes longer. Cut in squares; spoon beef juice or 'dish gravy' over top.

Mushroom Pot Roast

3½–4 lb. beef blade pot roast; salt and pepper; 2 cups sliced onion; 1/4 cup water; 1/4 cup catsup; 1/3 cup dry sherry; 1 clove garlic, minced; 1/4 tsp dry mustard; 1/4 tsp dried marjoram; 1/4 tsp crushed, dried thyme; 1/4 tsp crushed, dried rosemary; 1 medium bay leaf; 1 (10 oz) can sliced mushrooms, drained; 1/4 cup cold water; 2 tbsp. all-purpose flour.

Trim excess fat from roast. Coat meat with flour. In a Dutch oven with 2 tbsp. hot shortening, brown meat on both sides; season with salt and pepper. Add in onion. Blend together 1/4 cup water, catsup, sherry, minced garlic, mustard, marjoram, rosemary, thyme and bay leaf. Add to meat. Simmer, covered, for 2 hours, or until tender. Remove meat to plate. Discard bay leaf. Remove excess fat from pan juices. Add in drained mushrooms. Blend 1/4 cup cold water with flour and stir into juices. Cook, stirring, until thickened and bubbly. Pour a little gravy over roast; pass remaining gravy. *Serves 6 to 8.*

Tournedos With Eggplant

4 tbsp. olive oil or salad oil	freshly ground black pepper
4 small eggplant rings	3-1/2 tbsp. butter
12 cherry tomatoes (skinned, if desired), stems removed	2 tbsp. chopped shallots or green onions
4 tournedos (small filets mignons), each cut approximately 1-1/2 inches thick	1/3 cup Madeira wine
	1 cup brown sauce or tinned beef gravy
	1/3 cup water
	salt and pepper to taste
	parsley sprigs or watercress for garnish, if desired

In skillet, heat 3 tbsp. oil. Saute eggplant slices on both sides until tender and lightly browned. Remove from skillet; keep warm. Add remaining 1 tbsp. oil to skillet. Cook tomatoes for 2 minutes; remove from skillet; keep warm. In large skillet, heat 1-1/2 tbsp. butter until golden brown. Sprinkle meat with freshly ground black pepper. Cook meat on all sides until browned and desired degree of doneness (about 5 minutes each side for rare). Remove steaks from skillet to a warm serving platter. Add shallots or green onions to drippings in skillet. Cook briefly, then pour in wine. Add brown sauce and water. Season to taste with salt and pepper. Remove skillet from heat. Swirl in remaining 2 tbsp. butter. Top each "tournedo" with a sauteed eggplant slice and 3 tomatoes. Pour some of sauce over meat. Pass remaining sauce separately. If desired, garnish with parsley sprigs or watercress. *Makes 4 servings.*

Cooking

Canada's Beef

Beef Pot Roast with Vegetable

3-1/2 lb. beef pot roast	1 bay leaf
2 tbsp. all-purpose flour	1 tin (7-1/2 oz.) tomato sauce
salt and pepper to taste	6 medium potatoes, peeled and halved lengthwise
2 tbsp. salad oil (add more if necessary)	6 carrots, peeled and halved crosswise
1-1/2 cups sliced onion	
1 cup beef stock OR 1 beef bouillon cube dissolved in 1 cup boiling water	6 small white turnips, peeled and halved crosswise

Gravy

2-1/2 cups pan liquid (add water or beef stock to make up this amount, if necessary)	1/4 cup flour
	1/2 cup water
	salt and pepper to taste

Wipe roast well. In small bowl, place 2 tbsp. flour. Season with salt and pepper. Sprinkle mixture over roast and rub into surface. In large Dutch oven, heat salad oil. Add roast and brown well on all sides (this takes about 15 to 20 minutes). When meat is partially browned, add sliced onions and brown well (this gives good colour and flavour). Add beef stock (or bouillon cube dissolved in boiling water) and bay leaf. Reduce heat; cover and simmer for 1-1/2 hours. Turn roast. Add tomato sauce and prepared potatoes, carrots and turnips. Have vegetables covered with the liquid in pan. Cover and simmer for 1-1/2 hours longer or until meat and vegetables are tender. To serve, arrange roast and vegetables on warm serving platter. Keep warm. To make gravy, strain pan liquid. Skim off all fat. Measure; add water if necessary to yield 2-1/2 cups. Return liquid to Dutch oven. In small bowl, blend thoroughly 1/4 cup flour and 1/2 cup water. Slowly stir into liquid in Dutch oven. Season with salt and pepper to taste. Bring mixture to boiling, stirring constantly; reduce heat and simmer for 5 minutes. Serve gravy with meat and vegetables. *Makes 6 servings.*

Beef Tournedos

meat tenderizer	2 tablespoons lemon juice
1 1/2 pounds chuck roast, tender sections only	1/2 teaspoon dry mustard
1/4 cup dry white wine	dash cayenne
1 teaspoon tarragon, crumbled	1/2 cup butter or margarine
1 tbsp. onion, finely chopped	4 toast rounds, about 4 inches in diameter
3 egg yolks	artichoke cuttings or hearts

Sprinkle meat tenderizer on beef according to label directions. Divide meat into 4 equal pieces. Shape into compact rounds about 3/4 to 1 inch thick by tying with string. Simmer wine, tarragon and onion for 5 minutes, in a small saucepan; remove from heat; strain into a one cup measure. Combine egg yolks, lemon juice, mustard and cayenne in a blender; blend until ingredients are combined. Heat butter until melted and almost boiling. With blender at low speed, slowly pour about 1/3 of the hot butter, in a thin stream, into blender. Turn blender to high speed and slowly pour in remaining butter. Blend until mixture is smooth and thickened. Stir in wine mixture; mix well. Keep warm. Broil beef until desired doneness, 4 inches from heat. Heat, drain and season artichoke hearts or cuttings. Place one beef tournedo on each toast round; top with artichoke heart or cuttings; spoon over sauce. Garnish with parsley. *Serves 4.*

Basic Burger Mix

1 lb. ground beef; 1/4 cup fine bread crumbs; 1/4 cup minced onion; 1/2 tsp. salt; 1/8 tsp. pepper; 1 cup tomato sauce.

Combine first 5 ingredients and 1/4 cup of the tomato sauce; mix well. Form into patties. In a fry pan, brown both sides of meat; drain off excess fat. Simmer in any of the following sauces. *Makes 4 servings.*

Burger Variations

Western: To remaining 3/4 cup tomato sauce add 1/4 tsp. salt; 1/4 cup water; 1 tsp. Worcestershire sauce and 1 (4 oz.) can sliced ripe olives. Pour sauce over burgers; let simmer 15 minutes.

Mexican: To remaining 3/4 cup tomato sauce add 1/4 cup chopped onion, 1 tsp. chili powder and 1 (14 oz.) can kidney beans. Pour sauce over burgers; let simmer 15 minutes. Top with a sprinkling of grated Cheddar cheese just before serving.

German: To remaining 3/4 cup tomato sauce, add 1/4 cup vinegar, 1/3 cup water, 5 whole cloves and 5 crumbled gingersnap cookies. Pour sauce over burgers; let simmer 15 minutes.

Swedish: To remaining 3/4 cup tomato sauce, add 1/2 cup white wine, 1 tbsp. sugar and 1/4 tsp. nutmeg. Pour sauce over burgers; let simmer 20 minutes.

Italian: To remaining 3/4 cup tomato sauce, add 1/4 cup water, 1/4 tsp. basil and 1/4 tsp. oregano. Pour sauce over burgers; let simmer 15 minutes.

VARIATIONS

Mushroom Pizza Burger

Shape meat into 4 patties; broil several minutes on each side or until almost done. Remove from oven. Season meat lightly with salt and freshly ground black pepper. Top each patty with 1 to 2 tbsp. prepared bottled pizza, spaghetti or barbecue sauce; 1 thin slice mozzarella cheese; a dash of crushed oregano and several mushroom slices. Return to oven and broil just until bubbly. *Makes 4 servings.*

Bacon-Onion Burgers

Mix ground beef with 1/3 cup finely chopped sauteed onions and 1/3 cup crisp-cooked, crumbled bacon. Season to taste with salt, pepper and Worcestershire sauce. Shape into patties. Panfry, broil or barbecue until done.

Herbed Burgers

Mix ground beef with 1 tbsp. chopped chives, 1 tbsp. fresh dill, 1 tbsp. sour cream and 1 tbsp. capers (optional). Shape into patties. Season with salt and cracked black pepper to taste. Panfry, broil or barbecue until done.

Stuffed Bleu Cheese Burgers

Shape meat into 6 thin patties. Mash 1 to 1-1/2 tbsp. crumbled bleu cheese with just enough milk or cream to make an easy spreading consistency. Spread mixture over top of three patties. Top with remaining three patties and pinch edges to seal. Broil, pan-fry or barbecue patties until done.

Burgers Diane

Shape very lean ground beef into 4 patties. In skillet, melt 2 tbsp. unsalted butter; cook patties on both sides until desired degree of doneness. Remove to a warmed serving platter. Season with salt and pepper to taste. Keep warm. Into pan drippings, add 3 tbsp. dry sherry, 1 tbsp. unsalted butter, 1 tbsp. chopped parsley, 1 tbsp. chopped chives, 1 tbsp. cognac (optional), 1 tsp. Dijon-style mustard and 1 tsp. Worcestershire sauce. Heat, stirring in any crusty brown bits until bubbly. Pour sauce over cooked meat patties. Serve immediately.

Beef Stew with Red Wine

Mushrooms

1/4 cup butter
1 lb mushrooms, [whole
if small, sliced if large]

Melt butter over medium heat in 8-10 inch skillet of enamel or stainless steel. (The enamel or stainless steel pans keep the mushrooms light coloured). When butter is frothy, toss mushrooms lightly for 2-3 minutes or until slightly soft. Set aside and keep warm.

Onions

1/2 lb. side bacon, cut
into strips about 1 1/2"
long, 1/4" in diameter.
1 tbsp. butter
6-8 medium onions,
sliced in 1/4 inch slices

In heavy skillet, melt butter over moderate heat, brown bacon strips, stirring constantly, until crisp and golden. Remove bacon from pan with slotted spoon; set aside to drain on paper towels. In skillet brown onions slightly in bacon drippings over medium high heat, shaking pan to rotate to colour as evenly as possible. Transfer onions to dish, add warm mushrooms; set aside.

Beef

3 lbs beef [lean
boneless; chuck or
rump, cut in 1 1/2 inch
chunks]
Bouquet garni*
1/4 cup green onions,
finely chopped
Freshly ground
black pepper
1/2 cup carrots, finely
chopped
1/4 cup flour

2 cups dry red wine
1 tbsp. ketchup
1 clove garlic, finely
chopped
1 tsp. oregano
3/4-1 tsp. salt
3 tbsp. fresh parsley,
finely chopped
1 cup hot beef stock,
fresh or canned
[OR 1 beef boullion
cube dissolved in
1 cup boiling water].

Preheat oven to 350 degrees F. Use skillet with bacon drippings; fat should cover approx. 1/16" over surface of pan. Add a little oil or butter, if necessary. Over medium to high heat bring fat almost to smoking point. Dry beef with paper towels, then brown in fat.

Brown only 5-6 chunks at a time. Add more drippings or oil if necessary. When chunks are evenly browned on all sides remove with tongs to a heavy oven-proof 5-6 quart casserole. Bury bouquet garni in the meat. After meat is browned add chopped green onions and carrots to remaining drippings in pan. Cook over low heat, stirring constantly until lightly coloured. Stir in flour. If mixture looks dry add a little more oil. Return to low heat; stir constantly, until flour begins to brown lightly, being careful not to burn. Remove from heat, cool a minute, then add hot beef stock, blend quickly with wire whisk. Blend in wine and ketchup. Bring to boil, whisking constantly as sauce thickens. Mix in garlic, oregano, sauteed bacon strips, salt and a few twists of pepper grinder. Pour sauce over beef, stirring gently to coat each beef cube with sauce. The sauce should almost, but not quite cover beef in pan. If desired, add more wine. Bring to boil on top of stove; cover tightly. Place casserole in lower third of oven. Let meat simmer gently in the oven for 1 1/2 to 2 hours. Regulate oven temperature to guarantee continuous simmering of the beef.

Let beef cook until tender when pierced by sharp knife tip. Gently stir in browned onions and mushrooms, adding any juices which might have accumulated. With a large spoon gently mix beef and vegetables with sauce in casserole. Continue baking for another 15-20 minutes. To serve, remove bouquet garni; skim off any excess fat. Taste sauce; correct seasonings. Sprinkle beef with parsley. Serve directly from casserole.

*To make bouquet garni take 4 sprigs of parsley and 1 bay leaf; tie together with piece of cotton.

Note: To guarantee that no one ingredient in your beef stew is overdone cook the mushrooms, onions and beef separately before finally combining them.

Pressure Cooked Beef Stew

1 1/2 lbs. round
or chuck steak
2 tbsp. oil
1 tin (10 oz.)
tinned consomme, undiluted
2 small onions, diced
2 large potatoes,
cut in sticks

5 to 6 carrots,
cut in 2 inch pieces
1 small turnip,
cup in sticks
1 tsp. dehydrated
onion soup mix
1/2 cup dry red wine

Cut meat into 1 1/2 inch cubes; brown in oil in pressure cooker - approximately 10 minutes. Add consomme; cover and cook under pressure for 10 minutes. Allow steam to escape. Add onions, potatoes, carrots, turnips, soup mix and wine. Cook under pressure; another 10 to 12 minutes depending upon vegetables. Let steam escape. Thicken if desired. *Makes 4 hearty servings.*

Viennese Goulash

3 1/2 pounds beef, cut into cubes
(cross rib, chuck, rump or blade roasts are best)
1/2 cup flour
1 teaspoon salt
1/8 teaspoon pepper
1 tablespoon paprika
1/4 cup butter or margarine
3 medium onions, chopped

1 clove garlic, finely chopped
2 cups boiling water
1 beef bouillion cube
1 cup water
1 (7 1/2 ounce) can tomato sauce
1/2 teaspoon ground marjoram
1/2 teaspoon salt
1 tablespoon lemon juice

Combine flour, 1 teaspoon salt, pepper and paprika. Coat cubed beef with flour mixture. Saute onion and garlic in butter over medium heat, in a Dutch oven. Add floured beef, sprinkling any excess flour over beef in pot. Sear beef in Dutch oven along with onions and garlic. Dissolve bouillion cube in boiling water: Add to beef mixture in Dutch oven. Add remaining ingredients; mix well. Cover and place in a 325 degree F. oven for 3 hours. Serve over cooked rice or noodles. *Serves 6 to 8.*

Minute Steak Scramble

4 (4 oz. each) cube (or minute) steaks, cut in julienne strips	1 cup bias-cut celery
1 tsp. ground ginger	1/2 cup bias-cut green onions
1/4 tsp. salt	2 tbsp. cornstarch
1/4 tsp. garlic salt	1/3 cup soy sauce
1/4 cup salad oil	1 cup hot water
2 medium green peppers, cut in julienne strips	2 medium tomatoes, peeled and cut in eighths

Preheat electric skillet to 350 degrees. Season meat with ginger, salt, and garlic salt. Heat **half** the oil in skillet; add meat and brown quickly on all sides. Remove meat. Add remaining oil; heat. Add peppers, celery and green onion; cook just until tender - about 5 minutes. Lower heat to about 250 degrees. Combine cornstarch and soy sauce; stir in water. Add mixture to skillet. Cook and stir until mixture thickens and boils. Add meat and tomatoes; heat through for approximately 5 minutes. Serve with hot rice. Very easy, fast and colourful. *Makes 4 servings.*

Danish Steak Deluxe

4 lean beef sirloin steaks, about 1/3 pound each
1 tsp. Dijon-style mustard
4 thin slices cooked ham
4 thin slices Samsoe or Tybo cheese
1/3 cup flour
1 tsp. salt
1/2 tsp. pepper
1 egg, slightly beaten
2/3 cup bread crumbs
1/3 cup butter
sliced lemon, sliced tomato and
    parsley sprigs for garnish

Pound each steak to about 4 x 7-inches and 1/3-inch thick. Spread with mustard. Top each steak with a slice of ham and slice of cheese (be sure to cut ham and cheese slices smaller than the steak). Fold steak over to enclose ham and cheese; secure with skewers. Season flour with salt and pepper. Have flour, beaten egg and bread crumbs in three shallow dishes. Dip each steak on both sides, first in flour, then in egg and finally in bread crumbs. Heat butter in large frying pan until light brown. Saute steaks about 4 minutes on each side or until golden brown. Remove skewers. Garnish with lemon and tomato slices and parsley sprigs to serve. *Makes 4 servings.*

Swiss Steak

1 flank steak (approx. 2 pounds); 1 can tomatoes (14 ounce); 3 tablespoons fat; 1 medium-sized onion, finely chopped; 1 cup water; 1/4 teaspoon pepper; 1 teaspoon salt; 1/2 cup sifted flour.

Sprinkle a little water over steak. Sift flour into large bowl or onto large plate, then put steak into flour and press as much flour into the steak as you can. Put the fat into a large frying pan and when sizzling hot put the floured steak in. Brown the steak thoroughly on both sides. The steak can either be cooked on top of the stove or in the oven; whichever way you cook it the pot or baking pan should have a lid. Grease the pot or baking pan with a little fat and transfer the browned steak to it. Now put the cup of water into the frying pan the steak was browned in, and let the water boil while you run a fork over the pan to loosen up any of the steak juices and flour that may be sticking to the pan. Then pour the boiling water from the frying pan over the steak, add the onion, tomatoes, salt and pepper. Bring to a boil, reduce heat, cover the pan or pot with a lid, and allow to simmer for 2 hours. If cooked in the oven, cover the baking pan and bake in a slow oven (300–325 degrees F.) for 2 hours or until tender.

Sensational Pepper Steak

1 1/2 lbs. round steak, 1/2" thick, cut diagonally into thin slices, 1/4 cup salad oil, salt and pepper to taste, 1 clove garlic, peeled, 1 medium onion, finely chopped, 3 green peppers, cut into 1" chunks, 2 stalks celery, thinly sliced on the bias, 1 cup boiling water with 1 beef bouillon cube dissolved in it, 2 tbsp. cornstarch, 3 tbsp. water, 2 tsp. soy sauce, hot parslied rice, tomato wedges and lemon slices, for garnish, if desired.

Prepare meat. In skillet, heat oil. Add salt, pepper and garlic clove. Brown meat over high heat, stirring frequently until desired doneness. Remove meat from skillet. Keep warm. Discard garlic. In same oil cook onion until transparent; add green pepper, celery and water with bouillon cube. Cook, covered, until vegetables are tender-crisp. Combine cornstarch, water and soy; blend to make smooth paste. Slowly add to vegetable mixture. Stir until thickened. Return meat to skillet. Heat through. Serve immediately over hot parslied rice. Garnish with tomato wedges and lemon slices, if desired. *Makes 4 servings.*

Flank Steak Marinade

2/3 cup oil	2 cloves garlic, crushed (or 1/4 tsp. garlic powder)
1/3 cup soya sauce	
1/4 cup red wine	1-1/2 tsp. salt
2 tbsp. lemon juice	1/2 tsp. pepper
2 tbsp. Worcestershire sauce	1-1/2 tsp. parsley
2 tbsp. minced dried onion	flank steak
1 tbsp. dry mustard	

Combine all ingredients (except steak) thoroughly. Place steak in shallow pan and cover with marinade. Marinate steak overnight in refrigerator (or if at room temperature, for several hours). To cook meat, remove steak from marinade; pat dry with paper towels. Broil meat to medium rare. To serve, cut meat in thin slices diagonally across grain.

Note: This marinade is also great for use in barbecuing flank steaks.

Saucy Spaghetti and Meatballs

Sauce

3 tbsp. salad oil	2 cups water
1 medium onion, chopped	1-1/2 tsp. dried
1 large clove garlic,	oregano, crushed
crushed	1-1/2 tsp. salt
1 tin (28 oz.) tomatoes,	to taste
undrained - crush and	1 tsp. sugar
break up tomatoes	1/2 tsp. pepper
2 tins (5-1/2 oz.)	or to taste
tomato paste	1 bay leaf

Meatballs

4 slices bread	1 tsp. salt
1/2 cup water	or to taste
2 eggs	1/4 tsp. dried
1 lb. ground beef	oregano, crushed
1/4 cup grated	2 tbsp. salad oil
Parmesan cheese	hot, cooked spaghetti
2 tbsp. chopped parsley	extra grated
	Parmesan cheese

To make sauce, in skillet, in 3 tbsp. hot oil, cook onion and garlic until tender but not browned. Stir in tomatoes, tomato paste, 2 cups water 1-1/2 tsp. oregano, 1-1/2 tsp. salt, sugar, pepper and bay leaf. Simmer, uncovered, 30 minutes stirring occasionally. Remove bay leaf. Meanwhile, prepare meatballs.

Soak bread in 1/2 cup water for several minutes. Add eggs, mixing well. Combine with ground beef, Parmesan cheese, parsley, 1 tsp. salt and 1/4 tsp. oregano. Form mixture into small balls (approximately 24). Brown slowly in 2 tbsp. hot oil. Add meatballs to prepared sauce. Simmer, loosely covered for 30 minutes. Serve over hot cooked spaghetti; sprinkle with extra grated Parmesan cheese. *Makes 6 servings.*

Ground Beef Ring

1½ lbs. ground lean beef, 1 c. shredded carrot, 1½ tbsp. prepared horseradish, 1 (1½ oz.) pkg. dehydrated onion soup mix, 1¼ c. quick-cooking rolled oats, 1 egg, slightly beaten, 2/3 c. (1 small can) evaporated milk, ¾ tsp. salt, 1/8 tsp. pepper.

Butter a 4½ c. ring mold. Preheat oven to 350 F.

Turn meat into a bowl and break up with a fork. Add and mix in carrot, horseradish, onion soup mix, rolled oats, egg, evaporated milk, salt and pepper. Turn into prepared mold and pack lightly. Bake in preheated oven 40 to 45 minutes. To serve, unmold and fill center with mixed vegetables. Makes 6 servings.

Cabbage Rolls with Franks

8 to 10 large cabbage leaves; 1½ cups cooked or leftover rice; 1/2 cup shredded Cheddar cheese; 1/4 cup chopped onion; 1/4 cup reconstituted nonfat dry milk (OR fluid milk); 1/2 tsp paprika; 1/4 tsp salt; 1/2 lb. frankfurters; 1 (7½ oz) can tomato sauce; 1/2 cup water; 1 tbsp brown sugar; 1 tbsp prepared mustard; 1/2 tsp chili powder.

Place cabbage leaves (heavy center vein of leaf may be cut out about 2 inches) in boiling water just until limp, 3 minutes; drain. Blend together cooked rice, cheese, onion, milk, paprika and salt. Mix well. Cut frankfurters in half crosswise. In the center of each cabbage leaf, place 3 to 4 tbsp of the rice mixture; top with frank half. Fold in sides of each leaf and roll ends over meat-rice mixture, fasten with toothpicks. In a skillet, combine tomato sauce, water, brown sugar, mustard and chili powder. Place cabbage rolls in sauce. Simmer, covered, for 30 minutes, basting often. *Serves 4 or 5.*

Eastern Style Meatballs

1 lb. ground beef, 1 small onion, finely chopped, 1/4 cup uncooked long grain rice, 1 egg, 2 slices bread, torn in pieces, 4 tbsp. soy sauce, 1 can condensed tomato soup, 1 cup water, 1 tbsp. soy sauce.

Blend beef, onion, rice, egg, bread and 4 tbsp. soy sauce. Shape into 20 meatballs, In large frying pan blend tomato soup, water and 1 tbsp. soy sauce. Arrange meatballs, side by side, in soup mixture. Cover and simmer 1 hour, or until rice is cooked. Makes 4 servings.

Hungarian Goulash

1-1/2 lbs. beef round steak,	1/8 tsp. pepper
cut in 1/2-inch cubes	1/8 tsp. thyme
approximately 2 tbsp. salad oil	1-3/4 cups tinned tomatoes
(add more if necessary)	and their liquid
1 medium onion, chopped	1 bay leaf
1 large clove garlic, crushed	1/2 cup sour cream
2 tbsp. all-purpose flour	hot cooked noodles
3/4 tsp. paprika	chopped parsley for garnish,
3/4 tsp. salt or to taste	if desired

In skillet, brown meat in hot salad oil. Reduce heat. Add onion and garlic. Cook until onion is tender but not browned. Blend in flour. Stir in paprika, salt, pepper, thyme, tomatoes and bay leaf until seasonings are well distributed. Cover and simmer, for approximately 1 hour, or until meat is tender, stirring occasionally. Stir fairly frequently during last part of cooking time. Just before serving, blend in sour cream. Do not boil. Serve over hot cooked noodles. Garnish with chopped parsley, if desired. *Makes 4 servings.*

For even-sized meatballs, place meat mixture into a rectangle, then cut into squares of equal size, according to the size of meatballs desired. Roll each square into a ball.

Parisian Ground Steak

2-1/2 lbs. lean ground beef
salt and pepper
2/3 cup crumbled Roquefort
 or bleu cheese
1 tbsp. finely chopped
 green onion

1/4 cup butter
1/2 lb. mushrooms, sliced
1 tbsp. chopped parsley
1-1/4 cups dry red wine

Season ground beef lightly with salt and pepper to taste. Mix, handling lightly. Divide mixture into 12 balls; flatten. Combine Roquefort cheese and green onions. Spread mixture evenly over 6 patties. Place remaining 6 patties over cheese-topped patties; seal edges. In skillet, melt 2 tbsp. butter. Add mushrooms; saute until tender; remove mushrooms with slotted spoon, leaving juices in skillet. Add remaining butter to skillet. Brown stuffed meat patties well on both sides. Return mushrooms to skillet. Add parsley and wine. Simmer, uncovered, for 5 minutes or until done, basting constantly. Serve immediately. *Makes 6 servings.*

Beef-a-roni

1 lb. ground beef
1 large onion, chopped
3 stalks celery, sliced on bias
1/2 green pepper, slivered
1 large clove garlic, crushed
1 tin (28 oz.) tomatoes
2 tsp. chopped parsley
salt and pepper to taste

2 tsp. Worcestershire sauce
 (or to taste)
3 cups hot cooked elbow
 macaroni, well drained
1 cup shredded sharp
 cheddar cheese
1/4 cup grated Parmesan cheese

In large skillet, saute ground beef, onion, celery and green pepper until meat is no longer pink and vegetables are tender but not browned, (if meat is very lean, add a small amount of oil to prevent sticking). Add garlic and undrained tomatoes. Crush tomatoes with a fork. Add parsley, salt, pepper and Worcestershire sauce. Stir to distribute seasonings. Cover; allow to simmer for 5 minutes. Add hot, cooked and well drained macaroni; add cheddar cheese and Parmesan cheese. Stir to combine well. Cover; allow to simmer 10 to 12 minutes longer or until Beef-a-roni is piping hot and cheese has melted. Serve immediately. This dish re-heats very well. *Makes 6 servings.*

No Peek Stew

1-1/2 to 2 lbs. stewing beef
1/2 package dehydrated
 onion soup mix
1 tin (10 oz.)
 cream of mushroom soup

1 tin (10 oz.) mushrooms,
 undrained
1/2 cup Burgundy wine

Place meat in casserole; sprinkle with dry onion soup; cover with mushroom soup and mushrooms. Pour wine over all. Cover. Bake in 250 degree F. oven for 3 to 4 hours or until done. Do not peek during cooking time. *Makes 4 to 6 servings.*

Beef Stew

2 lbs. beef stewing meat
1 tin (28 oz.) tomatoes
3 tbsp. minute tapioca
salt and pepper to taste
2 carrots, peeled and sliced

2 onions, sliced
1 slice bread, broken into bits
1-1/2 cups frozen peas, cooked
 (hot)
seasoned mashed potatoes (hot)

In large casserole dish, place meat, tomatoes, tapioca, salt, pepper, carrots, onions and bread. Cook, covered, in 250 degree F. oven for 4 hours. To serve, place seasoned mashed potatoes (hot) on top of stew. In centre of dish mound hot cooked peas. Serve immediately. *Makes 4 to 6 servings.*

Cooking Canada's beef

Five Star Chili

1 lb ground beef
1 clove garlic, crushed
1 1/2 cups sliced onions,
 separated into rings
1 cup celery, cut on bias
1 green pepper, cut in
 1-inch squares
1 [28 oz.] can tomatoes,
 crushed and undrained
1 [7 1/2 oz.] can
 tomato sauce
1 tsp. salt
 [or to taste]

1/4 tsp. finely ground
 black pepper
1 to 3 tbsp. chili
 powder [according to
 preference]
1 1/2 tbsp. vinegar
2 tsp. Worcestershire
 sauce
2 [14 oz.] cans
 red kidney beans,
 well-drained

Heat large skillet; cook ground beef (if beef is very lean, add small amount of oil when cooking to avoid sticking), garlic, onions, celery, and green pepper. Crumble beef with fork or potato masher. Cook until meat is no longer pink and vegetables are tender but not browned. Reduce heat to simmer; add tomatoes and juice, tomato sauce, salt, pepper, chili powder, vinegar, and Worcestershire sauce. Stir to combine seasonings well. Allow mixture to simmer approx. 1 1/2 hours. Add kidney beans. Stir.

Simmer 30 minutes longer. Serve piping hot with cole slaw and - hot buttered buns. Makes 6 servings. **Note:** Freezes well. Makes a tasty "leftover" meal.

Lasagna

1-1/2 lb. ground beef; 1 clove garlic, minced; 1 medium onion, chopped; 1 tin (19 oz.) tomatoes; 1 tin (5-1/2 oz.) tomato paste; salt and pepper to taste; 1/2 tsp. oregano; 1 egg, slightly beaten; 1 lb. cottage cheese; 8 oz. lasagna noodles, cooked; 1 lb. Swiss cheese, thinly sliced; 1/2 cup grated Parmesan cheese.

Saute ground beef, garlic and onion in skillet until beef is crumbly and onion soft but not brown. Add tomatoes, tomato paste, salt, pepper and oregano. Cover and simmer gently for 20 minutes. Combine egg and cottage cheese. In 10 x 17 x 2 inch (or similar size) baking dish place several tablespoons of sauce, then 1/2 of each of the noodles, cottage cheese mixture, meat mixture and Swiss cheese.

Repeat layers with other half of ingredients ending with Swiss cheese and topping with Parmesan cheese. Bake at 350 degrees F. for approximately 35 minutes; allow to set for 10 minutes before serving. *Makes 10 servings.*

If using a very lean ground beef, add a little cooking oil.

Mere's Burgundy Oxtails and Glazed Onions

2 large oxtails, cut into 2-inch sections	a bouquet garni composed of 1 bay leaf and parsley sprigs tied with a string
1/4 cup oil	dash thyme
4 medium onions, finely chopped	salt and pepper to taste
1/2 cup red burgundy	18 small onions, peeled
1 cup well seasoned beef broth	6 tbsp. butter
1 tin (5-1/2 oz.) tomato paste	2 tsp. sugar

In large skillet or Dutch oven, brown oxtails on all sides in oil; pour off excess fat. Add finely chopped onions, burgundy, beef broth, tomato paste, bouquet garni, thyme and season to taste with salt and pepper. Cook mixture 3 to 3-1/2 hours at low temperature. Before serving, glaze the small onions, in separate skillet; melt butter; stir in sugar. Add onions and cook turning frequently to glaze nicely. Serve oxtails and sauce surrounded with small glazed onions.

Oriental Dinner

2 tbsp. oil	1/4" slices, separated into rings
2 cups beef [or poultry breasts], cut in 1/4" julienne strips	2 cups carrots, cut on the bias 1/4" thick
meat tenderizer [for less expensive beef cuts —chuck, shoulder]	1 beef boullion cube
2 cups turnips cut in 1/4" julienne strips	1/2 cup hot vegetable water
2 cups celery cut on the bias	1 1/2 tbsp. cornstarch
1 large onion cut into	1/4 cup vegetable water, cooled
	1 tbsp. soy sauce
	1 tsp. ground ginger [optional]

In skillet or wok, heat oil to almost smoking. Cut beef into strips; sprinkle inexpensive cuts of beef with tenderizer according to manufacturer's directions. Stir-fry meat until almost cooked.

Remove to warm platter. Keep warm. In large kettle or dutch oven, heat 10 to 12 cups of salted water to boiling point. Blanch turnips, celery, onion and carrots for 2 to 4 minutes (depending on age and size of vegetables) or until almost tender. Remove vegetables with sieve or slotted spoon (save vegetable water); shake well to remove moisture. Add a little more oil to drippings in pan if necessary. Stir-fry vegetables until each vegetable is lightly coated with drippings (colour of vegetables is vibrant). In a small bowl dissolve beef boullion cube in one half cup of hot vegetable water. Add to vegetables in skillet; mix well. Sprinkle meat with ginger if desired. Return meat to skillet toss with vegetables.

Cover; steam 4 to 5 minutes or until vegetables are tender crisp. Mix cornstarch with cooled vegetable water; add soy sauce. When vegetables are cooked, stir cornstarch mixture into meat-vegetable mixture; stir until liquid is thickened and sauce is bubbly. Correct seasoning by adding more soy sauce if desired. Serve with bowls of hot steaming rice and extra soy sauce. Makes 4 to 6 large servings.

Stuffed Green Peppers

6 green peppers; 1/2 to 3/4 lb. hamburger; 1 can kidney beans; 1 medium size onion, grated; 1/2 cup grated cheddar cheese; 1 beaten egg; 1 crushed wheat biscuit; salt to taste; pepper to taste; 1-1/2 tsp. chili powder; 1-1/2 tsp. cumin seed.

Remove seeds from green peppers and boil in salted water for approximately 10 minutes. Drain. Mix hamburger, kidney beans, onion, cheese, egg, crushed shredded wheat biscuit, salt, pepper, chili powder and cumin seed. Stuff peppers with filling. Place in shallow pan. Add a small amount of water. Bake 45 minutes at 350 degrees F.

Round Steak Italiano

1-1/2 to 2 lbs. beef round steak, cut 1-inch thick	1 jar (16 oz.) spaghetti sauce
2 tbsp. all-purpose flour	1/2 cup water
1/8 tsp. garlic powder	1/2 tsp. sugar
2 tsp. salt or to taste	1/2 tsp. oregano, crushed
1/4 tsp. pepper	2 tsp. chopped parsley
3 tbsp. salad oil (more if necessary)	12 thin slices salami
	6 slices onion

Cut meat into 6 serving-size portions. In small bowl, combine flour, garlic powder, salt and pepper. Pound mixture into both sides of steak. Heat oil in skillet; brown meat well on both sides then place meat in single layer in shallow baking dish. In bowl, combine spaghetti sauce, water, sugar, oregano and parsley.

Place 2 pieces salami (overlapping slightly) and one slice onion on each piece of meat. Pour sauce carefully over and around meat. Cover and bake in 350 degree F. oven for 1 hour. Remove cover and continue cooking 20 to 30 minutes longer or until meat is tender. Delicious served with fluffy mashed potatoes or hot parslied spaghetti and a crisp green salad. *Makes 6 servings.*

Chili Pie

1 tbsp. oil	1 - 10 oz. can tomato soup
1 medium onion, chopped	1 - 14 oz. can tomatoes, broken up
1 lb. ground beef	1 - 14 oz. can red kidney beans
salt and pepper to taste	
1 dry chili pepper, crushed	

Heat oil in a Dutch oven; saute onion. Add ground beef and brown. Season to taste with salt and pepper; add chili pepper. Stir in tomato soup and tomatoes mix well. Add kidney beans stirring carefully to mix well, but not break the beans. Place in a 300 degree F. oven for 2 hours. Make pastry.

Pastry

3/4 cup all-purpose flour	1/2 tsp. salt
1/2 cup instant mashed potato flakes	4 tbsps. butter or margarine
1 1/2 tsp. baking powder	1/3 cup milk

Mix dry ingredients together. Cut in butter blending until butter is size of small peas. Add milk stirring just to combine. Roll out on a lightly floured board to the size of the Dutch oven. After the chili has baked for 2 hours remove from the oven and cover the chili with the pastry, seal at the edge and make a slit in the centre for steam. Bake in a 400 degree F. oven 10 - 15 minutes or until crust is golden.

Beef Wellington

1 lb. beef tenderloin (without head or tail); 1 to 2 tbsp. shallots (onions); clarified butter; 1/2 to 2/3 cup fresh mushrooms, finely chopped; 1/2 (2 oz.) tin goose liver paste; dash of cognac; finely chopped fresh parsley; 1 egg yolk; rosemary; salt and pepper; puff pastry; 1 beaten egg.

Season 1 lb. piece of beef tenderloin with salt and pepper (do not use head or tail of tenderloin). Sear on all sides of meat in a hot skillet until brown, keeping meat rare. Set aside. Fry finely chopped shallots in a little clarified butter until golden brown; add finely chopped fresh mushrooms. Simmer until all moisture is evaporated. Cool. Mix with goose liver paste, dash of cognac, finely chopped fresh parsley, raw egg yolk. Season with rosemary, salt and pepper. Spread this mixture around tenderloin. Roll out puff pastry approximately 1/3-inch thick, large enough to cover the tenderloin completely. Brush with beaten egg.

Place over meat with brushed surface towards the meat. Fold pastry around meat with the two ends and two sides tucked underneath. Brush top with beaten egg. Bake in 350°F oven until crust is golden brown. (meat will be medium rare). With a sharp knife, cut slices across the grain of the meat; do not break crust. *Serves 3.*

Poor Man's Beef Wellington

8 slices bacon; 1 lb. ground beef; 1 medium onion, finely chopped; 3 tbsp. minced parsley; 2 eggs; 1/3 cup chili sauce; salt and pepper to taste; dash of garlic powder; dash of Worcestershire sauce; 1/4 lb. sharp cheddar cheese, grated; Sour Cream Pastry; 1 tbsp. milk.

In skillet fry bacon until crisp; drain, crumble, set aside. Pour off bacon fat. In skillet cook ground beef, onion and parsley, until meat has lost its red colour and onion is transparent. Transfer meat to a medium size mixing bowl, draining off as much liquid as possible. Allow to cool 15 minutes. In a small mixing bowl beat together 1 whole egg and 1 egg white until combined; add bacon, chili sauce, salt, pepper, garlic powder, Worcestershire sauce and cheese; stir thoroughly into cooled meat mixture.

Roll pastry into a 14 to 15 inch circle. Place on a foil-lined 15 x 10 inch (approximately) jelly-roll pan. Pile meat mixture on one half of the pastry. Gently fold other half over and pinch edges together to seal, using a little water on fingers. In small bowl beat remaining egg yolk and milk; brush over pastry. With fork prick top of loaf in several places to allow steam to escape. Bake in a 375 degree F. oven about 40 minutes or until golden brown. Cut into wedges and serve. *Makes 6 servings.*

Ravioli

Noodle Dough

2 cups sifted flour	*3 tablespoons water*
3 eggs	*2 teaspoons salt*

Sift flour and salt into bowl. Make hollow in centre of flour and break into this the 3 eggs and the water. Mix together until the mixture is combined in a heavy, dry dough. It may be necessary to add just a little water, but be sure to add only enough to make the flour and egg mixture combine. On a floured surface knead the dough until it does not stick to either the surface or your hands. Roll the dough into a 24 inch x 18 inch rectangle. Cut the dough into 9 (2-inch) wide strips. Cut each 9 inch strip into 6 equal parts so that you have 54 pieces of dough measuring 2 inches x 4 inches. Place about 1 teaspoon of filling on one end of each 2 inch x 4 inch strip. Fold the other end over the filling and seal by pressing the 3 sides together with a fork.

Filling

1/2 pound hamburger	*1 clove garlic, minced*
1 cup grated cheddar cheese	*1/8 teaspoon oregano*
1 egg	*1/2 teaspoon salt*
1/4 cup cracker or bread crumbs	*1/8 teaspoon pepper*

Combine all ingredients and mix well.

Cook the filled dough in fast boiling water dropping a few at a time so that the water does not stop boiling. (Use a large pot so that you can cook all the ravioli at one time.) Allow to boil for about 20 minutes. Remove from water and place in a large Dutch Oven. Pour sauce over and cook in the oven at 375 degrees F. for about 1 1/2 to 2 hours.

Sauce

1 can tomatoes (28-ounce)	*1 envelope dry onion soup mix (1 1/2-ounce)*
1 can mushroom soup (10-ounce)	*2 soup cans water*

Mix together in a bowl all ingredients until well combined. Pour over ravioli in Dutch Oven.

Meatzza Pie

1 lb. ground beef
1 tin [6 oz.]
    evaporated milk
1/4 cup fine dry
    bread crumbs
1/2 cup chopped onion
1 clove garlic, crushed
    salt and pepper
    to taste

1 cup tinned tomatoes,
    very well drained
1 1/3 cups shredded
    sharp cheddar cheese
1 tsp. oregano
    anchovy fillets [soak
    in milk to remove
    excess saltiness]
    optional

In bowl, combine beef, milk, bread crumbs, onion, garlic, salt and pepper. Mix well, handling lightly. Press mixture evenly along sides and on bottom of 9 inch pie plate to form a "shell." Crimp edges (flour fingers). Spread well drained and crushed tomatoes over meat. Sprinkle with cheese and oregano. Garnish with anchovy fillets, if desired. Bake in 400 degree F. oven for 25 to 30 minutes, or until done. Makes 6 servings.

SAUCES and RELISHES

Make-Your-Own Curry Powder

½ cup tumeric, ½ cup coriander, 4 tbsp. black pepper, 2 tbsp. cardamon, 1 tbsp. red pepper, 1 tbsp. ginger, 1 tbsp. cumin, ½ tsp. cayenne pepper.

This formula is for a fairly hot curry mix which can be blended and put away in a screw top jar.

Mère's Curry Sauce

3 tbsp. butter
2 tbsp. arrowroot
2 tsp. mei yen powder
1 tbsp. onion powder

2 tbsp. curry powder
1/4 tsp. salt
2 cups rich milk

In saucepan, melt butter. Stir in arrowroot, mei yen, onion powder, curry powder and salt until well blended. Add milk. Stir constantly until mixture is thickened.

Note: Use amount of seasonings according to personal preference. This sauce is great served with seafood, chopped meat, hard-cooked eggs or sauteed mushrooms. Use to fill cooked small pastry shells, pate shells or serve over hot cooked rice.

Spicy Horseradish Sauce

4 oz. cream cheese
1 1/2 tsp. sugar
1 to 1 1/2 tbsp. prepared
    horseradish
1/2 tsp. Worcestershire
    sauce

2 tsp. lemon juice
1/4 cup whipping cream,
    whipped

Soften cream cheese; blend in sugar, horseradish, Worcestershire sauce, and lemon juice. Fold in whipped cream. Serve with ham, corned beef, cold roast beef, or cold cuts.

Did you know...

Woodward's have spices in bulk packages?

Chow Chow

4 qts. sliced green tomatoes, 1 qt. chopped onions, 3 or 4 sweet red peppers, finely chopped, 1 qt. chopped apples, 3 c. vinegar, 3 c. white sugar, 1 tbsp. turmeric, 1 c. whole mixed pickling spices.

Cover vegetables with salt and ice water; let set overnight. Drain thoroughly. Add apples, vinegar, sugar, turmeric and spices in a bag. Bring to a boil; simmer 45 minutes. Remove spice bag. Pour mixture into hot, sterilized jars. Seal.

Blue Cheese Sauce

2 tbsp. butter, 2 tbsp. all-purpose flour, 1 chicken bouillon cube, 1 cup milk, ¼ cup dairy sour cream, ¼ cup crumbled blue cheese.

In a saucepan, melt butter; then blend in flour, add bouillon cube, and milk all at once. Cook stirring constantly until mixture is thick and bubbly. Remove from heat; stir in sour cream and blue cheese. Heat through but DO NOT BOIL. Serve with baked potatoes or green vegetables. Makes 1¼ cups.

Chili Sauce

24 large red-ripe tomatoes; 8 large onions, chopped; 6 green peppers, chopped; 2 cups vinegar; 1 tbsp. salt; 1 tsp. cinnamon; 1 tsp. cloves; 1 tsp. ginger; 1 tbsp. celery seed; 1 tsp. crushed red pepper; 1 tsp. dry mustard; 3 cups sugar.

Peel, core and chop tomatoes; combine with remaining ingredients. Gently boil, uncovered, 4 hours or until sauce is thickened, stirring frequently to prevent sticking. Pour into hot sterilized jars, leaving 1/4-inch head space. Seal. *Makes about 6½ pints.*

Freezer Tomato Sauce

3 tbsp. salad oil
4 medium onions, chopped
2 large garlic cloves, crushed
4 tins (28 oz.) tomatoes
4 tins (5 1/2 oz.) tomato paste
3/4 cup chopped parsley

1 lb. mushrooms, sliced
3 tbsp. sugar
1 tbsp. oregano
3 tbsp. salt
pepper to taste
2 bay leaves

In large saucepan, over medium heat, heat oil. Cook onions and garlic until tender but not browned. Add remaining ingredients; bring to a boil. Reduce heat to low; cover and simmer 2 hours. Remove and discard bay leaves. Place sauce into 1 pint freezer containers, leaving at least 1 inch head space. Cover and refrigerate until well chilled. Label and freeze. *Yields approximately 8 pints sauce.*

Marinated Beef Teriyaki

2/3 cup soy sauce	1 clove garlic,
1/4 cup dry sherry	crushed
2 tbsp. sugar	2 lbs. beef sirloin steak,
1/2 to 1 tsp.	1/2-inch thick, cut into
ground ginger	serving-size portions

In screw-top jar, combine soy sauce, sherry, sugar, ginger and garlic. Shake vigorously. Place steak in shallow dish; cover with soy mixture. Marinate at room temperature for approximately 30 minutes, turning meat several times. To cook, drain meat well, reserving marinade. Broil 3 inches from heat for 5 to 7 minutes on each side; baste with marinade several times while cooking. *Makes 6 to 8 servings.*

Teriyaki Beef Kabobs

1 beef top-round steak,	3 tbsp. soy sauce
approximately 2 lbs.,	1 clove garlic, minced
cut about 1-inch thick	1/8 tsp. ginger
1/4 cup brown sugar	1 small pineapple,
2 tbsp. lemon juice	cut into 1-inch chunks
1 tbsp. salad oil	hot, cooked rice

Trim excess fat from meat; cut into 1-inch chunks. In medium bowl, combine brown sugar, lemon juice, salad oil, soy sauce, garlic and ginger. Add meat cubes. Cover and refrigerate at least 4 hours, stirring meat frequently. Just before cooking, thread meat and pineapple chunks alternately on 12-inch metal skewers. Broil Kabobs for 12 to 18 minutes, or until desired degree of doneness, basting occasionally with marinade and turning once. Serve Teriyaki Beef Kabobs over hot, cooked rice and with a crisp green salad. *Makes 6 servings.*

Sukiyaki

1 lb. sirloin steak	2 large onions, thinly sliced
2 tbsp. salad oil	and separated into rings
1/2 cup beef broth	1 can bamboo shoots
1/3 cup soy sauce	(8-1/2 oz.), drained
2 tbsp. sugar	3 cups spinach,
1 bunch green onions, washed,	washed and trimmed
trimmed and cut	hot cooked rice
in 1-inch lengths	extra soy sauce for seasoning,
1/2 lb. mushrooms, thinly sliced	if desired
3 stalks celery, sliced on the bias	

Cut steak across the grain 1/4-inch thick; slice to approximately 2-inch long pieces. In large skillet or wok, brown prepared steak quickly in oil. Push meat to 1 section of skillet. In bowl, combine broth, soy sauce and sugar; stir to combine. Pour into skillet. In separate sections, place prepared green onion, mushrooms, celery, onion rings and bamboo shoots. Leave a good-sized section for spinach. Do not stir. Cover skillet. Simmer 8 to 10 minutes. Turn top vegetables in their own section. Add spinach in reserved section; simmer 5 minutes longer or until spinach is cooked. Serve over hot, cooked rice. Pass extra soy sauce, if desired. This dish looks very attractive served at the table in cooking utensil. *Makes 4 servings.*

Spicy Carbonated Marinade for Beef Steaks

1 medium onion, chopped	1/2 cup salad oil
1 clove garlic, crushed	7 ounces carbonated
1 tbsp. soy sauce	lemon-lime beverage
2 tsp. ground pepper or to taste	beef steaks
1 tsp. salt or to taste	

In bowl, stir onion and garlic with soy sauce, ground pepper and salt. Mix in oil then lemon-lime beverage. Stir thoroughly. Pour marinade over steaks in a shallow pan. Cover pan; refrigerate for several hours. To grill steaks, drain well, reserving marinade. Cook steaks over coals (or under broiler); brush occasionally with reserved marinade. *Yields approximately 2 cups marinade.*

English Mixed Grill

This recipe is very large. If desired, the steaks can be omitted.

3 veal kidneys	1 tbsp. vinegar
3 cups water	1 tsp. salt

Butter Sauce

1/2 cup butter or margarine	1 tsp. salt
2 tbsp. lemon juice	1/8 tsp. pepper
2 tbsp. finely chopped parsley	

Crumb Topping

2 tbsp. butter	1/4 tsp. dried basil leaves
or margarine, melted	1/4 tsp. dried rosemary leaves
1/3 cup soft bread crumbs	

Also:

12 slices bacon	6 club steaks,
6 link sausages	(approximately 2 1/2 lbs.)
6 loin lamb chops, 1 inch thick	instant meat tenderizer
(approximately 2 1/2 lbs.)	watercress or parsley sprigs
3 medium tomatoes, halved	for garnish

Rinse kidneys. Place in medium saucepan with water, vinegar and 1 tsp. salt; bring to boiling. Lower heat and simmer covered, 10 minutes, drain. Split lengthwise. Refrigerate, covered, until ready to use. Make Butter Sauce. In small saucepan, melt 1/2 cup butter. Add lemon juice, parsley, salt and pepper. Set aside.

Make Crumb Topping. In small bowl, combine 2 tbsp. melted butter, bread crumbs, basil and rosemary. Set aside. Pan-fry bacon in large skillet. Drain, one slice at a time, and immediately roll up and fasten with toothpick, to form curl. Place sausages in large skillet. Cover with cold water; bring to boiling over moderate heat. Drain; then saute; turning sausages occasionally until nicely browned. Meanwhile, arrange lamb chops on rack in broiler pan. Brush well with some of Butter Sauce. Broil 6 inches from heat 12 minutes. Turn chops. Arrange tomatoes, cut side up, on broiler rack. Brush chops and tomatoes with butter sauce. Broil 12 minutes longer or until chops are cooked. Meanwhile (optional) sprinkle steaks with meat tenderizer according to package directions. When sausages are brown; remove and keep warm. Discard drippings in skillet. Heat skillet; add steaks and cook over high heat 3 to 5 minutes. Brush with Butter Sauce; turn, brush again with sauce and cook 3 to 5 minutes longer, or until done as desired. Keep warm. Remove chops to serving platter. Keep warm. Divide Crumb Topping evenly over tomatoes. Arrange kidneys, cut side up, on broiler rack. Brush with Butter Sauce and broil tomatoes and kidneys 1 to 2 minutes longer, or just until crumbs are golden. Arrange bacon curls, sausages, steaks and tomatoes on platter with chops and kidneys. Garnish with watercress or parsley sprigs, if desired. *Makes 6 extra large servings.*

Ways With Liver

Remove membrane and veins from 1 pound calves liver, ⅜ to ½ inch thick. Cook in any of the methods mentioned below. (Makes 4 servings.)

Panfried: Cover slices of liver with seasoned all-purpose flour; brown quickly on one side in ¼ cup hot shortening *or bacon fat* (about 1 minute); turn over and cook other side 2 to 3 minutes. Do not overcook.

Braised: Cover liver slices in ¼ cup all-purpose flour, seasoned with salt and pepper; Quickly brown on both sides in 3 to 4 tablespoons hot shortening. Reduce heat. Dissolve 1 beef bouillon cube in ½ cup boiling water; add to skillet with 1 thinly sliced medium onion. Cook over low heat 15 to 20 minutes.

Broiled: Cover liver slices in 2 tbsp melted butter OR French salad dressing. Broil 3 inches from heat for 3 minutes. Turn and top with bacon slices; broil 3 minutes longer; turn bacon once.

French Fried: Cut liver in ½-inch wide strips. Let stand in ½ cup French salad dressing for 30 minutes; drain. Dip in 1 beaten egg, then roll in 1 cup salted cracker crumbs. Fry in deep hot fat (360F) about 2 minutes. Drain.

Kidney With Wine Sauce

2 lbs. beef kidneys; 1 (10 oz) can condensed beef broth; 1/2 cup chopped onion; 1 clove garlic, minced; 1/2 tsp salt; 1 cup coarsely chopped carrot; 1 cup coarsely chopped celery; 2 tbsp dry red wine; 2 tbsp cold water; 2 tbsp all-purpose flour; hot cooked rice.

Remove membranes and hard parts from kidneys; cut meat into 1-inch pieces. In a saucepan, mix together kidney, beef broth, onion, garlic and salt. Cover tightly; cook slowly 1½ hours. Add carrots and celery; cook until tender, about 25 minutes longer. Blend together wine, water and flour until smooth. Stir into kidney mixture. Cook, stirring, until thickened and bubbly. Serve over hot cooked rice. *Makes 4 to 6 servings.*

Cooking Canada's Veal

Wiener Schnitzel a la Holstein

1 1/2 lbs. veal cutlets	*2 tbsp. salad oil*
or round steak,	*2 tbsp. butter*
cut 1/2-inch thick	*2 tsp. lemon juice*
1/4 cup flour	*4 eggs*
salt and pepper	*2 tbsp. butter*
1 egg, beaten	*1 tbsp. water*
1 tbsp. milk	*lemon wedges and parsley*
1 cup fine dry bread crumbs	*for garnish, if desired*

Cut meat into 4 pieces; pound 1/4 to 1/8-inch thick with meat mallet or side of saucer. Make small slashes around edge of meat to prevent curling. Coat meat on both sides with flour; season with salt and pepper. Combine beaten egg and milk. Dip floured cutlets into egg mixture; then into bread crumbs. In hot skillet, place oil, 2 tbsp. butter and lemon juice. Cook meat 2 to 3 minutes on each side or until tender and golden brown. Meanwhile, in separate skillet, fry eggs in 2 tbsp. butter until whites are set. Add water. Cover and cook until eggs are done. Place 1 egg on each cooked veal cutlet. Garnish with lemon wedges and parsley, if desired. *Makes 4 servings.*

Veal Parmesan

This dish is also delicious made with turkey scallops.

1 1/2 lb. veal scallops, pounded thin, 2 eggs, 3/4 cup fine dry bread crumbs, 1/2 cup grated Parmesan cheese, 2 tbsp. salad oil, 1/2 lb. brick cheese or mozzarella cheese, thinly sliced, 1 recipe Tomato Sauce (below).

Pound veal until fairly thin. Slightly beat 2 eggs. In small bowl combine bread crumbs and 1/4 cup Parmesan cheese. Dip veal in egg then in bread crumb mixture. In large skillet, cook veal in heated salad oil until browned slightly on both sides. Remove veal from skillet and place in a 9 x 9 x 2 inch baking dish (or similar size). Cover with 2/3 of tomato sauce; cover this with brick or mozzarella cheese; top this with remaining tomato sauce and sprinkle remaining 1/4 cup Parmesan cheese over all. Bake in 350 degree F. oven for approximately 30 minutes or until bubbly. *Makes 5 to 6 servings.*

Tomato Sauce

1 tbsp. salad oil, 2 medium onions, finely diced, 3 cloves garlic, crushed, 1 tin (14 oz.) tomatoes, 1 tin (7 1/2 oz.) tomato sauce, 1 tbsp. parsley, 1/2 tsp. salt, 1/2 tsp. oregano, 1/4 tsp. thyme, pepper to taste.

Heat oil in skillet. Saute onion and garlic till tender but not browned. Add tomatoes (break them up), tomato sauce, parsley, salt, oregano, thyme and pepper. Simmer approximately 20 minutes.

Veal Cutlets Sicilian Style

	2 cloves garlic minced
	or 1/4 tsp. garlic
3 large, very thin cut-	*powder*
lets, cut across the	*chopped parsley*
leg	*1 tsp. basil*
1/4 lb. Hungarian or	*5 hard cooked eggs*
Italian salami	*Mazola oil*
1/2 lb. Mortadella	*salt and pepper*
1/4 lb. prosciutto or	*5 slices bacon*
ham	*2 c. tomato sauce*
1/4 c. fine bread crumbs	*1 whole garlic clove*

Leave veal slices in the whole piece, but remove bone. Pound until very thin. Arrange slices side by side (the long sides adjoining) so they overlap slightly. Pound overlapping areas thoroughly to press them together. On veal arrange rows of overlapping slices of salami. Top with rows of sliced mortadella and finally the sliced prosciutto or cooked ham.

Sprinkle surface with fine bread crumbs, garlic, chopped parsley and basil. Down the centre place a row of shelled hard cooked eggs. Sprinkle with oil, salt and pepper. Roll up very carefully as for jelly roll, making certain that the eggs stay in place in centre. Place roll in baking dish and top with bacon. Over all pour tomato sauce with clove of garlic added. Bake in 350 degree oven for one hour. Makes 8 servings.

NOTE: This dish is exceptionally good sliced cold the next day . . ideal for a buffet.

Cooking Canada's Pork

Tomato Oriental Cutlets

¼ inch slices of pork from boneless Boston butt (approx. 2 slices per serving), salt, pepper, M.S.G., milk, ¾ cup fine breadcrumbs, ¾ cup all purpose flour, oil.

Place pork cutlets in shallow dish and pour boiling water over them. Drain on paper towelling. Season pork with salt, pepper and M.S.G. Dip cutlets into milk, then into mixture of breadcrumbs and flour. Pan fry in a generous amount of oil at moderate heat till cutlets are dark brown. Drain on towelling. Serve on shredded lettuce on a platter. Serves 6.

SAUCE

1 onion, cut in half lengthwise; finely sliced to form ½ rings, 1 tbsp. oil, ¾ cup juice from canned tomatoes, 3 to 4 canned tomatoes, quartered, 2 tbsp. ketchup, 1 tbsp. H.P. sauce, 1 to 2 tbsp. honey or brown sugar, 1 tbsp. cornstarch AND ¼ cup cold water (mixed together), stir-fried broccoli or asparagus.

Brown onion in 1 tbsp. oil. Add tomato and other ingredients, bring to boil. Pour over pork. Garnish with stir-fried broccoli or asparagus.

Curried Meatballs

Meatballs

1 lb. lean hamburger; 1/2 lb. lean minced pork; 1 medium onion, finely chopped; salt and pepper to taste; 1/2 tsp. curry powder; 1 egg, beaten; 2 tbsp. oil.

Mix hamburger, pork, onion, salt, pepper, egg and curry powder until meats and spices are well blended. Handle lightly. Form into balls. Brown in heavy skillet which has been lightly coated with oil. Remove from skillet and drain.

Sauce

1 medium onion, chopped; 1 stalk celery, chopped; 3 tbsp. flour; 1 tbsp. curry powder; salt and pepper to taste; 1 tsp. sugar; 1-1/2 tbsp. lemon juice; 1 tin beef consomme; 3 tbsp. butter; 2 medium size apples, peeled and diced.

Cook onion and celery in butter until soft but not browned. Stir in flour, curry powder, salt and pepper. Gradually stir in consomme and lemon juice. Add sugar and apples. Allow to simmer gently for 1 hour. Add meat balls and simmer another 15 minutes or until meat is heated through.

NOTE: Additional curry may be added if a stronger curry flavour is desired. If a more delicate flavour of curry is wanted then omit curry from the meatballs and cut the amount of curry powder in the sauce to 1/2 tablespoon.

Country Style Ribs

5 lbs. country style spareribs; 1 lemon, unpeeled, thinly sliced; 1 onion, thinly sliced; Barbecue Sauce.

In shallow roasting pan, place ribs with meaty–side up. Don't crowd. Bake in 450°F oven for 45 minutes. Reduce heat to 350°F; remove ribs from oven. Drain off fat. Top each rib with a slice of lemon and onion. Pour 3 cups of Barbecue Sauce over top ribs. Return to 350°F oven and bake 1½ hrs., or until tender. Baste every 20 minutes, adding remaining sauce as needed.

BARBECUE SAUCE

2 tbsp. sugar; 1 tbsp. salt; 1/4 tsp. pepper; 2¼ tsp. chili powder; 1½ tsp. curry powder; 1/4 tsp. garlic salt; 1 tbsp. grated lemon peel; 6 tbsp. lemon juice; 6 tbsp. Worcestershire sauce; 2¼ cups catsup; 3¾ cups water.

Combine all ingredients; blend well. Bring mixture to a boil and quickly simmer, uncovered, over medium heat for 20 minutes or until reduced to about 4 cups of sauce. (This sauce is excellent for basting in rotisserie cooking; cook 5 to 10 minutes longer as sauce should be thick enough to cling to poultry or meat.)

Apple Stuffed Pork Chops

Sauce:

1 onion, finely chopped; 1/2 tsp. garlic powder; 1-1/2 tsp. oil; 1 tsp. flour; 1 small can stewed tomatoes; 1 cup hot water with 1 oxo or bovril cube dissolved in it; 1-1/2 tbsp. vinegar; 1-1/2 tbsp. Worcestershire sauce; 1 tbsp. sugar; 2 tsp. lemon juice; 1 tbsp. tomato chutney; 1-1/2 tbsp. parsley flakes; salt and pepper to taste.

Make sauce first. In skillet heat oil and brown onion. Add garlic powder and flour; stir constantly until a light brown. Add stewed tomatoes and stock. Heat mixture to boiling; add vinegar, Worcestershire sauce, sugar, lemon juice, tomato chutney, parsley flakes, salt and pepper. Simmer for 10 - 15 minutes; stir frequently to avoid burning. Strain, if desired, allow to cool.

4 large pork chops suitable for making a pocket for stuffing; 3 tbsp. butter; 1 medium onion, finely chopped; 1 stalk celery, finely diced; 1 apple, large, peeled and diced; 2 cups bread crumbs; 1/4 cup parsley flakes; 1 tbsp. lemon juice; salt and pepper to taste; 1 small egg, beaten; oil; dash of poultry seasoning.

Stuffing:

Melt butter in frying pan. Cook onion and celery until soft but not browned. Add bread crumbs, apple, parsley flakes, lemon juice, salt, pepper and poultry seasoning. Bind mixture with egg. If too dry add a little milk.

Chops:

Make a cut in centre of side of each chop. Be sure to use a sharp knife and not to pierce the top or bottom of the chop. Insert stuffing into pocket of chop. Sew or skewer slit. Dry chops and brown in oil. Place stuffed chops in casserole dish. Brush chops generously with barbecue sauce. Bake at 350 degrees F. for 1 hour, covered. Baste at frequent intervals. Heat remaining barbecue sauce and use as gravy. Serve with mashed potatoes and crisp salad. Remove thread or skewer before serving. An excellent company dish. Economical but very special.

Pork Chop Dinner

3 cups uncooked noodles; 1 (16 oz) can tomatoes; 1 tsp. salt; 6 pork rib chops, cut 1/2-inch thick; 1/2 cup chopped onion; 1 beef bouillon cube; 1/2 tsp. dried thyme leaves, crushed; dash pepper.

Cook noodles in boiling, salted water just until tender; drain. Drain tomatoes, reserving 3/4 cup juice. Quarter tomatoes and stir into noodles, adding 1/2 tsp. salt. Place noodles in an 11¾x7½x1¾-inch baking dish. Trim fat from chops, and cook in skillet until 2 tbsp. fat accumulates. Discard trimmings. Brown chop in hot fat. Place chops over noodles; sprinkle with onion. In small saucepan combine reserved tomato juice, bouillon cube, remaining salt, thyme and pepper. Cook, stirring, until bouillon cube is dissolved. Pour mixture over chops. Bake, covered, in 350°F oven about 1¼ hrs., until meat is tender. *Makes 6 servings.*

Barbecued Pork Chops

1 tin (7-1/2 oz.) tomato sauce	2 tbsp. brown sugar
1/2 cup water	3/4 cup diced celery
1 tsp. mustard	4 lean pork chops, well trimmed
1/2 tsp. Tabasco or to taste	(use fat trimmings to
1 tsp. Worcestershire sauce	brown chops)

In saucepan, mix and heat tomato sauce, water, mustard, tabasco, Worcestershire sauce, brown sugar and celery. In skillet, brown pork chops in trimmed fat; remove any excess fat from chops. Place chops in casserole. Cover with hot barbeque sauce. Cover. Bake in 350 degree oven for 1 to 1-1/4 hours. Remove cover; then bake 15 minutes longer. *Makes 4 servings.*

Pork Chops Dijonnaise

2 tbsp. butter or margarine	1 chicken bouillion cube dissolved in
4 loin or rib pork chops, approximately 1-inch thick	1˙ cup boiling water OR 1 cup chicken broth
salt and black pepper to taste	2 tbsp. brown sauce or tinned beef gravy
2 tbsp. chopped green onions	2 to 3 tsp. Dijon-style mustard
1 tbsp. flour	2 tbsp. chopped sweet pickle

In skillet, heat 1 tbsp. butter. Brown chops on both sides. Season meat with salt and pepper to taste. Reduce heat; cover and simmer over low heat until chops are cooked and tender, turning occasionally. When chops are completely cooked, remove to a warm serving platter. Keep warm. Pour off all but 1 tbsp. drippings in skillet. Add green onions. Cook, stirring constantly, until green onions are wilted. Sprinkle with flour and stir. Dissolve chicken bouillion cube in boiling water (or use hot chicken broth). Gradually add broth and brown sauce (or beef gravy) to flour mixture in skillet; stir constantly with a wire whisk until sauce is blended and smooth. Return chops to sauce in skillet and cook about 5 minutes per side. Return chops to warm serving platter. To sauce, add mustard, sweet pickle and remaining 1 tbsp. butter. Stir to distribute ingredients. Do not boil. Spoon sauce over chops and serve piping hot. *Makes 4 servings.*

Onion Glazed Pork Chops

6 to 8 (1/2-inch to 3/4-inch) pork chops; 2 (1 1/2-ounce) packages of dehydrated onion soup mix; 2 cups water.

Combine soup mix and water in saucepan. Heat to boiling and simmer for 3 minutes. Place pork chops in 1 layer in baking dish. Pour soup mixture evenly over pork chops and bake at 375 degrees F. for 1½ to 2 hours or until pork chops are tender and glazed.

Lime Tenderloin Bits

1-1/2 lbs. pork tenderloin; 1/3 cup lime marmalade; 1/4 cup soy sauce; 1/4 cup cider vinegar; 3 tbsp. brown sugar.

Cut tenderloin into generous bite-size pieces. Place in foil-lined broiler pan or shallow roasting pan. Bake at 450 degrees F. for approximately 30 to 40 minutes or till browned. Remove meat from oven and drain fat, if any, from pan. Reduce oven temperature to 350 degrees F. Combine **thoroughly** lime marmalade, soy sauce, vinegar and brown sugar. Pour sauce over meat and return to oven. Bake 30 minutes longer, or until tender, basting occasionally. Serve over fluffy rice. If desired, spoon sauce over meat before serving. *Makes 4 servings.* Orange marmalade can be substituted for lime marmalade.

Baked Pork Chops with Beans

4 large loin or thin shoulder pork chops	1/2 tsp. dry mustard
salt and pepper	1 tin (10 oz.) lima beans, drained
1 medium onion, chopped	1 tin (14 oz.) red kidney beans, drained
1/2 cup chopped green pepper	1/3 cup chili sauce
1 clove garlic, crushed	1 tbsp. vinegar
2 tsp. brown sugar	

Trim excess fat from chops. In skillet, melt trimmed fat. Brown chops on both sides; season with salt and pepper. Remove chops; drain. To drippings in skillet, add onion, green pepper and garlic. Saute until tender but not browned. Add brown sugar, dry mustard, lima beans, kidney beans, chili sauce and vinegar. Mix well. Pour bean mixture into 2 qt. casserole. Arrange chops on top. Cover. Bake in 350 degree F. oven 45 minutes or until beans are piping hot and chops are tender. *Makes 4 servings.*

Pork of Three Kingdoms

(Sweet 'n' Sour Pork with Pineapple)

3 lbs. pork (pork tenderloin or boneless Boston Butt) cut into squares 1-inch square, ½ inch thick, 1 tsp. sugar, ¼ c. rye, gin, saki or other spirits (optional), ¼ tsp. salt, 1 tsp. salad oil, 2 eggs, ¾ c. cornstarch, ¼ c. flour, peanut oil for frying.

Marinate pork squares in a mixture of sugar, spirits, salt and 1 tsp. oil for at least 2 hours for the tenderloin, or for 4 hours for Boston Butt. Beat eggs and dip pork first in eggs, then in the cornstarch and the flour which have been mixed together. Deep fry in peanut oil at 400 F. (to make crispy, cook in oil for 1 or 2 minutes, remove from oil to let steam escape and let oil return to temperature, put back into oil and fry till golden). Drain on paper towels. Serves 6.

Sauce: ½ c. white vinegar, ½ c. water, 7/8 c. sugar, 1 tsp. ketchup, ½ c. drained, crushed pineapple, ¼ lemon, skin and pulp included, ½ c. drained lichees (optional), ¼ c. water, 2 tbsp. cornstarch.

In a blender, blend crushed pineapple and lemon. Mix vinegar and water. Bring to a boil. Add sugar, ketchup and pineapple-lemon mixture. Bring to a boil. Thicken with cornstarch which has been blended with water. Add pineapple chunks and lichees. Serve with fluffy rice.

Oriental Style Pork Chops

6 pork chops, cut 3/4-inch thick	1/2 cup finely chopped onion
1/2 cup water	1/8 to 1/4 tsp. ground ginger
1/4 cup soy sauce	1/8 tsp. pepper
3 tbsp. honey	1-1/2 tbsp. toasted sesame seeds
1 tbsp. catsup	

Trim any excess fat from chops. Place trimmings in skillet; melt, (if necessary, add a small amount of salad oil). Brown pork chops on both sides. Place in a 13 x 9 x 2-inch baking dish. In bowl, combine water, soy sauce, honey, catsup, chopped onion, ginger and pepper. Stir well. Pour mixture over chops in baking dish. Sprinkle sesame seeds over meat. Cover. Bake in 350 degree F. oven for approximately 45 minutes or until chops are tender. *Makes 6 servings.*

Spicy Spareribs

2 lbs. country style spareribs	salt to taste
1 clove garlic, crushed	dash tabasco
1 tbsp. lemon juice	3 tbsp. vinegar
pepper	1/8 tsp. dry mustard
1 cup catsup	dash chili powder
3 tbsp. Worcestershire sauce	1 cup water
	1 lemon, thinly sliced

Place spareribs in single layer in large casserole dish. Top with crushed garlic, lemon juice and pepper. Bake in 450 degree F. oven for 35 to 40 minutes or until nicely browned. Drain off fat. Meanwhile combine catsup, Worcestershire sauce, salt, tabasco, vinegar, dry mustard, chili powder and water. Stir to blend well. Pour sauce over spareribs. Reduce oven to 350 Degrees F. and bake for 1 hour, basting occasionally. Remove spareribs from oven; top with lemon slices. Baste lemon slices. Bake 15 minutes longer or until spareribs are tender. *Makes 4 servings.*

Orange Pork Chop

6 pork chops, 3/4-inch thick
salt and pepper
milk
flour
3 tbsp. salad oil
1/2 tsp. allspice
1 tsp. freshly squeezed lemon juice
1 tsp. grated orange peel
3/4 cup freshly squeezed orange juice
2 tbsp. honey
2 oranges, peeled and sliced
   into 6 thick cartwheels

Season chops well on both sides with salt and pepper. Dip in milk; coat lightly with flour. Brown chops well in hot salad oil. Transfer chops to casserole. Combine allspice, lemon juice, orange peel and juice. Pour mixture over chops. Cover and bake in 350 degree F. oven for 35 minutes. Remove cover; bake 10 minutes longer. Remove chops to warm serving platter. Blend honey into pan drippings; add orange slices and glaze 1 or 2 moments on each side. Top each chop with orange slice; pour over remaining sauce. Serve at once. *Makes 4 to 6 servings.*

Sausage Combo

8 slices bacon, diced in 1 inch pieces	2 tsp. Worcestershire sauce
1 lb. sausages, cut in 1 inch pieces	1 clove garlic crushed
1 1/2 tbsp. reserved drippings	1/2 tsp. dry mustard
2/3 cup thinly sliced celery	salt and pepper to taste
1 large onion, chopped	1 large tomato, coarsely chopped
1 small green pepper, chopped	1 1/2 cups sharp cheddar cheese, grated
1 tin (28 oz.) baked beans	

In skillet, saute bacon and sausages until cooked. In reserved drippings, saute celery, onion and green pepper until tender but not browned. In large casserole dish combine beans, Worcestershire sauce, garlic, dry mustard, salt and pepper. Stir to combine. Add cooked bacon, sausages, celery, onion, green pepper and chopped tomato. Combine well. Place in 375 degree F. oven, covered, for 25 to 30 minutes. Remove dish from oven; sprinkle with cheese; return to oven uncovered and cook 10 to 15 minutes longer or until cheese is melted and beans are piping hot. *Makes 4 servings.*

PORK AND LAMB FREEZING GUIDE

Freeze good quality lamb and pork. Careful slaughtering and handling of meat is essential.

Prepare meats in cuts of size and weight to suit family needs.

Package roasts individually in freezer wrappings or bags.

Cover sharp bones with pieces of crumpled aluminum foil, to prevent puncturing of wrappings.

For easy separation of frozen chops, steaks, or ground meat patties, place folded pieces of waxed paper between layers of meat.

Use freezer cartons for bulk minced meat, stew meat, leftover meat, stews, gravy, etc.

Good packaging of meats is necessary for successful results. Containers and wraps must be moisture-vapour proof, odourless, and tasteless.

Seal prepared packages well; label, date, and freeze.

Maximum storage times at 0°F are:

Bacon	1 to 2 months
Lamb chops	4 to 5 months
Lamb roasts	6 to 8 months
Pork chops	3 to 4 months
Pork (cured, smoked)	1 to 2 months
Pork roasts	4 to 5 months
Sausages, wieners	2 to 3 weeks

For best results when thawing lamb and pork, allow meat to defrost in original wrapper in refrigerator (approx. 12 hours per lb.). Meats will require 2 to 3 hours per lb. at room temperature.

Never refreeze meat that has **completely** thawed. It may be cooked and then refrozen. Meat that has only partly thawed can be refrozen.

Meats that have been thawed will cook more quickly and brown more readily than when cooked from frozen state.

For accurate results when cooking partially thawed roasts, use a meat thermometer.

BEEF FREEZING GUIDE

Use only good quality beef.

Careful slaughtering and handling is especially important when meat is to be frozen.
Prepare (or have butcher prepare) meat in cuts of weight and size to suit family needs.

Use recommended freezer wrap only. Re-wrap all pre-packaged meat. Trim bones and excess fat to save on freezer space. Package carefuly to exclude as much air as possible.

Pad sharp bones with crumbled aluminum foil to avoid puncturing outer wrap.

Separate prepared patties, steaks, etc. by placing folded pieces of freezer wrapping or waxed paper between layers for easy separation while still frozen.

Slice cooked leftover meat; cover with gravy or make into a casserole to retain flavour and natural moisture.

Label each package (meat type and cut, date, and weight).

WHEN USING FROZEN MEAT

For shortest and most even cooking time (especially with large cuts) let meat thaw before cooking, steaks will brown more easily; breading (of liver, etc.) will adhere better.

Thaw in freezer wrapping to prevent evaporation of juices.

Thawing times vary (according to shape, size, and thickness of meat). For each lb. allow approx. 12 hours in refrigerator or 2 to 3 hours at room temperature.

Never refreeze meat that has been completely thawed. Always cook promptly to avoid spoilage, then refreeze, if desired.

If meat has been completely thawed, cook as for fresh meat.

If cooking meat unthawed, the cooking time must be increased. The length of extra time is dependent upon size, shape, and thickness of meat. For roasts, **increase** cooking time by approx. half that required for fresh roasts (for accuracy, use a meat thermometer). To pan-fry or broil steaks, allow approx. twice the length of cooking time as for fresh steaks.

Cooking
Canada's Lamb

Spring Lamb Stew

2 lbs. lamb stewing
    meat
3 tbsp. flour
3 tbsp. oil [or more
    if needed]
1 clove garlic, crushed
2 medium onions, sliced
1/3 cup soy sauce
    pepper to taste
    water

4 medium potatoes,
    peeled & cubed
1 turnip, peeled
    & cubed
4 carrots, peeled and
    sliced on bias
3 stalks celery,
    sliced on bias
2 tbsp. parsley, chopped

Coat lamb with flour. In large Dutch oven heat oil, add garlic and meat; brown on all sides. Add onions; saute gently. Add soy sauce, pepper and enough water to cover meat. Cover pan tightly, bring to boil; lower heat; simmer 1 hour. Add potatoes, turnip, carrots, celery and parsley. Simmer 45 to 60 minutes longer or until meat and vegetables are tender. Add more water if necessary during cooking process. Thicken gravy if desired. Makes 6 servings.

Curried Lamb with Condiments

2 lb. boneless lamb, cut
    into 1-inch cubes
1/4 cup all-purpose flour
2 tbsp. salad oil
1 clove garlic, crushed
1 1/2 cups sliced onions
    [separated into rings]
1 to 3 tbsp. curry powder
    [according to taste]
1 1/2 tsp. salt [or to taste]

dash freshly ground
    black pepper
1/8 tsp. cinnamon
1/8 tsp. ground cloves
1 beef boullion cube
    [dissolved in 1 cup
    boiling water]
1/2 cup tomato juice
1 tbsp. snipped pasley
    hot cooked rice
    condiments

Coat prepared meat with flour. In large skillet, heat oil. Cook lamb until well-browned on all sides (add more oil, if necessary). Remove meat from skillet; set aside. Into drippings, place garlic, onion rings and curry powder. Cook over medium heat, stirring frequently until onions are tender, but not browned. Return meat to skillet; add salt, pepper, cinnamon, cloves and beef bouliion cube dissolved in boiling water. Reduce heat to low. Cover tightly; simmer for 1 3/4 to 2 hours or until meat is tender stirring occasionally. Stir in tomato juice and parsley; heat through. Serve on fluffy hot cooked rice and condiments. Makes 4 servings.

Condiments: Set out several condiments attractively in separate small dishes, from list below. Sprinkle over curried lamb. Fried onion rings; crisp, crumbled bacon; chopped hard-cooked eggs; tomato wedges; chopped apple; raisins, salted peanuts; flaked coconut; chutney; chopped green onion; diced green pepper.

Lazy Day Lamb Pilaf

1 lb. boneless lamb stew meat, 1 tbsp. butter or margarine, 3 tbsp. Teriyaki sauce, 2 tbsp. onion soup mix, 4 tbsp. Teriyaki sauce, 2 cups boiling water, 3/4 cup uncooked long-grain rice, 2 tbsp. chopped pimiento.

Cut lamb into 3/4-inch cubes. Melt butter in frying pan with cover. Add lamb and brown. Stir in 3 tbsp. Teriyaki sauce, cover and simmer 50 to 60 minutes, or until lamb is tender (stir occasionally and if, necessary, add some water). Meanwhile, combine soup mix, boiling water, rice, 4 tbsp. Teriyaki sauce and pimiento in 1½ qt. baking dish. Cover and bake in 350°F oven 25 to 30 minutes, or until rice is tender. Remove lamb from sauce and add to hot rice. Toss gently to combine. Makes 4 servings.

Savory Lamb Steaks and Vegetable Dinner

4 lamb steaks, cut 1/2"
    thick
1/2 tsp. dried rosemary, crushed
    salt and pepper [to taste]
1 to 2 tbsp. salad oil
1 medium onion, thinly sliced,
    separated into rings
1 clove garlic, crushed

1/4 cup chopped green pepper
1/2 cup sliced mushrooms
1 large tomato, cut in thin
    wedges
1/3 cup dry white wine
1 tbsp. all-purpose flour
2 tbsp. cold water

Remove any excess fat from steaks; season with rosemary n' salt and pepper to taste. In large skillet, heat oil; brown steaks on both sides. Add onion, garlic and green pepper. Cook until tender, but not not browned. Reduce heat to low. Add mushrooms, tomato wedges and wine. Cook, covered, 35 minutes. Uncover; cook over low heat 10 minutes longer or until meat is tender. Remove meat and vegetables to warmed serving platter, leaving juices in skillet. Keep warm. Measure juices; add enough water to yield 1 cup liquid. Return juices to skillet. In cup blend 1 tbsp. flour and 2 tbsp. water; stir into meat juices. Cook, stirring constantly, until mixture thickens and bubbles. Serve gravy with lamb steaks and vegetables. Makes 4 servings.

Ways With Leftover Ham

Cooking Canada's

Ham and Bacon

There are many varied and delicious ways to use leftover ham:

Hot Appetizers — *Slice leftover ham paper-thin; heat and serve with thin raw onion rings in small hot biscuits. Great for a late night snack!*

Chef's Salad — *Toss thin strips of ham with Swiss cheese and crisp salad greens. Top with your favourite dressing.*

Ham Spread or Dip — *Blend ground ham with cream cheese. Season with garlic salt and Worcestershire sauce. Thin if for dip with pickle juice. If using as a spread, spread over crisp crackers and top with olives, cheese, hard cooked egg slices or whatever is in your fridge that is suitable.*

Ham and Melon — *Arrange thinly sliced pieces of ham on melon wedges or other fruit to serve with breakfast, lunch or as first course at dinner.*

Hearty Soups — *Use ham bone to make split pea, bean or lentil soup. Serve with crusty bread and carrot and celery sticks and you have a nourishing and hearty supper.*

Satisfying Sandwich — *Tuck a thin slice of ham into a turkey or chicken sandwich. Also delicious broiled with cheese on toast. Ham lends itself to cucumber and tomato sandwiches as well. The varieties are endless.*

Omelet Filling — *Use finely chopped ham and minced green pepper or chopped green onion to fill an omelet.*

Bacon Rarebit

6 slices bacon; 1/2 cup chopped onion; 1/2 cup chopped celery; 1/4 cup flour; 1 cup milk; 1 (7½ oz) tin tomato sauce; 1 cup shredded sharp cheese; 1 tsp Worcestershire sauce; 6 English muffins, toasted and split.

Cook bacon until crisp; drain and set aside. Cook onion and celery until tender in about 5 or 6 tbsp of the bacon drippings. Blend in flour; add milk, tomato sauce. Cook, stirring until thickened. Add in cheese and Worcestershire sauce. Continue stirring until cheese melts. Spoon mixture over toasted English muffin halves; top with a bacon strip. *Makes 6 servings.*

Crispy Eggs and Bacon

6 slices bacon; 1/2 cup small croutons; 6 eggs; 1/3 cup milk or light cream.

Cook bacon until crisp, then drain and crumble coarsely. Save bacon drippings; measure 1 tbsp of drippings into frypan. Add croutons. Heat and stir until brown and crisp; remove. Add another 1 tbsp of drippings to pan. Slightly beat eggs, milk, 1/4 tsp salt and dash pepper together; pour into pan. Cook and stir until almost set; then gently stir in crumbled bacon and croutons. Cook until just set. *Makes 4 to 6 servings.*

Hearty Ham Soup

1 lb. package dried large white navy beans; 6 cups boiling water; 1 shank end fully cooked or cook before eating ham (about 3 lbs.); 4 cups shredded cabbage; 1 large onion, chopped; 1 green pepper, chopped; 2 cups thinly sliced carrots; 2 celery stalks, chopped; 1 minced garlic clove; 1 package pepperoni, sliced thin; 1 can tomatoes (14 oz.); 1½ tsp. salt; 1 tsp. pepper; 1 tsp. Worcestershire sauce; 1 tbsp. lemon juice; 2 tbsp. parsley; 1 cup macaroni; 6 cups water.

Put beans in a large bowl and pour boiling water over. Cover Allow to stand 1 hour. Trim fat from ham (several pieces) and melt in large soup kettle. Add cabbage, onion, carrots, celery, green pepper, and minced garlic. Simmer gently, frequently stirring, for approximately 15 to 20 minutes. Remove from heat and set aside. Pour beans and liquid into kettle (Not vegetables) add ham, sliced, pepperoni, tomatoes, salt, pepper, Worcestershire sauce, lemon juice and parsley.

Add 6 more cups water. Bring mixture to a boil; cover and simmer for 1½ hours. Remove ham from kettle and cut off excess fat. Dice ham. Place ham with vegetables that had been set aside. Mix both preparations together (vegetable and bean) and cook another 30 - 45 minutes or until beans are tender. Add macaroni and continue cooking another 15 minutes or until macaroni is tender. Sprinkle with more parsley or a slice of lemon when serving, if desired. Very good reheated. A meal in itself with French bread.

Party Ham with Orange Glaze

6 to 7 lb. rolled boneless ready-to-eat ham.

Slice ham into 1/4-inch thick slices, keeping ham together by running a long skewer through the center. Place ham in large shallow baking pan. Bake in 350°F oven, allowing 15 minutes per pound (or about 1½ hours). After 30 minutes' baking, spread top generously with Orange Glaze. Continue baking, and basting every 10 minutes with additional Orange Glaze; 1 hour longer, or until richly glazed. To serve, place ham with skewer still in place, on serving tray or platter.

Orange Glaze: Combine 1 (6 oz.) can frozen concentrated orange juice, 1/4 cup firmly packed brown sugar, 1/2 tsp. dry mustard, and 1 tsp. Worcestershire sauce in a small saucepan. Heat, stirring constantly, until sugar dissolves. Sufficient glaze for a 6 to 7 lb. ham.

Glazed Ham Slice with Cranberry Raisin Sauce

1 slice ready-to-eat ham (approximately 2 lbs. - 1 1/2 inches thick)	dash salt
whole cloves to stud (optional)	dash ground cloves
1/2 cup brown sugar	1 1/2 cups cranberry juice cocktail
2 tbsp. cornstarch	1/2 cup orange juice
	1/2 cup seedless raisins

Slash fat edge of ham at 2-inch intervals. If desired, insert whole cloves in fat. Place ham in shallow baking dish. Bake in 325 degree F. oven for 30 minutes. Meanwhile, make sauce. Mix sugar, cornstarch, salt and ground cloves. Add cranberry juice cocktail, orange juice and raisins. Cook, stirring constantly until mixture thickens and comes to a boil. Remove ham from oven. Spoon some of sauce over ham; bake 20 minutes longer or until glazed. Pass remaining sauce with the ham. *Makes 6 servings.*

Ham Glazes

Golden Glaze
In small bowl, combine well 1 cup light molasses and ½ cup prepared mustard. Brush on prepared ham for final hour of baking time. Baste with glaze. *Yields 1½ cups (enough glaze for a 10 to 15 lb. ham).*

Honey-Orange Glaze
In small bowl, combine well 1 cup brown sugar, ½ cup honey and ½ cup orange juice. Brush on prepared ham, during the last half hour of baking time. Baste with glaze. *Yields approximately 2 cups.*

Tutti-Frutti Glaze
In small bowl, combine 1 cup peach jam, ¼ cup frozen orange juice, ¼ cup brown sugar and 2 tbsp. flour. Spread glaze on prepared ham during the last 35 to 40 minutes of cooking time. Baste with glaze. *Yields approximately 1½ cups glaze.*

Cooking Canada's Ham

Ham is a great favourite during the festive season. As a rule of thumb for a party, count on a minimum of ¼ lb. for each serving of boneless ham and ½ lb. for the bone-in type. It is best to be generous with these allowances. Bake ham as the label directs or place ham, fat side up on rack in shallow roasting pan. Do not add water or cover. Insert meat thermometer. Bake in 325 degree F. oven. Approximate cooking times are as follows: (for a fully cooked ham).

Size of Ham	Minutes Per Pound	Total Time
Half, 6 to 8 lbs.	15 to 17 min. per lb.	2 to 2¼ hours
Whole, 12 to 14 lbs.	12 to 15 min. per lb.	3 to 3¼ hours
Round, Boneless Half, 8 lbs.	20 min. per lb.	2½ hours
Round, Boneless Whole, 12 to 14 lbs.	14 to 16 min. per lb.	3 to 3½ hours

The meat thermometer should read 130 degrees for all types of fully cooked ham.

Roughly half an hour before cooking time is up, (unless glazing recipe directs otherwise) remove ham from oven and pour fat drippings from pan. Score ham fat in diamonds. Cut only ¼ inch deep and approximately 1 inch apart. Stud with whole cloves. Spoon your favourite glaze or one from *above* over ham. Continue baking 30 minutes longer, basting at 10 minute intervals.

Mona says . . .

Be sure to wipe body cavity thoroughly before stuffing to avoid a soggy stuffing. Do not refreeze completely thawed poultry. Once fresh frozen poultry has been cooked it may be refrozen.

Always wash cutting board or work surface thoroughly with cold water and then scrub with hot water and soap after cutting raw poultry.

POULTRY FREEZING GUIDE

Never freeze stuffed poultry. Always store stuffing separately.

Truss before freezing to make carcass more compact, saving on storage space.

Prepare and package poultry ready for oven straight from freezer. Freeze giblets in separate package.

To eliminate air when packaging, place bird in freezer plastic bag; lower ¾ of way into **hot** water. The water will collapse the plastic firmly around the bird and expel the air. DO NOT let any water seep into the bag. Twist top of bag to make tight closure; secure.

When freezing whole chicken or pieces with freezer foil wrap, pad protruding or bony parts before wrapping.

Use drug store fold to wrap; gently press down to expel air. Seal by folding ends in tightly using freezer tape, if necessary.

Check the wrap of commercially frozen poultry. Rewrap if torn or ripped.

Cook thawed poultry immediately or keep refrigerated and cook within 24 hours.

Completely thaw whole birds for uniform cooking and best results. Cook same as fresh poultry allowing extra time for poultry that has not completely thawed.

It is easier to cut bird while only partially defrosted when cut-up pieces are required for specific recipes. Thaw whole poultry either one of two ways:

(1) Place unopened chicken (in freezer bag) in refrigerator on rack in shallow pan. When pliable, remove chicken from wrapper; wipe with clean damp cloth. Remove giblets and neck (if not frozen separately). Cover loosely with plastic wrap, wax paper or foil. Refrigerate until completely thawed; allow 5 hours per pound to thaw. Cook immediately.

(2) Place unopened chicken in shallow pan at room temperature (allow approximately 1 hour per pound at room temperature). Leave until partially thawed. Remove from wrapper; wipe chicken. Remove neck and giblets. Place on rack in shallow pan. Cover **loosely** with foil, plastic wrap or wax paper. Refrigerate until completely thawed.

DOMESTIC POULTRY AND OTHER BIRDS

Classes of Chicken

Classes of Chicken	Weight	How Much To Buy
Cornish Hens	up to 1 pound	1 bird per serving
Broiler-Fryers	1½ to 3½ pounds	¼ to ½ bird per serving
Roasters	over 3½ pounds	¾ to 1 pound per serving
Capons	up to 8 pounds	¾ to 1 pound per serving
Fowl (Stewing Chickens)	2½ to 6 pounds	½ to ¾ pound per serving

Roasting Times

To roast chicken cover loosely with tent of foil. Remove foil during last 30 to 40 minutes of cooking to brown bird.

Eviscerated Weight	Oven Temp.	Approx. Time Stuffed Birds
Up to 2½ lbs.	350°F.	35 min. per lb.
1½ to 2½ lbs.	325°F.	1¼ to 2 hours
2½ to 3½ lbs.	325°F.	2 to 3 hours
3½ to 4¾ lbs.	325°F.	3 to 3½ hours
4¾ to 6 lbs.	325°F.	3½ to 4 hours

Rock Cornish Hens

6 Rock Cornish Game hens
1 1/2 cups rice*
1 1/2 cup finely chopped celery
1/2 cup finely chopped mushrooms
3 Tbsp. butter or margarine
3/4 tsp. salt
3/4 cup sauterne or apple juice
1 tsp. sage or poultry seasoning.
*Cook rice according to package directions

Saute onions, celery and mushrooms in butter for 5 minutes or until golden. Combine vegetables with drained rice; add salt, sauterne and sage. Stuff 6 hens and truss. Place in shallow baking pan, brush with oil or melted butter. Roast, uncovered, in preheated oven at 400 degrees F. for 1 hour

Variations: Hens may be oiled sprinkled with paprika and seasoned salt. Cook on rotissiere for about 1 hour or until tested done, OR stuff hens lightly with bread stuffing. Baste during the last 15 minutes with a mixture of 1/4 cup corn syrup and 1/4 cup consomme.

Cornish Game Hens roasted to perfection are a practical dinner choice of homemakers cooking for one or two. These one pound birds are available from the freezer section at your food store.

Photo courtesy Markets Branch, British Columbia Ministry of Agriculture

Broiled Chicken

4 pieces chicken breasts; 4 tbsp. butter; 1 tbsp. parsley; 2 tbsp. parmesan cheese, grated (prepared); 1 tbsp. lemon juice; 1 tsp. paprika; salt and pepper to taste.

In small pan melt butter and add parsley, parmesan cheese, lemon juice, paprika, salt and pepper. Remove skin from chicken breasts. Place chicken meat side down on cookie sheet that has been covered with foil and lightly brush with oil. Brush bone side with marinade and place 6 to 7 inches from broiler. Cook approximately 10 minutes and then turn. Place remaining marinade on the meaty side liberally and broil approximately 10 to 15 minutes more.

Calcutta Chicken

1 (2½ to 3 lb.) ready-to-cook broiler-fryer chicken, cut-up, 1/3 cup all purpose flour, 1 tsp. paprika, ¼ cup butter or margarine, 1 medium onion, thinly sliced, 4 chicken bouillon cubes, 3½ cups boiling water, 1 cup uncooked long grain rice, ½ cup light raisins, ½ cup flaked coconut, ¼ cup coarsely chopped peanuts, 1 tsp. curry powder.

With a mixture of flour, 1 tsp. salt, dash pepper and paprika, coat chicken. Brown chicken in butter, in a skillet; remove. Also in skillet cook onion in remaining butter till tender but not brown. Dissolve bouillon cubes in boiling water; add to onions. Stir in remaining ingredients. Turn rice mixture into 12 x 7½ x 2 inch baking dish. Top with chicken. Bake covered at 350 F. about 1¼ hours or until rice is cooked and chicken is tender. Serves 4.

Chicken Kiev

Herb Butter
3/4 cup softened butter
2 tbsp. chopped parsley
1 tbsp. chopped chives
1/2 tsp. dried tarragon leaves
1 clove garlic, crushed
salt and pepper to taste

3 boned whole large chicken breasts, split and skinned
2 eggs, well beaten
1/3 cup flour
1 1/4 cups fine dry bread crumbs
salad oil or shortening for deep frying
lemon wedges and parsley sprigs for garnish, if desired

To make Herb Butter - in small bowl, thoroughly mix butter, parsley, chives, tarragon leaves and garlic. Season with salt and pepper to taste. Refrigerate until firm. Meanwhile, wash prepared chicken; dry well. To flatten chicken, place each half breast, smooth side down, on sheet of waxed paper; cover with second sheet. Using a mallet or side of saucer, pound chicken to approximately 1/4 inch thickness, being careful not to break the meat.

Divide hardened butter into 6 balls. Place butter ball in centre of each piece of chicken. Fold over 2 short ends, then the long ends, making sure no butter is showing. Fasten each piece with toothpicks or skewers. This is important to keep the herb butter inside during frying. Roll each chicken piece in flour. Dip each in eggs and then roll in crumbs, coating evenly. Refrigerate, covered, approximately 1 hour. In a Dutch oven or large heavy saucepan, slowly heat salad oil or shortening (3 inches deep) to 360 degrees F. on deep-frying thermometer. Add chicken pieces, 3 at a time. Fry, turning with tongs, until browned - approximately 5 minutes. Do not pierce chicken. Keep warm in 200 degree F. oven (no more) in pan lined with paper towels. Remove skewers or toothpicks carefully. Garnish with lemon wedges and parsley sprigs, if desired. *Makes 4 to 6 servings.*

Pick-Up Chicken Sticks

3 lbs. chicken wings (about 25); 1½ cup sifted all-purpose flour; 1 tbsp salt; 1 cup margarine or butter; 1/3 cup finely crushed toasted almonds; 1/2 tsp ground ginger.

Divide each chicken wing in half by cutting through joint with a sharp knife. Wash and drain on paper towels. Melt margarine in large shallow baking pan. Mix together flour, crushed almonds, salt and ginger in pie plate. Roll chicken pieces, one at a time, in butter letting excess drip back. Then roll in flour mixture to coat generously. Set aside on waxed paper until all is coated. Arrange, without touching, in a single layer in the pan which contained the margarine.

Bake in 350°F oven for 1 hour or until tender and golden on bottom. Brown under broiler for 3 to 5 minutes.

Tarragon Chicken Treat

½ lb. fresh mushrooms, sliced,
¼ cup butter,
salt and pepper to taste,
6 chicken breasts,
1 tsp. MSG,

½ tsp. tarragon,
1 cup dry white wine,
1 cup sour cream,
3 green onions, chopped,
tomato wedges for garnish.

Prepare mushrooms; in large Dutch oven saute mushrooms in 2 tbsp. butter until tender but not browned. Season with salt and pepper. Remove mushrooms with slotted spoon, leaving juices in pan. Add remaining butter to pan and saute chicken gently until golden on all sides. Sprinkle with MSG. Return mushrooms to Dutch oven; sprinkle with tarragon. Pour wine over chicken. Cover and simmer 45 minutes or until tender. Spoon sour cream into pan juices.

Heat gently. Do not allow to boil. Sprinkle with green onions and garnish with tomato wedges. Serve immediately. Delicious over hot, parslied noodles. *Makes 6 servings.*

Crunchy Chicken-nut Saute

2 whole chicken breasts boned, 1 tsp. sake or dry white wine, 1 tsp. grated fresh ginger root, 1 tbsp. cornstarch, 1 cup cashews or peanuts, 1 tbsp. salad oil, 2 tbsp. soy sauce, 2 tbsp. salad oil, 1 tbsp. sake, 1 tsp. sugar, 1/2 tsp. cornstarch, 1 tbsp. water.

Remove and discard skin from chicken. Cut meat into 1/2 inch cubes. Sprinkle 1 tsp. sake and ginger over chicken and coat with 1 tbsp. cornstarch. Saute nuts in 1 tbsp. oil until golden brown over low heat. Remove from pan and set aside. Heat remaining oil, add chicken and stir-fry about 5 minutes, or until chicken is cooked. Season with soy sauce, 1 tbsp. sake and sugar. Dissolve cornstarch in water; stir into chicken mixture and cook until sauce thickens. Remove from heat and stir in nuts. Makes 3 to 4 servings.

Crunchy Chicken

1 (10 oz.) can cream of mushroom soup; 3/4 cup milk; 1 tbsp. finely chopped onion; 1 tbsp. chopped parlsey; 2 lbs. chicken parts; 1 cup bread crumbs, finely crushed; 2 tbsp. melted butter or margarine.

Mix 1/3 cup soup, 1/4 cup milk, onion and parlsey. Dip chicken in soup mixture; then roll in bread crumbs. Place in shallow 12x8x2-inch baking dish. Drizzle butter over top chicken. Bake in 400°F. oven for 45 min. Mix remaining soup and milk together. Heat thoroughly, stirring occasionally. Serve over chicken. Makes 4 servings.

Napoleon's Chicken

1 frying chicken [3 to 3-1/2 lb.] cut in serving-size portions	1 cup chicken broth*
3 tbsp. olive oil	2 cloves garlic, crushed
1/4 cup butter	1 tbsp. chopped parsley
3/4 lb. mushrooms [slice if large]	4 slices white bread [crusts removed]
1/2 cup white wine	2 tbsp. butter
2 tomatoes, chopped [peel and seed tomatoes, if desired]	4 eggs salt and pepper
	1 tbsp. butter

In large skillet, saute chicken pieces in olive oil over medium heat until completely cooked and golden brown on all sides. Remove the white portions before dark meat so it will not be dry. When chicken pieces are fully cooked, remove from skillet; place on large warmed serving platter. Keep warm. Drain olive oil from skillet. Add 1/4 cup butter to pan; saute mushrooms until tender.

Remove mushrooms from pan with slotted spoon, leaving juices and butter in pan. Keep mushrooms warm. To pan juices, add wine. Simmer 1 minute. Add prepared tomatoes, chicken broth, garlic, and parsley. Simmer quickly to reduce. Keep tomato mixture warm. In another skillet, saute bread in 2 tbsp. butter until golden on both sides. Keep warm. Fry eggs in 1 tbsp. butter. Season with salt and pepper. Place eggs on fried bread. Spoon sauce over chicken. Arrange eggs on bread around chicken. Garnish with prepared mushrooms. Serve immediately. Makes 4 servings.

Note: Substitute 1 chicken boullion cube dissolved in 1 cup boiling water.

54

Snow Peas with Chicken

3 whole chicken breasts, skinned, sliced horizontally in 1/8-inch thick slices, then cut in 1-inch squares	1 can [8-1/2 oz.] bamboo shoots, drained
	1/2 cup water chestnuts, sliced
1/2 lb. snow peas [Ho Long Dow] tips and strings removed	3 tbsp. soy sauce
	1 tbsp. water
	2 tbsp. cornstarch
	1/2 tsp. sugar
1/2 cup green onions cut in 1" lengths	1/2 tsp. salt
	1/4 cup salad oil [or peanut oil]
1 cup sliced mushrooms	1/4 cup cashew nuts
	1 cup well-seasoned chicken broth

Prepare chicken, snow peas, green onions, mushrooms, bamboo shoots, and water chestnuts; arrange on tray. In small bowl, mix throrughly, soy sauce, water, cornstarch, sugar and salt. In wok or electric skillet over moderate heat, heat 1 tbsp. oil; saute, stirring constantly cashews, until lightly toasted (approx. 1 minute); remove from pan. Add remaining 3 tbsp. oil; heat. Add chicken; cook quickly. Add snow peas, green onions, and mushrooms; pour in broth; stir. Cover and simmer 2 minutes. Add bamboo shoots and water chestnuts. Stir in soy-cornstarch mixture to pan juices. Cook, stirring constantly, until sauce is thickened; simmer 1 minute. Sprinkle with prepared cashews. Serve immediately. Makes 6 servings.

Stan's Jamaican Chicken

3 to 4 pounds chicken, cut up; 1 tablespoon Worcestershire sauce; 1/2 teaspoon garlic powder; 2 tablespoons soy sauce; 1/2 teaspoon thyme; 1 tablespoon ketchup; salt and pepper to taste; 1½ teaspoons ginger powder; 1 egg; 1 tablespoon milk; 1 teaspoon soy sauce; 1½ cups (about) bread crumbs.

Combine Worcestershire sauce, garlic powder, 2 tablespoons soy sauce, thyme, ketchup, salt, pepper and ginger. Place chicken in a large bowl and pour mixture over. Cover and let marinate in fridge overnight, turning occasionally. Beat egg and milk together and add 1 teaspoon soy sauce. Dip marinated chicken in egg/milk/soy mixture and roll in bread crumbs. Fry in pan over moderate heat until done or place in a 375 degree F. oven for about 1 hour. Serves 6 to 8.

Kikko Broiled Chicken

1/4 cup soy sauce, 1/4 cup lemon juice, 1/2 tsp. onion powder, 1/4 tsp. tarragon leaves, crushed, 2 (approx. 2 lbs. each) broiler fryers, halved or quartered.

Combine soy sauce, lemon juice, onion powder and tarragon. Place chickens, skin side down, in broiler pan. Broil 5 to 7 inches from heat about 20 minutes. Brush with sauce, turn over and broil 20 minutes longer or until chicken is tender, brushing frequently with sauce. Makes 4 servings.

Chicken Stroganoff

1 broiler-fryer chicken
   [2-1/2 to 3 lbs.], cut up
   in serving size
   portions
   salt and pepper
1/4 cup butter
1 medium onion, chopped
1 cup sliced mushrooms
3 tbsp. flour
1/4 tsp. salt
1/4 tsp. thyme
 3 chicken boullion cubes
1 3/4 cups boiling water
1/2 pt. sour cream
   paprika
   chopped parsley
   hot cooked rice or
   noodles

Sprinkle chicken pieces with salt and pepper. In large skillet, melt butter; brown chicken on all sides. Cover skillet; cook chicken over low heat for 30 to 40 minutes or until tender, turning occasionally. Remove chicken from skillet; keep warm. Saute onions and mushrooms in pan drippings until tender but not browned. Remove from heat; blend in flour, 1/4 tsp. salt and thyme.

Dissolve bouillon cubes in boiling water; gradually add to flour mixture. Cook over medium heat, stirring constantly, until smoothly thickened. Stir in sour cream; heat gently. Do **not** boil. Pour one half of sauce over chicken. Sprinkle lightly with paprika and chopped parsley. Serve immediately with remaining sauce as gravy. Delicious with hot cooked rice or noodles. Makes 4 servings.

Chicken Veronique

1 broiler-fryer chicken
   [2 1/2 to 3 lbs.], cut up
   in serving-size
   portions
1 small lemon, halved
   salt [to taste]
1/3 cup butter[approx.]
1/3 cup sauterne
1 cup grapes [washed,
   halved; seeds removed]
   chopped parsley
   [optional]

Rub chicken pieces well with cut lemon; set lemon halves aside. Sprinkle salt over chicken. Allow to stand and dry on rack for 15 minutes. In skillet, melt butter, squeeze juice from retained lemon halves; add to butter. Brown chicken well on all sides. Reduce heat to simmer; add sauterne; spoon sauce over chicken. Cover; simmer for 35 to 40 minutes or until chicken is tender (spoon sauce over chicken occasionally). Several minutes before serving, add prepared grapes; heat thoroughly. Garnish with parsley, if desired. Serve immediately. Makes 4 servings.

Chicken Kabobs

2-1/2 to 3 lbs. chicken breasts
1 lb. chicken livers
1 bunch green onions
1 cup soy sauce

1/4 cup sugar
1 tbsp. salad oil
2 cloves garlic, crushed
1/2 tsp. ground ginger

Remove skins and bones from chicken breasts, keeping meat in one piece; cut into 1 inch squares. Cut livers into 1 inch pieces and onions into 1 inch lengths. Thread metal skewers each with a piece of chicken, piece of green onion (spear through side) and piece of chicken liver.

Blend together soy sauce, sugar, oil, garlic and ginger.

Country Good Chicken

3/4 cup sour cream, 1 tbsp. lemon juice, 1 tsp. salt, 1 tsp. paprika, 1/2 tsp. Worcestershire sauce, dash garlic powder, 1 broiler-fryer chicken (2-1/2 to 3 lbs.), cut up, 1 cup fine dry bread crumbs, 1/4 cup butter.

Preheat oven to 350 degrees F. Combine sour cream, lemon juice, salt, paprika, Worcestershire sauce and garlic powder. Dip chicken in mixture; roll in crumbs; place in broad, shallow baking dish. Dot with butter. Bake covered for 45 minutes. Remove cover and continue baking another 40 to 50 minutes or until chicken is golden brown and tender. Baste occasionally with pan drippings. Makes 4 to 5 servings.

Curry Chicken Breasts

3 large chicken breasts
   skinned & halved lengthwise
3/4 tsp. seasoned salt
   or to taste
paprika
1 chicken bouillon cube dissolved in 1 cup boiling water
1/4 cup sauterne
1/2 cup finely chopped onion
1/2 tsp. curry powder
   or to taste
dash pepper
1 cup sliced mushrooms
1 tbsp. butter or margarine
2 tbsp. all-purpose flour
1/4 cup cold water
2 to 3 tbsp. toasted
   slivered almonds
watercress

Sprinkle chicken with salt and paprika. Place in single layer in shallow baking dish. In bowl, combine chicken bouillon cube that has been dissolved in 1 cup boiling water, sauterne, onion, curry powder and pepper. Pour mixture over chicken. Cover with foil. Bake in 350 degree F. oven for 30 minutes. Uncover and continue cooking 45 minutes longer or until tender. Meanwhile, in skillet, saute mushrooms in butter until just tender. Set aside.

When chicken is tender, remove from baking dish to a warm serving platter. Keep warm. Strain juices; reserve for sauce. To make sauce, blend flour with 1/4 cup cold water in saucepan; slowly stir in pan juices. Cook and stir until sauce thickens; boil and stir several minutes. Add the sauteed mushrooms (with juices); heat through. Spoon over chicken breasts (reserving some sauce to pass). Sprinkle toasted, slivered almonds over top. Garnish with watercress. Makes 6 servings.

Place kabobs in large shallow baking pan; pour sauce over. Brush each kabob thoroughly with sauce. Marinate kabobs about 1 hour and remove; reserve marinade. Broil kabobs 5 inches below preheated broiler 3 minutes on each side; brushing with marinade after turning. Serve immediately. If desired for a main course, alternate ingredients several times on larger skewers.

Makes about 4 dozen kabob appetizers.

Cooking Canada's

Chicken

Chinese Pineapple Chicken

1 whole large
  chicken breast (bone
  and skin removed)
1 egg, beaten
1 tbsp. flour
1/2 tsp. salt
1 tsp. MSG
approximately 1/3
  cup salad oil
1 cup tomato juice
1 clove garlic,
  crushed
2/3 cup fresh or
  canned pineapple chunks
  (drain thoroughly,
  if using canned)

1/3 cup sliced celery
  (cut on the bias)
1/4 cup green
  pepper strips
1 tbsp. cornstarch
1/4 cup honey
1/2 tsp. ground ginger
  or to taste
1 tbsp. soy sauce
1 tbsp. sherry
hot cooked rice

Cut the meat into long slivers. In a bowl, combine egg, flour, salt and MSG. Roll chicken pieces in egg mixture to coat evenly. In large skillet, heat oil. Add prepared chicken. Cook, stirring constantly, over medium heat until chicken is lightly golden. Add tomato juice, garlic, pineapple chunks, celery and green pepper. Mix well. Cover and simmer 15 minutes. In bowl, combine thoroughly, cornstarch, honey, ginger, soy sauce and sherry. Pour over chicken mixture. Stir until sauce is creamy - approximately 2 minutes. Serve immediately over hot cooked rice. *Makes 4 servings.*

Chicken-Asparagus Stir-fry

3 whole chicken breasts
6 tbsp. salad oil
1/2 lb. asparagus
2/3 cup thinly sliced green onions
1 cup sliced mushrooms
2 chicken bouillon cubes
  dissolved in 1-1/3 cups boiling
  OR 1-1/3 cups well seasoned
  chicken broth

Jean's Favourite Chicken

5 chicken breasts, halved, 1 pkg. dry onion soup mix, 1 can mushroom soup, 1/2 pt. sour cream, salt and pepper, 1 1/2 tsp. dill seed, 2 tsp. lemon juice, butter, dash of paprika.

Place chicken breasts in buttered baking dish, skin side up. Rub with butter, sprinkle with salt, pepper and a dash of paprika. Combine rest of ingredients and pour over chicken. Bake in 350 F. oven for approximately 1 1/4 hours or until done.

Mandarin Chicken

4 whole large chicken
  breasts, skinned, boned
  and halved lengtnwise
6 green onions
1 stalk celery
1 large green pepper
2 tbsp. cooking oil
1-3/4 cups well
  seasoned chicken broth
1 tin (10 oz.) mandarin
  oranges, drained,
  reserving syrup

1/4 cup soy sauce
1/4 cup packed
  brown sugar
3 tbsp. vinegar
1/3 cup cornstarch
dash ground ginger
hot, cooked rice
extra soy sauce

Cut chicken breasts in 1/2-inch wide strips; bias-cut green onions in 1/2-inch lengths; bias cut celery; thinly cut green pepper into julienne strips. Heat oil in wok or skillet over medium-high heat; stir fry chicken strips until golden brown. Add green onions, celery, green pepper and broth. Bring mixture to a boil. Cover, reduce heat. Simmer 2 to 3 minutes. Meanwhile, drain mandarin oranges; set oranges aside. In bowl combine reserved orange syrup, soy sauce, brown sugar and vinegar; blend mixture slowly into cornstarch until smooth. Add ginger. Add soy sauce mixture to chicken mixture; cook, stirring constantly, until mixture is thickened and bubbly. Add reserved mandarin orange segments. Cover and heat through. Serve Mandarin Chicken immediately over hot, cooked rice with extra soy sauce, if desired. *Makes 8 servings.*

1/2 tsp. ground ginger
salt to taste
1 tsp. sugar
1/4 tsp. garlic powder
2 tbsp. cornstarch
1/3 cup dry sherry
3 tbsp. soy sauce
hot cooked rice

Skin and bone chicken breasts; cut in half. Slice chicken into thin strips approximately 1-1/2 inches long. In large skillet or wok heat 4 tbsp. oil. Add chicken; stir-fry until chicken is lightly golden. Remove from skillet; keep warm. Reserve drippings. Break tough, woody ends from asparagus; wash well. Split each stalk lengthwise, then cut into 1-1/2 inch lengths (on the bias). Heat remaining 2 tbsp. oil in skillet or wok along with chicken drippings. Stir in asparagus, green onions and mushrooms. Stir-fry for 2 minutes. Dissolve bouillon cubes in boiling water. Add to asparagus mixture along with cooked chicken, ginger, salt, sugar and garlic powder. Cover, simmer 3 minutes. In small bowl, blend cornstarch, sherry and soy sauce until smooth. Stir into mixture in skillet. Cook, stirring constantly, until mixture thickens and bubbles. Cook 1 minute longer. Serve immediately over hot, cooked rice. *Makes 6 servings.*

Company Chicken Wings

2 lbs. chicken wings
2-3 tsp. sugar
1/2-3/4 cup soy sauce
2 tsp. minced ginger
1 clove garlic, minced
1/4 tsp. pepper
1/2 tsp. paprika
1/2 tsp. chili powder

Trim tips off wings. Sprinkle chicken wings with sugar and allow to sit at room temperature for 15-20 minutes. Place chicken wings on baking sheet. In a 2-cup measure or small bowl add soy sauce, ginger, garlic, pepper, paprika and chili powder.

Stir to combine. Pour over chicken and allow to sit 30 minutes, turning occasionally to completely coat chicken with the soy mixture. Place in 350 degree oven for 45 minutes to 1 hour or until done.
Delicious served hot or cold.

Note: Chicken wings can be left in one piece after the tips have been cut off or cut in two.

Mix gravy ingredients in a screw-top jar and shake. No lumps!

Left-over soup or soup stock can be put into ice-cube trays and frozen; then wrap and store frozen soup cubes in freezer. Can be used in small amounts or for another meal.

Other Birds

Roast Duck Apricot Glace

3 to 5 lb. ready-to-cook duck; 1 small orange; 1 medium onion, cut into wedges; 1 small apple, halved and cored; apricot glaze *

Peel and quarter orange, saving the peel; set orange aside. Scrape white membrane from peel; cut remaining peel portion into thin strips. Lightly salt cavity of duck. Stuff loosely with onion, apple and quartered orange. Tie legs of duck to tail. Prick legs and wings with fork to allow fat to escape. Place duck on rack in a shallow roasting pan. Roast in 375°F oven for 1½ to 2 hours, spooning off excess fat.

Brush duck with Apricot Glaze. Roast 15 minutes more or until done. Serve remaining glaze as an accompaniment with duck. *Makes 3 to 4 servings.*

*Apricot Glaze: In saucepan, combine 1½ cups apricot nectar, 2 crumbled chicken bouillon cubes, reserved orange peel and 1 tbsp. cornstarch. Cook and stir until thick and bubbly.

Did you know ...
    the Woodward's Brands of canned fruits, juices and vegetables are really choice quality.

Mona says . . .

Chicken and turkey lend themselves to festive dining. When roasting the whole bird try a different and glamorous stuffing.

Add a touch of colour: A bouquet of parsley, nasturtium leaves, flowers, orange slices, or other favourite garnish . . . just enough to accent the bird.

Do carve at the table so that everyone may enjoy the occasion to its fullest.

To estimate roasting time of unstuffed turkeys, deduct 5 minutes per pound. Use a meat thermometer as an accurate guide as to whether meat is cooked or not. If using a thermometer, insert it into middle of thick, thigh muscle or breast. Be sure thermometer does not touch bone. When cooked, thermometer should read 185 to 190 degrees F. If not using a meat thermometer, pinch thick muscle of drumstick or breast between cloth or paper towel protected fingers. It should feel soft. Leg will move easily when twisted.

As a rough guide, allow approximately ¾ to 1 cup of stuffing per pound of eviscerated (ready-to-cook) turkey. Pack stuffing lightly into turkey to permit dressing to expand. Any leftover dressing can be cooked separately — bake, covered in a greased casserole for approximately 30 to 60 minutes (depending upon quantity of stuffing) to heat through and blend flavours. A spoonful or two of pan drippings can be drizzled over stuffing, before baking for additional flavour.

Carving Hints — Let turkey stand 15 minutes before carving; keep warm. With fingers, pull leg away from body; cut through meat between thigh and backbone. With tip of knife, disjoint leg bone from backbone. Holding leg vertically, large end down, slice meat parallel to bone (and under some tendons), turning leg for even slices. Or first separate thigh and drumstick; slice thigh meat by cutting slices parallel to bone. Before carving breast meat, make a deep horizontal cut into breast close to wing (have wing tips folded behind back before roasting so carving can be done without removing wings). Cut thin slices from top of breast down to horizontal cut. Follow curve of breast bone for final smaller slices. Repeat for other side of turkey.

Turkey Chunks — Use in hot or cold salads, souffles, casseroles, turkey tetrazzini, or curried turkey. As an appetizer (cubed, on a toothpick) with a spicy dunking sauce.

Turkey Slices — Serve heated in gravy or zesty barbecue sauce over hot toasted buns with a salad. Serve in club sandwiches or open-face sandwiches; make your favourite turkey sandwich; dip it in an egg-milk mixture then grill it "french toast" style; serve with cranberry sauce.

Small Turkey Pieces — Use in recipes for hashes, croquettes, turkey loaf, or patties. Use in omelets, "a la king" recipes, or add to homemade or appropriate canned soups.

Turkey Bones — Make turkey stock. Use as base for soup; or strain to use as liquid or part liquid in gravies, sauces, creamed mixture, casseroles, or as liquid for canned soups or for cooking vegetables.

Cooking Canada's Turkey

There are two methods used to thaw frozen turkey:

Slow Method

Slit the bag along the back; place turkey on rack in pan. Thaw in refrigerator allowing approximately 5 hours per pound. When bird is pliable, remove it from the freezer bag and remove giblets and neck out of body and neck cavities. Rinse turkey under cold running water; dry inside and out. Place on rack in pan; cover loosely with waxed paper, plastic wrap or aluminium foil; refrigerate to complete thawing. Cook turkey within 48 hours. If giblets are not to be cooked as soon as thawed, rinse, dry, cover loosely and store in refrigerator and cook within 24 hours.

Faster Method

Thaw turkey at room temperature in original unopened bag. Make 3 or 4 small holes in bottom of the bag and set turkey on rack in shallow pan or in sink. Allow approximately 1 hour per pound. When turkey is pliable, proceed as directed in slow method.

TIME TABLE FOR ROASTING WHOLE TURKEYS
(Cleaned, Ready-to-Cook, & Stuffed)

Weight in Pounds	Time in Hours (approx.)
6 — 8	3¾ — 4
8 — 10	4 — 4½
10 — 12	4½ — 5
12 — 14	5 — 5¼
14 — 16	5¼ — 6
16 — 18	6 — 6½
18 — 20	6½ — 7½
20 — 24	7½ — 9
over 24	add 15 min. per lb.

Oven Temperature — 325°F

Guide To Quantity

Whole Turkey - over 12 pounds
Allow approximately 1/2 to 3/4 pound per serving when roasted, braised or stewed.

Whole Turkey - under 10 pounds
Allow approximately 3/4 to 1 pound per serving when roasted, braised, stewed, fried or broiled.

Boned Turkey Roll or Roast - 2-1/2 pounds and over
Allow approximately 1/4 to 1/3 pound per serving when roasted, as a fondue, or cutlets.

Cut-up Turkey - Thighs and Breasts
Allow approximately 1/2 to 3/4 pound per serving when roasted, baked, braised, steaks, cutlets or for fondue.

Cut-up Turkey - Drumsticks and Wings
Allow approximately 3/4 to 1 pound per serving when baked, braised or stewed.

Turkey Cutlets or Ground Turkey
Allow approximately 1/4 to 1/2 pound per serving when pan-fried or baked.

Applesauce Turkey Bake

1 turkey (approximately 6 lbs. or equivalent in turkey pieces), cut-up
1 cup apple sauce
1/3 cup soy sauce
1 tbsp. brown sugar
1/4 tsp. garlic powder

Place turkey in baking pan. In bowl, combine apple sauce, soy sauce, brown sugar and garlic powder; spoon mixture over turkey. Cover and bake in 350 degree F. oven for 1 1/2 hours or until turkey pieces are tender. Thicken juices and serve with turkey as a sauce or gravy.

Zip up your favourite turkey recipes with one of these suggested spices:

Turkey Casseroles — *Thyme, sage, rosemary, saffron, garlic, or savory.*

Turkey Sauces — *Dill, savory, or mace.*

Turkey Stuffings — *Parsley, basil, marjoram, sesame seed, thyme, rosemary, oregano, celery seed or poppy seed.*

Creamed Dishes — *Rosemary, parsley, dill weed, allspice, mace, or curry powder.*

Turkey Soups — *Tarragon, thyme, savory, parsley, rosemary.*

Turkey Salads — *Poultry seasoning, sesame seed, thyme, tarragon, parsley, chives, or dill.*

Turkey Stews — *Basil, bay leaf, cumin, allspice, parsley, oregano, or dill.*

Parmesan Turkey and Broccoli Bake

A great recipe to use up leftover turkey!

2 packages (10 oz.) frozen broccoli spears,	1 cup light cream,
boiling salted water,	¾ cup grated Parmesan cheese,
1 chicken bouillon cube,	¼ tsp. dry mustard,
1 cup boiling water,	2 tsp. chopped parsley,
4 tbsp. butter or margarine,	12 thin wide turkey slices,
4 tbsp. flour,	paprika.

Prepare broccoli according to package directions in boiling salted water (use fresh, cooked broccoli if available); drain well. Place in bottom of greased 1½ qt. casserole dish; keep warm. Dissolve bouillon cube in boiling water; set aside. In medium-size saucepan over low heat, melt butter, stir in flour until mixture is smooth. Add prepared bouillon and cream. Cook over medium heat stirring constantly until mixture is thickened and bubbly. Remove from heat. Stir in ½ of the cheese; add mustard and parsley. Combine well. Arrange turkey slices over broccoli so vegetable is covered completely. Pour sauce over all covering turkey completely. Sprinkle with remaining cheese and dust with paprika. Broil moderately slowly until hot through and top is browned — approximately 10 minutes. Serve with a crispy salad and hot rolls. *Makes 6 servings.*

Dorothy's Gougere

3 tbsp. turkey drippings butter or margarine	salt and pepper
4 tbsp. all-purpose flour	1 to 2 cups diced cooked turkey
2 cups turkey giblet broth, consomme or milk	1/2 cup water
	1/4 cup butter or margarine
2 tbsp. capers (optional)	1/2 cup all-purpose flour
1/4 tsp. sage	pinch of salt
	2 eggs

To make sauce, melt the drippings and blend in 4 tbsp. flour. Slowly stir in the 2 cups liquid and cook, stirring constantly, until sauce is bubbly and creamy. Remove from heat and add capers. if desired, and sage. Season with salt and pepper to taste. Fold in turkey. Set aside. To make choux pastry, place water and 1/4 cup butter in saucepan and bring to a boil. Add 1/2 cup flour and pinch of salt. Cook, stirring hard, until paste leaves side of pan.

Remove from heat and beat in eggs; one at a time, stirring vigorously after each addition. With a knife, shape pastry into a circle around a shallow baking dish. Fill centre with creamed turkey mixture. Take a fork and gently pull the choux pastry slightly over the turkey mixture. Place in 375 degree F. oven and bake for 30 to 40 minutes or until pastry is light, fluffy and golden, and creamed turkey is bubbly.

Tasty Turkey Maryland

1 turkey [fryer-roaster, approx. 5 to 6 lb.]	1 1/2 tsp. salt [or to taste]
1 egg	1/4 tsp. pepper dash poultry seasoning
1/3 cup milk	3 tbsp. water
1/3 cup all-purpose flour	2/3 cup cream
1 1/2 cups fine dry bread crumbs	2 tbsp. flour
1/4 cup salad oil [more, if desired]	1/2 cup water

Cut turkey into serving-size portions. In bowl, beat egg with milk. On separate sheet of waxed paper, place flour and bread-crumbs. Dip turkey pieces and giblets, first into flour, then egg mixture, then crumbs. In large skillet, over medium heat, heat salad oil.

Cook turkey pieces, several at a time until golden brown on all sides. Arrange turkey in shallow roasting pan. Season with salt, pepper and dash of poultry seasoning. Add 3 tbsp. water. Cover pan with foil. Bake in 350 deg. F. oven for approx. 1 1/2 to 1 3/4 hours or until fork-tender. Remove foil cover during last 30 minutes of cooking time. When turkey is cooked, remove from pan; place on warm serving platter. Keep warm. To make sauce, stir cream into pan drippings (loosen any crusty brown bits in pan); in cup, blend flour and 1/2 cup water until smooth.

Gradually stir into hot liquid in pan; cook over medium heat, stirring constantly, until mixture is thickened. Makes 6 to 8 servings.

Basic Stuffing for Chicken or Turkey

1/4 cup chopped onion
1/4 cup thinly sliced celery
1/4 cup butter
4 cups dry bread cubes
  [approx. 6 slices
  bread cut in 1/2"
  cubes]
1/4 tsp. salt [or to taste]
  dash pepper
1 tbsp. chopped parsley
1/2 tsp. poultry seasoning
1/2 tsp. sage
2 to 4 tbsp. water
  [or chicken broth]

Saute onion and celery in butter until tender but not browned. Combine with bread cubes, salt, pepper, parsley, poultry seasoning, and sage. Toss lightly with enough liquid to moisten. Makes about 3 cups stuffing, sufficient for a 4 to 5-lb. chicken.

VARIATIONS:
Mushroom Stuffing: Prepare bread stuffing. Saute 1 cup sliced mushrooms in butter; sprinkle with MSG. Toss with stuffing.

Giblet Stuffing: In small saucepan, cook giblets in lightly salted water until tender. Drain, reserving broth. Chop giblets finely. Prepare bread stuffing using giblet broth as liquid. Toss chopped giblets with stuffing.

Stuffing the Bird

Stuffings and Coatings

Gourmet Rice Stuffing

1/2 cup butter; 2-1/4 cups finely-chopped onion; 2 cups finely-chopped celery; 1 green pepper, finely chopped; liver, gizzard & heart, finely chopped or ground; 1 tbsp. salt; 1/4 tsp. pepper; 1 tsp. marjoram; 1/2 tsp. savory; 1 tsp. sage; 1/2 tsp. thyme; 8 cups cooked rice (2-2/3 cups raw or 4 cups quick-cooking); 1 cup chopped pecans; 1/2 cup finely-chopped celery leaves; 2 eggs, well beaten.

Melt butter in large frying pan; saute onion, celery, green pepper, liver, gizzard and heart until thoroughly cooked. Blend in salt, pepper, marjoram, savory, sage and thyme. Add rice, nuts and chopped celery leaves. Stir in beaten eggs; mix thoroughly. Loosely stuff turkey. Any extra stuffing can be baked in a covered casserole or in aluminum foil during the last 45 minutes of roasting.

(NOTE: When storing left-over turkey in freezer or refrigerator, remove dressing from bird and store separately.)

Crumb Coating

To 1 c. of very fine bread crumbs, add mixing well: 1/4 c. flour, 1/2 tsp. sugar, 1 tsp. paprika, 1 tsp. m.s.g., 1/4 tsp. white pepper or cayenne, 1/2 tsp. salt or seasoned salt.

Buzz dry bread crumbs in a blender or through finest blade of a food chopper as the crumbs must be very fine. If you wish, a pkt. of spaghetti sauce mix may be blended into the crumbs.

Variation: Omit salt and use celery salt; garlic salt, thyme and rosemary. A hint of curry is a pleasant seasoning with chicken.

Sausage Apple Stuffing

1 lb. pork sausage meat,
1 large onion, chopped,
1 cup chopped celery,
1 large tart apple, peeled,
  quartered, cored and
  chopped,
6 cups bread cubes, day
  old, (approximately 11
  to 12 slices bread),
2 eggs, slightly beaten,
1 tsp. poultry seasoning,
1½ tsp. salt or to taste,
pepper to taste,
1 tbsp. chopped parsley.

In large skillet, brown sausage meat over medium heat until cooked; break sausage meat apart with spoon or fork until crumbly. Remove from skillet; drain meat well. Pour pork drippings from skillet. Return ¼ cup drippings to skillet. Gently saute, onion and celery until almost tender but not browned. Add apple during last few minutes; simmer gently, stirring frequently. Remove from heat. Stir in bread cubes; add eggs, poultry seasoning, salt, pepper and parsley. Mix well. Add reserved sausage. Stir until ingredients are well distributed. Stuff turkey just before roasting.

Makes enough stuffing for a 13 to 15 lb. turkey.

Turkey Giblet Stuffing

turkey giblets,
½ cup butter or margarine,
1 cup shredded carrot,
1 cup chopped celery,
¾ cup chopped onion,
7 cups dry bread cubes
  (approximately 14
  slices bread),
1 tbsp. chopped parsley,
2 tsp. ground sage,
salt and pepper to taste.

In small saucepan, cook giblets in salted water until tender — approximately 1 hour. Drain giblets reserving ½ cup liquid. Chop giblets. In large Dutch oven, melt butter; saute carrot, celery and onion until tender. Remove from heat; add bread cubes, parsley, sage, salt, pepper and giblets. Add giblet liquid. Combine well. Stuff turkey, just before roasting.

Mona says . . .

Did you know . . . *eggs are delivered to all Woodward's Stores daily?*

To get the very best results possible keep in mind that eggs should be cooked at a very low temperature.

Egg White Hints and Leftover Suggestions

When using egg white in recipe remove eggs from refrigerator several hours before needed. Egg whites beat up lighter and more readily when at room temperature and give increased fineness of grain and delicacy of texture to angel food cakes.

Top a one crust pie, baked pudding or fruit crisp with a 2 or 3 egg white meringue. Bake dessert until almost cooked. Top with meringue and continue baking until meringue is lightly browned.

Poach egg whites in hot water until firm. Drain and shred. Add to casseroles, soups, sauces and salads.

Beat egg whites slightly and brush over bread dough and pastries to make crust shiny.

Egg Yolk Leftover Suggestions

For creamier icings, replace part of the liquid by adding 1 or 2 yolks (especially chocolate icing).

Add 1 or 2 egg yolks to oil and vinegar salad dressing. Place in screw top jar and shake well.

Make up a dessert that calls for yolks only, such as custard pies, some Bavarian creams, French ice creams, souffles, mousses and lemon meringue pie. Replace meringue topping with ice cream or whipping cream.

Drop egg yolks into boiling water and turn heat low. Cook until yolk is firm; drain. Mash or chop yolk for use in sandwiches, fish sauces and casseroles.

For a golden crust on breads and pies — to each egg yolk add 1 tbsp. milk, cream or water. Combine and beat. Brush on before baking. Also use as a coating before frying such foods as chicken and fish. Coat, dip in crumbs and fry.

Using up leftover egg whites or egg yolks — add either one to whole eggs for scrambled eggs and omelets.

COOKING CANADA'S EGGS

Eggs are a versatile food because they can be prepared in so many ways and used with such a variety of other foods.

Eggs are very satisfactory foods in reducing diets because they have high nutritive value but a low calorie value (75 Calories per egg).

Eggs are an excellent source of highest quality protein — so good that this protein is used as a standard for evaluating proteins in other foods.

EGG FREEZING GUIDE

Because frozen egg yolks become gummy when not mixed with sugar or salt, one of these must be added for successful freezing of whole eggs and egg yolks, but nothing need be added to egg whites frozen separately. (For only two or three weeks of storage whole eggs may be frozen without sugar or salt.)

Prepare eggs as follows:

Whole Eggs — Break eggs out of shell. When eggs are to be used as a Breakfast Dish, in a Meat Loaf or a Salad Dressing — add ½ teaspoon salt to 1 cup eggs (about 6 eggs); when used in Baking and Desserts — add ½ tablespoon sugar to 1 cup eggs. Mix thoroughly with a fork. Package and freeze.

Egg Yolks — Break all egg yolks. When egg yolks are to be used in Mayonnaise — add ¼ teaspoon salt to ¼ cup of egg yolks (about 4 yolks); in Baking and Desserts — add 1 teaspoon sugar to ¼ cup egg yolks. Mix thoroughly with a fork. Package and freeze.

Egg Whites — No mixing required. Package and freeze.

PACKAGING
For best results freeze in small packages containing specific amounts for certain purposes. (Examples: 6 eggs for scrambling for breakfast; 12 egg whites for angel cake; 3 egg yolks for mayonnaise; 4 whole eggs for cream puffs; 1 whole egg for muffins; 2 egg whites for meringue, etc.)

Use freezer cartons or glass jars for large amounts of eggs, leaving ¼-inch headspace at the top of cartons and 1-inch headspace at the top of glass jars. For smaller quantities, use paper baking cups, custard cups, individual ice cube forms, etc., or use a spare ice cube tray to make "square eggs", allowing one or two eggs for each division in the tray. When eggs are frozen remove carefully from custard cups or ice cube containers and pack in freezer bags.
Note: Leave space in package for expansion.

STORAGE TIME
Eggs may be stored 4 months.

THAWING AND COOKING

Thaw eggs in the refrigerator or at room temperature, allowing the eggs to warm to room temperature before using so that they will whip or mix better. If thawed egg yolks appear to have a thicker consistency than fresh yolks, add a little water. Use thawed eggs promptly. Do not refreeze.

Use frozen eggs in place of fresh eggs in regular recipes. Use 1½ tablespoons thawed egg white for 1 white of egg; 1 tablespoon thawed egg yolk for 1 yolk of egg; 2½ tablespoons thawed whole egg mixture for 1 whole egg.

Basic Omelet

4 eggs, 4 tbsp. milk, water, or tomato juice, ½ tsp. salt, dash pepper.

Whole eggs are beaten enough to blend white and yolk, then dilute slightly with liquid and season. The mixture is cooked in a greased pan until set, after which the omelet is folded. (Use a spatula occasionally to lift the omelet in the setting, letting the liquid portion flow underneath onto the pan.)

Variations: Add in ¼ c. drained, sliced canned mushrooms; 1 tbsp. chopped onions or dried onions; ½ cheese slice, broken into small bits; OR 3 cooked bacon slices, crumbled.

Fried Eggs

Have skillet coated with fat or oil. Add eggs. Season to taste with salt and pepper. Add ½ tsp. water per egg when the whites of the egg are set and the edges are cooked. Cover; continue cooking until eggs reach desired consistency.

Soft-Cooked Eggs

For 4 eggs or less, place eggs in saucepan; cover with cold water to a depth of at least 1 inch above the eggs. Bring water rapidly to boiling. Turn off heat and cover. Start timing now — leave in water for 2 to 4 minutes depending upon desired degree of doneness. When cooking more than 4 eggs, follow above procedure but do not turn off heat but cook just below simmering for 4 to 6 minutes. To stop cooking and allow for easy handling, promptly cool eggs in cold water for a few seconds.

Baked Eggs

Butter custard or ramekins. Place 1 tbsp. cream in each. Carefully break 1 egg into each. Season to taste with salt and pepper. Place cups in shallow pan. Carefully pour hot water around them to a depth of 1 inch. Bake in 325 degree F. oven for approximately 20 minutes or until eggs are firm. For a special touch, after 15 minutes of cooking time, sprinkle some grated sharp cheddar cheese and/or chopped green onions over top of eggs. Continue cooking approximately 5 minutes longer or until cheese has melted and eggs are done.

Poached Eggs

Have water in pan about 3 to 4 inches deep. Let water come just to boiling. Stir the simmering water to make a swirl. (Have egg in cup or small bowl). Slip the egg right into the middle of the swirl. Make sure to follow the motion of the swirl with the dish so that the egg goes into the water in the same direction as the swirl. Turn heat down. Cook until egg is done to the desired degree of doneness — approximately 3 to 5 minutes. Carefully remove egg from water with a slotted spoon.

Gourmet Spanish Eggs

3 medium onion, chopped
2 large green peppers, chopped
3 tbsp. butter
2 tbsp. salad oil
3 large tomatoes, chopped peeled,
   if desired
1/2 cup chili sauce
1/8 tsp. chili powder
salt and pepper to taste
garlic sausage rings
   and cooked shrimp
5 to 6 eggs
1 tbsp. finely chopped green onion

In skillet, saute onion and green pepper in mixture of butter and oil until almost tender. Add tomatoes and continue cooking just until tomatoes are heated through and softened. Add chili sauce and chili powder. Season with salt and pepper to taste. Spread cooked vegetables and sauce in bottom of wide shallow 1-quart casserole. Around edge of dish arrange garlic sausage slices and shrimp. Carefully break eggs into casserole over prepared layer. Sprinkle with green onions. Bake in 350 degree F. oven for approximately 10 to 15 minutes or until eggs are done according to personal preference. Serve with hot buttered rolls. *Makes 5 to 6 servings.*

"Scotch" Eggs

1 lb. pork sausage meat	2 tbsp. milk
1/2 cup finely chopped onion	6 hard-cooked eggs,
2 tbsp. bottled steak sauce	shelled
1/2 tsp. salt [or to taste]	1 raw egg, slightly beaten
1/4 tsp. pepper	1 cup fine dry bread-crumbs
1 tbsp. chopped parsley	vegetable shortening [or
	oil for deep frying]

In bowl, lightly mix sausage meat, onion, steak sauce, salt, pepper, parsley and milk until well-blended. Divide mixture into six mounds; shape each around one hard-cooked egg to cover completely. Roll each meat-covered egg in slightly beaten egg; then roll in bread crumbs to coat well. Into deep saucepan, melt enough shortening to make a 2-inch depth. Heat to 365 deg. F.

Fry Scotch eggs, two or three at a time, turning once or twice until crumb coating is golden-brown (approx. 5 minutes). Lift eggs out with slotted spoon and drain thoroughly. Keep hot. Serve with french fries and crisp green salad. Makes 3 to 6 servings.

Variation: Substitute ground beef for sausage meat; or a combination of half ground beef and half sausage; or add chopped bacon to sausage meat or ground beef. **Note** — To cook Scotch eggs in oven, omit shortening; place breaded eggs in shallow baking dish. Bake in 400 deg. oven for 30 to 40 minutes or until meat is cooked and crumbs are golden.

Eggs Mornay

6 thin slices cooked ham
1 tbsp. butter or margarine
3 English muffins
1/2 cup whole cranberry sauce
6 eggs
salt and pepper
3 tbsp. butter or, margarine

3 tbsp. all-purpose flour
3/4 tsp. salt
dash pepper
1 cup light cream
1/4 cup dry white wine
1/3 cup shredded
    Swiss cheese

Lightly brown ham in 1 tbsp. butter. Split English muffins; toast and lightly butter. Place ham slice on each muffin half; top each ham slice with 1/6 of cranberry sauce. Poach eggs; place on top of cranberry sauce. Season with salt and pepper. Pour Mornay Sauce over top. To make Mornay Sauce - in saucepan, melt butter; blend in flour, salt and dash pepper. Add cream all at once. Cook and stir until mixture is thickened and bubbles. Stir in wine; add cheese and stir until melted. *Makes 6 servings.*

Cheese Egg Bake

2 cans condensed cream of chicken soup; 1 cup milk; 4 tsp. instant minced onion; 1 tsp. prepared mustard; 2 cups (8 oz) shredded process Swiss cheese; 12 eggs; 12 - 1/2-inch thick French bread, buttered and halved.

Combine soup, milk, onion and mustard in saucepan. Cook and stir until smooth; and heated through. Remove from heat; stir in cheese until melted. Pour 1 cup of the sauce into each of two 10x6x1¾-inch baking dishes. Break 6 eggs into sauce in each casserole. Carefully spoon remaining sauce around eggs. Stand French bread slices around edges of casseroles, crusts up. Bake in 350°F oven for 20 minutes or until eggs are set. Garnish with a sprinkle of snipped parsley, if desired. *Makes 12 servings.*

Perfect Scramble

6 eggs
1/3 cup milk or light cream
1/2 tsp. salt or to taste

dash pepper
1 1/2 tbsp. butter, margarine
    or bacon drippings

Combine eggs, milk, salt and pepper, (mix lightly for gold and white effect or mix thoroughly for all over yellow). Heat butter in skillet just until hot enough to make a drop of water sizzle. Pour in egg mixture. Reduce heat - this is important for tender eggs. Do not disturb mixture until it starts to set on bottom and sides, then lift and fold over with wide spatula so uncooked part goes to bottom. Avoid breaking up eggs more than necessary. Cook until eggs are just set - about 5 to 8 minutes. Remove skillet from heat just before all the moist part is cooked. Do not allow eggs to stand in skillet - the hot pan continues to cook them. Serve at once on warm platter. *Makes 3 to 4 servings.*

Note: To scramble eggs in top of double boiler, omit butter; use a spoon to stir. The water in bottom of double boiler should only simmer and not touch top pan. This method takes approximately twice the time as in a skillet.

Stuffed Eggs

6 hard-cooked eggs, peeled, 1 tbsp. mayonnaise, 1 tbsp. soy sauce, 1 tbsp. minced parsley, 1 tsp. dry mustard, dash paprika.

Cut eggs in halves crosswise in a decorative sawtooth pattern. Remove yolks gently. Mix yolks with mayonnaise, soy sauce, parsley and mustard. Refill whites with yolk mixture. Garnish with paprika. Makes 12 stuffed eggs.

Yummy Cheese Omelet

1 tbsp. butter or margarine, 1 cup cottage cheese, 3/4 cup shredded Swiss Cheese, 1 medium tomato, diced, 1 tbsp. flour, 1 tsp. dill weed, 1 tsp. chopped parsley, dash salt, Sprinkle freshly ground black pepper, 4 eggs, garnish with chopped parsley and tomato wedges, if desired.

Melt butter in 9'' pie plate. In bowl slightly beat cottage cheese; stir in Swiss cheese, tomato, flour, dill weed, parsley, salt, and pepper. Beat eggs slightly; add cheese mixture. Pour into prepared pie plate. Bake at 350 degrees F. oven for 25 to 30 minutes. Cut into wedges and serve immediately. Garnish with chopped parsley and tomato wedges, if desired. *Makes 4 to 6 servings.*

Mashed Brown Omelet

4 slices bacon
2 cups shredded
    cooked potatoes
1/3 cup chopped onion
1/3 cup chopped green pepper
4 eggs

1/4 cup milk
1/2 tsp. salt
pepper to taste
1 cup shredded
    sharp cheddar cheese

In large skillet, cook bacon until crisp. Remove bacon from skillet, crumble. Set aside. Into bacon drippings add potatoes, onions and green peppers. Mix well. Pat into the skillet. Cook over low heat until the underside is crisp and brown. In bowl, blend eggs, milk, salt and pepper. Pour egg mixture over potatoes. Top with cheese and reserved bacon. Cover; cook over low heat. When egg is done, loosen omelet. Fold. *Makes 4 servings.*

Lemon Omelet Souffle

6 eggs, separated, 6 tablespoons sugar, 3 tablespoons lemon juice, 1 teaspoon grated lemon rind, 1 1/2 teaspoons fine granulated sugar.

Beat egg yolks until light and lemon coloured. Beat in the sugar one tablespoon at a time. Add lemon juice and rind. Beat egg whites until firm. Gently fold them into yolk mixture. Heat a heavy ovenproof 7 to 8-inch skillet then butter it well. Sprinkle with 1 teaspoon of the fine granulated sugar. Pour the souffle mixture into the skillet and bake in a 375 degree F. oven for about 15 minutes. Sprinkle with the remaining 1/2 teaspoon of fine granulated sugar and serve at once.

Spanish Omelet

2 tbsp. salad oil; 3 tbsp. chopped onions; 3 tbsp. chopped celery; 3 tbsp. chopped green pepper; 1 tbsp. flour; 1 cup canned tomatoes; 1/4 tsp. chili powder; 1/4 tsp. salt; 1/4 tsp. MSG; 4 eggs; 1/4 cup milk; 1/2 tsp. salt; few grains pepper.

Sauce: Saute onions, celery and green pepper in oil until tender. Blend in flour and add tomatoes gradually; stir until thickened. Add chili powder, salt and MSG; simmer slowly for 5 minutes, stirring occasionally. Keep hot while preparing omelet.

Omelet: Mix eggs, milk and seasoning together. Pour mixture into moderately hot, buttered skillet. As egg cooks at edge, lift with spatula to let uncooked portion flow to sides. Do not stir. When mixture has set but moist (about 3 minutes), increase heat to brown bottom quickly. Add Spanish Sauce on one half of omelet and fold over. Serve at once. 3 servings.

Mona says . . .

Casserole dinners are a favourite at our house for a number of reasons.

— *Delicious and simple family budget stretchers. Avoid buying fancy quality when it really isn't necessary. For example, buying fancy, whole tomatoes when they are to be broken up and cooked into a sauce or casserole; or buying expensive, white tuna meat to be flaked and baked in a casserole. Suit the style of food to the purpose.*

— *Time-savers when prepared in advance and frozen.*

— *Elegant company fare enhanced by a variety of garnishes.*

Casserole Garnish Ideas — *Cut sliced bread into quarters diagonally. Form a star by arranging slices, points in, around edge of casserole.*

Cut bread slices into cubes. Place in checkerboard style on top of casserole.

Place mashed potato into pastry bag and add piping decoration to casserole.

Cut slices of cheese into strips to make cheverons.

Cut cheese slices into triangles. Place around a whole cheese slice to form a whirling star.

Cut flower motif from pastry and place on top of casserole.

To freeze casserole dishes

Don't overcook foods. There is more cooking time after the dish comes out of the freezer. Cook vegetables until just tender. Cook rice or noodles until just barely tender.

Add toppings such as grated cheese or potato chips when casserole is ready to be baked for serving.

Remove casserole from freezer to food compartment of refrigerator 12 to 24 hours before serving.

Do not keep casserole dishes in home freezers for longer than 2 months, or more than 2 weeks in freezing compartment of refrigerator.

If not freezing casserole in casserole dish itself, use metal or glass containers, waxed cartons, or plastic boxes for storing. Ensure the package is airtight.

If freezing food in casserole dish, cover or overwrap completely with aluminium foil, cellophane, saran or laminated freezer paper.

CASSEROLES
RICE and PASTA

Turkey Cacciatore

Cheddar Scalloped Onions

4 large onions [approx. 1/2-inch thick slices]	**Crumb Topping**
boiling, salted water	2 tbsp. butter, melted
1 clove garlic, crushed	1 tsp. lemon juice
1/4 cup butter	1 tbsp chopped parsley
1/4 cup flour	1/3 cup bread-crumbs
salt and pepper [to taste]	
1/2 tsp. dry mustard	
2 1/4 cups milk	
2 cups shredded sharp cheddar cheese	
2 tsp. Worcestershire sauce	
paprika	

In saucepan, cook onion slices in boiling salted water, to which crushed garlic clove has been added, until tender but still firm. Drain well. Arrange onion slices in well-buttered casserole dish. In medium saucepan, melt 1/4 cup butter; blend in flour, salt, pepper and dry mustard; cook, stirring constantly until bubbly. Stir in milk; cook, stirring constantly until bubbly and thickened. Allow to bubble for 2 minutes. Stir in cheese and Worcestershire sauce.

Stir until cheese melts. Pour sauce over prepared onions. Gently stir to combine. Sprinkle top lightly with paprika. **Crumb Topping:** In saucepan, melt 2 tbsp. butter; add lemon juice and parsley. Toss with bread-crumbs until well-coated. Sprinkle crumbs over top of onions and sauce. Bake in 350 deg. F oven for 30 minutes or until "scallop" is piping hot and crumbs are golden. Serve immediately. Makes 4 servings.

Variations: Add 1 1/2 cups cooked, cubed ham, chicken, or turkey to cheese sauce; or toss bread-crumbs with cooked, crumbled bacon; or add 1/2 pint coarsely chopped oysters to sauce. Serve piping hot over toast points or toasted English muffins.

1 skinned, boned, split turkey breast [about 3 lb.]	1 [19-oz.] can tomatoes, undrained [crush tomatoes]
flour	2 tsp. chopped parsley
3 tbsp. butter [more, if necessary]	1 tsp. salt [or to taste]
3 tbsp. salad oil	1/4 tsp. pepper
2 cloves garlic, crushed	1/2 tsp. dried oregano [or to taste]
2 medium onions, sliced 1/4-inch thick, separated into rings	1/2 tsp. celery seed
	1 bay leaf
1 [7 1/2-oz.] can tomato sauce	1/4 cup sauterne

Slice turkey into serving-size portions (cutlets). Coat with flour. In skillet, heat butter and oil; brown turkey pieces until golden on both sides. Remove from skillet. In drippings (add more butter, if necessary) cook garlic and onion slices until tender but not browned. Add tomatoes with their liquid, tomato sauce, parsley, salt, pepper, oregano, celery seed and bay leaf. Stir to blend seasonings. Cover; simmer 15 minutes. Add turkey (baste with sauce); cover; continue simmering 20 minutes longer, basting occasionally. Add sauterne; cook turkey 15 minutes longer or until tender, turning occasionally. Remove bay leaf; skim off any excess fat. Ladle sauce over turkey on serving platter. Serve with hot cooked spaghetti noodles, topped with grated Parmesan cheese. Makes 4 to 6 servings. **Note**—Cooking time depends upon the thickness of turkey cutlets; make appropriate allowances.

Chiliburger Casserole

1 tbsp. oil	1 tsp. chili powder
1 lb. ground beef	2 cups cooked shell macaroni
1/2 cup chopped onion	1 tin (14 oz.) creamed corn
1/2 tsp. salt	2 tbsp. tomato catsup
1/2 tsp. pepper	1 tsp. Worcestershire sauce
1/2 tsp. garlic powder	1/2 cup grated sharp cheddar cheese

In skillet, heat oil. Brown meat; add onion, saute until just tender. Add remaining ingredients except the cheese. Mix well. Place mixture into greased baking dish. Bake in 325 degree F. oven for 25 minutes. Sprinkle all over with grated cheese; return to oven until cheese is melted and casserole is piping hot. *Makes 4 servings.*

Tuna Pacific Pie

2 cups tuna, drained,
1 can condensed cream of
   chicken soup (10 oz.),
1 pkt frozen peas (10 oz.),
3 medium tomatoes,
   skinned, seeds removed
   and sliced,

2 cups potato chips,
2 tablespoons finely grated
   cheese (Parmesan is
   ideal),
Dash lemon juice.

Cook the peas and drain. Preheat oven to 350 degrees F. Drain and flake the tuna, sprinkle with lemon juice. Place layer of tuna on bottom of ovenproof casserole. Cover with half the soup, half the peas, half the tomatoes, and half the potato chips. Repeat the layers finishing with the remaining potato chips and grated cheese. Put the pie into the oven for 30 minutes. Broil under the grill to finish . . . the pie is ready when the cheese and potato chips are golden.

Serve with savoury rice or creamed potatoes.

Turnip Casserole

1 large turnip
salted water
1 tbsp. butter
2 large apples
1/4 cup lightly
   packed brown sugar

pinch cinnamon
1/3 cup flour
1/3 cup brown sugar
2 tbsp. butter

Cook turnip in salted water until tender; drain. Mash turnips add 1 tbsp. butter. Peel, core and slice apples; toss with 1/4 cup brown sugar and cinnamon. Arrange alternate layers of turnip and apples, beginning and ending with turnips. Mix together flour, 1/3 cup brown sugar and 2 tbsp. butter until crumbly. Sprinkle mixture over top of casserole. Bake in 350 degree F. oven for approximately 1 hour. Serve hot. *Makes 6 to 8 servings.*

Moussaka

2 large eggplants
1 cup flour
6 tbsp. oil
2 large onions, chopped
6 tbsp. butter or margarine
2 lbs. ground lamb or beef
1/2 cup dry red wine
1/4 cup finely chopped parsley
3 tbsp. tomato paste
2 tsp. salt or to taste

dash pepper to taste
1/4 tsp. cinnamon
2 cups milk
1/2 tsp. salt
1/8 tsp. ground nutmeg
1 cup cottage cheese
2 eggs
1/4 cup dry bread crumbs
1 cup grated Parmesan cheese

Cut unpeeled eggplant into 3/4 inch slices. Coat lightly on both sides with about 2/3 cup of the flour. Saute in oil on both sides until golden brown. Drain on paper towels. Saute onions in 2 tbsp. butter until soft but not browned. Add ground meat; cook 10 minutes longer, or until meat is browned and crumbly. Add wine, parsley, tomato paste, 2 tsp. salt (or to taste) pepper and cinnamon. Cover and simmer about 30 minutes or until sauce is very thick, stirring occasionally. Melt remaining 4 tbsp. butter in a saucepan, blending in remaining 1/3 cup flour, stirring constantly. Gradually stir in milk, 1/2 tsp. salt and nutmeg. Continue cooking over low heat until smooth and thickened. Remove from heat and stir in cottage cheese and eggs (stir vigorously).

Grease a 13 x 9-inch baking pan. Sprinkle with bread crumbs. Cover with meat sauce and sprinkle with 1/4 cup grated Parmesan cheese. Cover with prepared eggplant. Spoon white sauce over top and sprinkle with remaining 3/4 cup grated cheese. Bake in 350 degree F. oven for 1 hour, or until set and lightly browned. Let stand 10 minutes or longer before cutting into squares. *Makes 6 to 8 servings.*

Hamburger Bean

1 tin (14 oz.) baked beans; 1 tin (14 oz.) kidney beans; 1 package (10 oz.) frozen green beans, thawed; 1/4 cup brown sugar; 1 tbsp. dry mustard; 1 tsp. salt; pepper to taste; 1 medium onion, chopped; 1 lb. hamburger; dash of garlic powder; 2 tbsp. vinegar.

In a large casserole dish mix all ingredients together taking care to distribute spices evenly. Bake, covered, at 350 degrees F. for 1½ hours or until cooked. Serve with crusty rolls and salad. A quick nutritious dish for cold weather. *Makes 4 servings.*

Sweet Onion Bake

7-1/2 cups sliced large
   sweet onions
4 tsp. butter
1/2 cup raw rice

2 cups boiling salted water
1 cup grated Swiss cheese
2/3 cup cream

Saute onions in butter. Cook rice in water for 5 minutes. Drain rice. Mix with onions. Place mixture in casserole dish. Add cheese and cream. Bake, covered in 300 degree F. oven for 1 hour or until done. *Makes 8 servings.*

Tuna Cheese Casserole

1½ cups elbow macaroni, 1/4 cup butter or margarine, 1/4 cup flour, 1¾ cups water, 2 tbsp. soy sauce, 1 cup cheddar cheese, shredded, dash black pepper, 1 (7 oz.) can tuna, drained and flaked, 1/2 cup finely chopped green pepper.

Cook macaroni in boiling salted water until tender, yet firm. Drain. In saucepan, melt butter, blend in flour. Add 1¾ cups water and soy sauce all at once. Stir until well blended; simmer until sauce thickens, stirring constantly. Remove from heat and blend in black pepper and 3/4 cup cheese. Combine tuna, macaroni and green pepper in ungreased 1½ qt. baking dish. Stir in cheese sauce. Sprinkle remaining 1/4 cup cheese over top. Bake in 425°F oven until top is golden brown, about 15 minutes. Makes 4 servings.

Mashed Potato Casserole

6 medium-size potatoes, 1 medium onion, boiling, salted water, 2 eggs, well beaten, 1 tbsp. chopped parsley, 1 tbsp. chopped chives, salt and pepper to taste, 1 tsp. Worcestershire sauce, 1/4 cup butter, 1 1/4 cups grated cheddar cheese, freshly cracked black pepper, chopped parsley and cherry tomato halves for garnish, if desired.

Peel and quarter potatoes and onion. Place in salted water and cook until tender. Meanwhile, in medium bowl, beat eggs; add parsley, chives, salt and pepper and Worcestershire sauce. Beat to combine well. Drain potatoes and onion thoroughly. Add butter and 1 cup grated cheese. Mash until smooth consistency. Add egg mixture and combine well. Pour mixture into greased 1 1/2 qt. casserole dish. Sprinkle with remaining 1/4 cup cheddar cheese and black pepper; cover. Approximately 1 hour before serving time preheat oven to 350 degrees F. Bake potato casserole, covered, for 30 minutes; remove cover and bake 15 minutes longer. Garnish with chopped parsley and cherry tomato halves, if desired. *Makes 6 servings.*

Duchesse Potatoes — beat 2 or 3 yolks into hot, fluffy mashed potatoes. Bake until lightly browned.

Baked Pork Chops with Beans

4 large loin or thin
   shoulder pork chops
salt and pepper
1 medium onion, chopped
1/2 cup chopped green pepper
1 clove garlic, crushed
2 tsp. brown sugar

1/2 tsp. dry mustard
1 tin (10 oz.)
   lima beans, drained
1 tin (14 oz.)
   red kidney beans, drained
1/3 cup chili sauce
1 tbsp. vinegar

Trim excess fat from chops. In skillet, melt trimmed fat. Brown chops on both sides; season with salt and pepper. Remove chops; drain. To drippings in skillet, add onion, green pepper and garlic. Saute until tender but not browned. Add brown sugar, dry mustard, lima beans, kidney beans, chili sauce and vinegar. Mix well. Pour bean mixture into 2 qt. casserole.

Arrange chops on top. Cover. Bake in 350 degree F. oven 45 minutes or until beans are piping hot and chops are tender. *Makes 4 servings.*

Wiener and Bean Bake

1 - 28 oz. tin baked beans; 1 pkge. of weiners, sliced and halved (4 pieces from each weiner); 1 pkge. dehydrated onion soup; 2 tbsp. ketchup; 2 tsp. prepared mustard; dash pepper; 1 tbsp. brown sugar; 1/2 cup water.

Brown weiners in frying pan. Combine beans, onion soup, ketchup, mustard, pepper, brown sugar and water in a 2 quart casserole. Add weiners. Bake uncovered, at 350 degrees approximately 30 minutes. An economical, satisfying dish. Excellent with a crisp salad and buns. Requires very little preparation time.

Lazy Cabbage Rolls

1 tin (approximately 28 oz. or
   equivalent) sauerkraut, drained
   and rinsed in cold water
3/4 cup quick-cooking rice
1 large onion, finely chopped

1/2 lb. bacon, cut up
salt and pepper to taste
1/2 cup water
   (add more, if necessary)

Mix above ingredients together in Dutch oven. Bring mixture to boiling; then allow to simmer (or put in oven) for approximately 1 hour or until rice is soft but not mushy; add more water during cooking process if casserole becomes too dry.

Spinach-Rice Casserole

1 package (12 oz.) frozen spinach, thawed and chopped
1-1/2 cups cooked rice
3/4 cup shredded sharp cheddar cheese
1 tin (10 oz.) cream of mushroom soup

1/2 tsp. dry mustard or to taste
dash Worcestershire sauce
1/4 cup shredded sharp cheddar cheese (for topping)

In buttered casserole dish, layer chopped spinach, rice and 3/4 cup cheese. In bowl, combine cream of mushroom soup, dry mustard and Worcestershire sauce. Pour mixture over cheese layer. Top with remaining 1/4 cup cheese. Bake in 350 degree F. oven for approximately 30 minutes or until bubbling. *Makes 4 servings.*

This is a good dish with steak or fish.

Curried Rice With Ham

8 slices thinly sliced cooked ham; 1 tin asparagus, or frozen, cooked; 1 package curried rice mix; 1 cup white sauce; 1/2 cup Swiss cheese, diced.

Prepare the curried rice according to package directions. Put mixture in 1-1/2 quart casserole dish. Take ham slices and roll asparagus up. Place rolls, seam side down on rice in casserole dish. Make up white sauce according to standard recipe below and add diced cheese. Stir until cheese is completely melted. Pour sauce over ham rolls. Place in 400 degree F. oven for approximately 15 minutes, or until sauce is bubbly. Garnish with parsley, wedges of tomato, or chopped green onion if desired.

NOTE: Could make up own curried rice. Whole cooked green beans could be substituted for asparagus.

White Sauce: *Medium*
2 tbsp. butter; 2 tbsp. flour; dash salt; dash white pepper; 1 cup milk.

Melt butter over low heat. Blend in flour, salt and pepper. Add milk all at once. Cook quickly, stirring all the time until the mixture thickens and bubbles. Do not over-cook.

Corn Noodle Bake

2 cups noodles; 1/2 to 1 lb. ground beef; 2 celery stalks, chopped; 1 medium onion, chopped; 1 can cream corn; 1 can undiluted cream of mushroom soup; 1 can sliced mushrooms, drained; salt and pepper to taste; dash of Worcestershire sauce; dash garlic powder (optional); 1/2 lb. grated cheddar cheese.

Cook noodles in boiling salted water according to package instructions. Drain. Brown ground beef, celery, and onions. In large casserole dish add noodles, meat mixture, creamed corn, mushroom soup, mushrooms, salt, pepper, Worcestershire sauce, and garlic powder. Mix all ingredients together thoroughly. Top with grated cheddar cheese. Bake at 350 degrees F. approximately 30 minutes or until cheese has melted and casserole is bubbly. Delicious with a crisp green salad or coleslaw.

To prevent gummy noodles, rice, macaroni and spaghetti, add two teaspoons of cooking oil to the water before cooking and your problems will be solved. You'll find it makes the noodles glisten and stand apart.

Spaghetti Milano

2 tbsp. salad oil
1 lb. boneless pork loin,
  cut in 1 inch strips
1/2 cup chopped onion
1/2 cup chopped celery
1 medium green pepper,
  cut in thin strips
1 tin (4 1/2 oz.)
  sliced mushrooms, undrained
1 tsp. Worcestershire sauce
1 tsp. salt
1/8 tsp. pepper
1/2 tsp. basil
1 tin (10 oz.) condensed cream
  of mushroom soup, undiluted
1/2 cup milk
1 package (16 oz.) spaghetti
2 tomatoes, peeled, thinly
  sliced then cut in half
1 1/2 cups bread cubes
2 tbsp. melted butter
1 cup grated sharp cheddar cheese

In large skillet, heat oil; brown pork. Add onion, celery and green pepper. Cook until tender. Mix in mushrooms, Worcestershire sauce, salt, pepper and basil. Simmer, covered, 25 minutes. Blend in mushroom soup and milk; simmer, covered, 5 minutes. Cook spaghetti according to package directions; drain. In an ungreased 2 qt. baking casserole; combine pork mixture with drained spaghetti. Overlap tomatoes around edge of casserole. Toss bread cubes with melted butter and sprinkle over casserole. Bake, covered, in 350 degree F. oven for 20 minutes. Remove from oven and top croutons with cheese.

Bake, uncovered, 10 minutes longer or until cheese melts and casserole is piping hot. *Makes 6 to 8 servings.*

Ham and Noodle Bake

1 cup egg noodles; 2 tbsp. butter; 1/4 cup chopped green pepper; 1/2 cup chopped celery; 1 small onion, chopped; 2 tbsp. flour; 1/2 tsp. salt; 1/4 tsp. pepper; 2 cups milk; 1 cup diced cooked ham; 1-1/2 cups creamed cottage cheese.

Cook noodles in boiling salted water until tender. Rinse and drain. Melt butter in saucepan. Saute green pepper, celery, and onion in butter. Blend in flour and seasonings. Gradually add milk and mix until well blended. Cook, stirring constantly, until smooth and thickened. Remove from heat; add ham, cottage cheese and noodles. Pour into buttered 2 quart casserole and bake at 350 degrees F. for 30 minutes or until top is bubbly and brown. *Serves 6.*

Cheesy Spaghetti Casserole

2 strips bacon, diced
1 medium onion, chopped
1/2 lb. ground beef
2 tins (7-1/2 oz. each) tomato sauce
2-1/2 cups water
1 tsp. chili powder
6 olives, sliced (optional)
1 clove garlic, crushed
salt and pepper to taste
1 lb. spaghetti, uncooked
3/4 lb. cheddar cheese, grated

In skillet, saute bacon and onion. Add minced meat and cook until meat is light brown. Add remaining ingredients except spaghetti and cheese. Simmer for 20 minutes, stirring occasionally. Into buttered casserole, break spaghetti into pieces. Pour prepared sauce and grated cheese over spaghetti. Stir well. Cook, covered, for 30 minutes in 375 degree F. oven. Uncover. Stir well. Cook 15 minutes longer or until casserole is piping hot and spaghetti is cooked. *Makes 4 servings.*

Spaghetti Sauce from Leftovers

3 tbsp. salad oil, 1 large onion, chopped, 2 cloves garlic, minced, 2 stalks celery, thinly sliced, 1/2 green pepper, coarsely chopped, 1 cup mushrooms, sliced, 2 cups cooked beef, ground medium fine, 1 tin (28 oz.) tomatoes, undrained 1 tin (7 1/2 oz.) tomato sauce, salt and pepper in generous amounts - to taste, 1/2 tsp. oregano, 2 tbsp. parsley, 1/4 cup Parmesan cheese, Hot, cooked spaghetti, extra Parmesan cheese.

In large skillet heat oil; saute onion, garlic and celery until tender but not browned. Add green pepper, mushrooms and cooked beef; saute quickly, stirring constantly. Add tomatoes, tomato sauce, salt, pepper, oregano, parsley and Parmesan cheese. Allow to simmer gently, covered for 45 minutes, stirring occasionally. Add a little water if necessary. Serve over hot spaghetti noodles. Pass extra Parmesan cheese around. *Makes 6 servings.*

Devilled Spaghetti

1 (8 ounce) pkge. spaghetti; 1 onion, cut fine; 1 small clove garlic; 2 tbsp. fat; 2-1/2 cups cooked tomatoes; salt and pepper; 1 tbsp. sugar; dash cayenne; 1/2 cup diced cooked chicken; 1 cup mushrooms, sauteed; grated cheese.

Cook spaghetti in boiling salted water until tender. Drain and place in greased casserole. Saute onion and garlic in fat until tender but not brown. Add tomatoes, salt, pepper, sugar and cayenne. Heat to boiling, then add chicken and mushrooms and pour over spaghetti. Toss with a fork.

Sprinkle with grated cheese and bake in moderate oven (350 degrees F.) until mixture is heated through and cheese is melted. *Serves 6 to 8.*

Savory Rice

1 cup long grain rice, cooked	1 cup sliced mushrooms
2 tbsp. butter or margarine	1/4 tsp. poultry seasoning
1 medium onion, chopped	salt and pepper to taste
1 stalk celery, chopped	

Cook rice until tender, according to package directions; set aside. In medium saucepan, melt butter; saute onion and celery until onion is transparent and celery is tender-crisp. Add mushrooms; saute until tender. Stir in prepared rice and seasonings. Heat through. A delicious accompaniment to poultry dishes. *Makes 4 to 6 servings.*

Rice Extra-Ordinary

To 4 servings of hot fluffy rice (prepared according to label directions), add any of the following, tossing until well mixed.

Celery: 1 small celery stalk, chopped.

Mushroom: 1/4 to 1/2 cup mushroom slices, caps or stems and pieces (canned or cooked, drained).

Carrot-Parsley: 1 shredded raw carrot and 2 tbsp chopped parsley.

Cheese: 1/2 cup shredded mild or sharp Cheddar

Olive: 1/4 cup sliced ripe or pimento-stuffed olives.

Chutney: 1/4 cup drained, diced chutney and 1/4 cup seedless raisins.

Spanish Rice

Brown ½ lb. bacon, chopped and ½ c. chopped onion in skillet; drain excess oil. Combine 1 can tomato sauce and 1 can water; season with salt and pepper. Fold in 2 c. cooked long grain rice and 1 c. (or more if desired) grated sharp Cheddar cheese. Place into buttered casserole and top with bacon and onion. Bake in 350 F. oven about 1 hour. (Leftovers can be reheated.) Spices (chili powder, tabasco sauce, garlic, thyme, oregano or bay leaf) can be added, to taste, if desired.

Chinese Fried Rice

3 slices bacon, diced	2 cups cold, cooked
2 tbsp. finely chopped onion	long grain rice
2 tbsp finely chopped	2 eggs, slightly beaten
green pepper	soy sauce

In skillet, cook bacon until crisp. Using slotted spoon, remove bacon from skillet and drain on paper towels; set aside. Pour off all but 2 tbsp. hot bacon drippings from skillet. In remaining drippings, stir-fry onions, green pepper and rice for approximately 5 minutes - then add eggs and bacon bits. Cook, stirring constantly, until eggs are firm shreds. Sprinkle with soy sauce. Serve piping hot. *Makes 3 to 4 servings.*

Garden Flavoured Rice

3/4 cup chopped onions; 1½ lbs. zucchini, thinly sliced; 3 tbsp butter or margarine; 1 (12 oz) can whole kernel corn, drained; 1 (14 oz) can tomatoes; 3 cups cooked rice; 1½ tsp salt; 1/4 tsp. pepper; 1/4 tsp. ground coriander; 1/4 tsp. leaf oregano.

Saute zucchini and onions in butter until tender. Add in remaining ingredients. Simmer, covered, 15 minutes. (This dish will freeze well.) *Makes 8 servings.*

Mona's Guide to Chinese Vegetables

Bok Choy
Also called "Chinese Cabbage".
Clump of white stocks ending in wide, dark-green leaves.
Store in refrigerator crisper up to one week.
Use in stir-fried vegetable, meat, poultry, or seafood dishes.

Ho Long Dow (Snow or Sugar Peas)
Pale green flat pea pod with tiny peas; entire pod is tender and edible.
Remove strings and tips before cooking.
Store in refrigerator crisper; use as soon as possible.
Requires very short cooking-time.
Use in stir-fried meat, poultry, vegetable, and seafood dishes.

Lo Bak (Chinese Radish)
White in colour; approx. 5 to 10 inches long, 2 to 4 inches in diameter.
Peel before using.
Store in refrigerator crisper up to one week.
Use in stir-fried dishes, steamed with butter; raw in salads.

Sui Choy
Also known as "Celery Cabbage" in Chinese recipes.
White stalks tipped in light green, in celery shape, about 10 to 12 inches long.
Store in refrigerator crisper.
Use raw in salads; in stir-fried vegetables, meat, poultry, or seafood dishes.

Yen Sai (Chinese Parsley)
More tender and stronger flavour than North American variety.
A coriander spice plant.
Store in refrigerator crisper approx. 1 week.
Use as garnish or flavour in soups, poultry, and meat dishes; use sparingly.

Ngah Choi (Bean Sprouts)
Tiny white shoots about 2 inches long with pale green hoods.
For salads, blanch for an instant in boiling water, then plunge into cold water; drain.
Use in salads, omelets, soups, seafood, meat, and poultry dishes.

VEGETABLES AND SAUCES

Sour Cream Mustard Sauce

A great topping for your favourite vegetables. Try using this sauce also to brighten up heated, leftover vegetables.

1 cup sour cream	1/4 tsp. salt
1 tbsp. minced onion	dash pepper
1 tbsp. prepared mustard	1 tbsp. chopped parsley

In small saucepan, over *very low heat*, heat sour cream, minced onion, prepared mustard, salt and pepper, just until hot. Sprinkle with parsley. *Yields - approximately 1 cup.*

Quick Melted Butter Sauces

Try one of these melted butter sauces to perk up your menu.

Clarified or Drawn Butter
- great for sauteing chicken or fish. Serve with broiled shrimp or lobster.

Melt 1/2 cup butter over moderate heat. Skim off foam. Pour off clear yellow butter; leaving milky residue in bottom of pan.

Lemon Butter
- delicious on vegetables.
Add 3 tbsp. lemon juice to above recipe for Clarified Butter.

Brown Butter
Heat 1/2 cup clarified butter until a delicate brown colour.

Crunchy Crumb Butter
- delicious over broccoli or cauliflower and topped with chopped hard-cooked egg.
Saute 1/3 cup toasted bread crumbs in 1/2 cup Brown Butter; add 1 1/2 tbsp. lemon juice and 1 tbsp. chopped parsley.

White Butter
- wonderful on salmon.
Simmer 2 tbsp. finely chopped green onions, 2 tbsp. white wine vinegar, and 1/4 cup chicken bouillon until reduced to 2 tbsp. Remove from heat. Gradually add 1/2 cup chilled butter (cut into pieces) beating until light and creamy. Season to taste with salt and pepper.

Mushroom Butter
- great on vegetables.
Saute 2 cups sliced mushrooms and 2 tbsp. finely chopped green onion in 1/2 cup butter until lightly browned.

Nut Butter
- try this recipe on green beans, squash or sweet potatoes.
Saute 2/3 cup sliced nuts (almonds, Brazil nuts, peanuts, walnuts) in 1/2 cup butter until golden brown. Season to taste with salt and pepper.

Spicy Cheese Spread

2 cups sharp cheddar cheese, grated
  medium-fine
    1/3 cup pimiento-stuffed green olives,
    chopped medium-fine
    1/2 cup chopped walnuts
  2 tbsp. finely chopped green onions
  1 tbsp. chopped parsley
  1/2 cup mayonnaise
2 tbsp. prepared mustard
1 tbsp. horseradish
dash pepper

In a medium-size bowl combine all the ingredients. Mix well. A versatile spread to have on hand. Serve on crackers, with hamburgers, as a stuffing for baked tomatoes, a baked potato topper, stuffing celery stalks or as a sandwich spread. *Makes approximately 2 cups.*

Vegetable Platter with Fluffy Hollandaise Sauce

Vegetables

2 lbs. fresh broccoli or	2 lbs. fresh carrots,
2 packages (10 oz.)	boiling salted water.
frozen broccoli spears,	

If using fresh broccoli, trim and discard outer leaves and tough ends. If stalks are large, split lengthwise. Cook in boiling, salted water until tender. If using frozen broccoli, cook according to package directions. Drain well and keep warm. Peel carrots; cut into julienne strips. Cook in boiling salted water until tender — approximately 20 minutes; keep warm. Arrange attractively on warmed serving platter and spoon Fluffy Hollandaise Sauce over.

Sauce

½ cup butter or margarine,	2 tbsp. lemon juice,
¼ cup hot water,	¼ tsp. salt, or to taste,
4 egg yolks,	dash cayenne.

In top of double boiler, over simmering water, melt butter. When butter is melted, add hot water; stir; remove top of double boiler from heat (keep water in bottom of double boiler simmering). Add unbeaten egg yolks all at once; beat with electric or rotary beater until egg-butter mixture is almost double in bulk — several minutes. Stir in lemon juice, salt and cayenne. Return to stove and place over simmering water. Cook, stirring constantly, until thickened — approximately 5 minutes. Remove from heat. Serve immediately over prepared vegetables.

Tips on Sauce
- Ensure water in bottom part of double boiler never boils during cooking time.
- Do not allow water to touch bottom of upper pan of double boiler.
- If cooking sauce in advance, let it stand uncovered after cooking. To reheat, place pan over simmering water again and stir gently for several minutes. Sauce may lose some of its fluffiness in reheating but will still be creamy and delicious.

French Fries (oven style)

Place 2 tbsp of oil in shallow pan. Add frozen French Fries. Bake in 325°F oven for 1 hour OR in a 350°F oven for 40 minutes. NOTE: If potatoes are not quite browned or crisp enough, turn on the broiler for a few minutes.

Rakott Burgonya (layer potatoes)

1 cup sour cream; 1/2 cup whipping cream; 1-1/2 tsp. salt; 6 medium potatoes, cooked, cooled and thinly sliced; 3 hard-cooked eggs, sliced; 1 cup finely diced, fully cooked ham; 1 cup fresh bread crumbs; 2 tbsp. melted butter or margarine; 1/4 tsp. onion salt.

Preheat oven to 350 degrees F. In small bowl blend together sour cream, whipping cream and salt. In a greased 1-1/2 qt. casserole, arrange one third of potatoes, top with egg slices, then one half of cream mixture. Add another one third of potatoes; sprinkle with ham; pour over remaining cream mixture; then top with remaining potatoes. Toss crumbs with butter and onion salt, sprinkle evenly over potatoes. Bake 30 minutes or until bubbly. Serve with a crisp green salad. *Makes 6 to 8 servings.*

Baked Potato Variations

6 baked potatoes	*1/4 to 1/3 cup milk*
2 tbsp. butter	*salt and pepper to taste*

Bake potatoes; cut a slice from top of each potato; scoop out centre (leave shell intact). Mash potatoes; add butter and milk; season to taste with salt and pepper. Refill shells. Place stuffed potatoes in shallow baking dish. Place potatoes in 400 degree F. oven for 15 minutes or until done. *Makes 6 servings.*

Variations

- add 2 to 4 tbsp. raw or sauteed onion to potato filling
- mix mashed potatoes with sour cream instead of milk, add chopped green onions or chives
- add crumbled Roquefort cheese to taste to potato mixture when mashing
- add 2/3 cup grated sharp cheddar cheese to potato filling
- add 3/4 to 1 cup finely diced cooked ham into potato filling
- add 6 to 8 slices crisp-cooked, crumbled bacon to potato mixture
- add 1 cup sliced, sauteed mushrooms to potato filling

Egg Stuffed Potatoes

Refill potato shells, forming a 1/2-inch high ring around opening (leaving a depression in centre). Into this place 1 tsp. butter (for each potato); sprinkle with salt and pepper. Break an egg into centre of each hollow. Bake in 350 degree F. oven for about 15 minutes - or until egg is done as you like it. Garnish with chopped parsley or green onions and serve with bacon, sausages or sauteed ham slices.

Sweet Potatoes on Pineapple Rings

2 cups mashed cooked sweet potatoes; 1/2 tsp. salt; 1/2 cup brown sugar; 4 tbsp. butter; 4 slices canned pineapple; 4 marshmallows; 4 maraschino cherries.

Combine sweet potatoes, salt, sugar and 3 tablespoons butter in a mixing bowl and beat until light and fluffy. Place slices of pineapple on a baking sheet. Dot with remaining butter. Force sweet potato mixture through a pastry bag, using the rose tube, onto the slices of pineapple for individual servings. Top each serving with a marshmallow and a cherry. Bake in a hot oven (400 degrees F.) until heated through, about 10 minutes. *Serves 4.*

Cottage Hashed Brown Potatoes

1 1/2 lb. potatoes [approx. 4 medium], peeled	*1/2 tsp. salt [or to taste]*
3/4 cup finely chopped onion	*1/8 tsp. pepper [or to taste]*
1/2 cup finely chopped celery	*3 tbsp. butter*
2 tsp. finely chopped parsley	*2 tbsp. salad oil*

Peel and cook potatoes in boiling, salted water until tender. Allow to cool. Shred potatoes. In bowl, toss together potatoes, onions, celery and parsley. Season to taste with salt and pepper. In skillet, heat butter and oil. Pack potato mixture firmly in skillet, leaving a 1/2-inch space around edges. Cook over low heat for 10 to 15 minutes or until bottom crust is browned. Cut potato mixture into fourths; turn each portion. If necessary, add more butter. Cook 10 to 15 minutes longer or until browned. Makes 4 servings.
Variation; Cooked, cubed beef or ham can be added as a budget dinner.

Potato with Onion Caps

12 medium potatoes, pared and cut up; 1/2 cup butter or margarine (for potatoes); 1 cup milk, scalded; 3 tbsp. parsley flakes; salt and pepper to taste; 2 Bermuda onions, peeled and cut in 6 thick slices each; 3 tbsp. melted butter or margarine (for onions); olives and pimiento to garnish if desired.

Cook potatoes in salted water until tender. Drain well. Mash well and stir in the 1/2 cup butter or margarine; then beat in scalded milk slowly as needed until creamy smooth. Add parsley flakes, salt and pepper. Cover pan and keep hot. Broil onion slices, that have been brushed with the 3 tbsp. melted butter, without turning, approximately 8 to 10 minutes or until tender and lightly browned. Spoon hot potatoes in 12 even mounds on platter around roast, steak, or turkey. Top each with an onion slice. Rings will separate to make cap and then garnish with sliced olives and pimiento if desired. *Makes 12 servings.*

Gourmet Sherry Onion Rings

6 medium-size onion, sliced and separated into rings, 1/4 cup butter or margarine, 1/2 tsp. MSG, 1/2 tsp. salt, 1/2 tsp. freshly ground black pepper, 1/2 cup cooking sherry, 1 tbsp. chopped parsley, 1/4 cup grated Parmesan cheese.

Prepare onions. In medium-size saucepan, melt butter. Add onions; season with MSG, salt, and pepper. Cook onions, stirring frequently until tender but not browned — approximately 7 to 9 minutes. Add sherry and parsley.

Cook quickly several minutes longer. Sprinkle with Parmesan cheese and serve immediately. *Makes 8 servings.*

Rainbow Corn

*1 cup celery,
thinly sliced on bias
1/4 cup butter or margarine
1 tin (12 oz. or 14 oz.)
kernel corn, drained*

*1/4 cup chopped canned pimiento
salt and pepper to taste*

In skillet, combine celery and butter. Cook gently for 5 minutes; add drained corn and pimiento. Season with salt and pepper. Cover and cook 10 minutes longer over low heat, stirring occasionally. Serve immediately. *Makes 6 to 8 servings.*

Scandinavian Cabbage

*6 cups shredded cabbage
boiling salted water
1 cup sour cream*

*1/2 tsp. caraway seed
1 tsp. salt or to taste
1/4 tsp. pepper*

Cook cabbage in boiling, salted water, covered, just until tender - approximately 5 to 8 minutes. Drain very well. In top of double boiler, toss cabbage, sour cream and season with caraway seed, salt and pepper. Cook, covered, over boiling water until heated through - approximately 10 minutes. *Makes 4 servings.*

Marinated Cucumbers

*⅓ cup water,
¼ cup vinegar,
1 tbsp. salad oil,
½ tsp. sugar,
½ tsp. salt,
freshly ground black
pepper,
⅛ tsp. garlic powder,*

*1 tsp. chopped parsley,
1 large cucumber, unpeeled,
scored with tines of fork
and thinly sliced,
finely chopped green
onions, for garnish,
if desired.*

In medium bowl, beat until very well blended, water, vinegar, salad oil, sugar, salt, pepper, garlic powder and parsley. Add prepared cucumber slices and toss gently. Cover and refrigerate. To serve, drain marinade. Sprinkle with chopped green onion, if desired.

Ratatouille (vegetable stew)

*1/4 cup oil
1 clove garlic, thinly sliced
1 medium onion thinly sliced
1 green pepper, seeded and thinly sliced*

*1 medium eggplant, peeled and sliced 1/4 inch thick
1 medium (2 small) zucchini, sliced 1/4 inch thick
2 medium tomatoes, thinly sliced
salt and pepper to taste*

Saute garlic in oil over medium heat in a large frying pan with a lid. Remove and reserve 1 tablespoon of garlic flavoured oil. Layer vegetables in order given, seasoning each layer with salt and pepper. Sprinkle reserved tablespoon of oil over layered vegetables; cover and cook over medium-low heat (simmer) for 30 minutes. Uncover and cook for additional 10 minutes to reduce liquid to desired thickness. *Serves 6 to 8.*

Squash — an interesting selection

Winter Squash
Winter squash comes in many sizes, colours and shapes, but all have a yellow-orange flesh. Good winter squash is heavy for its size, free from blemishes and has a hard shell. A pound of fresh squash makes approximately 1 cup when cooked. Descriptions of the most popular kinds are:

Acorn Squash is small, has a hard dark green or orange rind with distinct ridges and is shaped like an acorn. The flavour is faintly sweet and nutty. This squash bakes well, or when peeled or cubed, can be boiled and mashed or added to stews.

Butternut Squash is gourd shaped, may be as small as an acorn squash or as long as 10 to 12 inches. Its rind is smooth and thin, and ranges in colour from light-tan to dark yellow. The flesh varies from creamy-yellow to orange. The flavour is slightly nutty. This squash is best when baked or steamed.

Hubbard Squash is large with a thick, warty rind. Its colour varies from dark green to slate blue to orange-red. The flesh is thick, deep yellow and sweet. Delicious baked or steamed, or peeled, cubed and boiled until tender then mashed with butter. Delicious in stews.

Hubbard Squash Squares in Sour Cream

4 cups cubed, pared Hubbard squash, 2 tbsp. butter or margarine, 1 medium onion, sliced and separated into rings, 1 cup sour cream, salt and pepper to taste, 2 tsp. chopped parsley, 1/2 tsp. dill seed.

Cook squash in boiling, salted water 15 minutes or until tender; drain well. Keep hot. Meanwhile, melt butter and gently saute onion until tender but not browned; remove from heat; add sour cream and season with salt and pepper. Add parsley and stir well. Place hot squash on platter; pour sour cream mixture over. *Sprinkle with dill seed and serve immediately. Makes 4 to 6 servings.*

Yam Stuffed Apples

5 to 6 large apples
3 fully cooked yams, mashed
1 tbsp. lemon juice
1/4 cup brown sugar
2 tbsp. melted butter
1/2 tsp. cinnamon
1/8 tsp. ground nutmeg

Hollow out apples, leaving about 3/4-inch shell of apple. Thoroughly combine cooked yams, lemon juice, brown sugar, melted butter, cinnamon and nutmeg. Stuff prepared apples with filling. Bake in a 350 degree F. oven for approximately 25 minutes. *Makes 5 to 6 servings.*

Marinated Asparagus Platter

2 lbs. fresh asparagus spears, trimmed (or use frozen or tinned equivalent)
1 cup well seasoned oil and vinegar salad dressing
1/4 cup finely chopped green pepper
1/4 cup finely chopped dill pickle
2 tbsp. finely chopped parsley
1 tbsp. finely chopped green onion
1 tbsp. chopped capers, optional
1 hard cooked egg
bed of lettuce
1 hard cooked egg, sliced and pimiento strips for garnish

Cook fresh or frozen asparagus until tender (if using tinned, drain thoroughly). In screw-top jar, combine dressing, green pepper, dill pickle, parsley, green onion and capers (if desired). Cover; shake vigorously. Chop 1 hard-cooked egg; stir into dressing. Place asparagus in shallow dish. Pour prepared dressing over spears. Cover and refrigerate until well chilled. To serve, place drained asparagus attractively over bed of lettuce. Garnish with hard-cooked egg slices and pimiento strips. *Makes 6 to 8 servings.*

Cabbage, Parsnips and Potatoes

3 qts. water
1 tbsp. salt
6 medium potatoes
2 1/2 to 3 lbs. parsnips
1 head cabbage (approximately 2 1/2 lbs.)
1/2 cup butter or margarine
2 tsp. lemon juice
salt and pepper to taste
1 tbsp. chopped parsley

Place water and salt in large kettle; bring to boiling. Meanwhile, pare potatoes; pare parsnips and halve lengthwise; cut cabbage into 6 wedges. Add vegetables to boiling water; return to boiling.

Lower heat and simmer, covered, 25 minutes or until vegetables are tender. Drain vegetables and place in serving dish. Keep warm. Meanwhile, in small saucepan, melt butter; add lemon juice and season with salt and pepper; add chopped parsley. Drizzle butter mixture over cooked vegetables. Serve immediately. *Makes 6 servings.*

Cabbage in Cream

3 cups finely shredded cabbage
3/4 cup milk
1/4 cup cream
1/2 tsp. salt or to taste
1/8 tsp. pepper
1 tbsp. butter, softened
1 tbsp. flour
1/4 tsp. paprika

Prepare cabbage. In saucepan, bring milk just to boiling. Add cabbage; boil for 2 minutes. Stir in cream, salt and pepper. Blend butter with flour and paprika. Add to cabbage mixture and stir to combine. Cook, over medium heat until cabbage is tender - approximately 3 to 5 minutes. *Makes 6 servings.*

Jigg's Corned Beef and Cabbage

2 cups chopped canned corned beef
1 medium onion, chopped
2 tbsp. oil
salt and pepper to taste
2 tbsp. chopped parsley
1 cup diced, cooked potatoes
1 cup tinned tomatoes
1/2 cup chili sauce
2 cups shredded cabbage

In Dutch oven, brown chopped corned beef and onion in oil. Season to taste with salt and pepper. Sprinkle with chopped parsley. Add potatoes, tomatoes, chili sauce and cabbage. Stir to combine well. Bake, covered, in 350 degree F. oven approximately 45 minutes, or until piping hot and cabbage is tender. *Makes 4 servings.*

Broccoli Italiano

2 lbs. fresh broccoli (OR 2 (10 oz) pkgs. frozen broccoli); 1/2 tsp. oregano, crushed; 1/2 cup mayonnaise or salad dressing; 1/4 cups shredded sharp process cheese; 1 tbsp. milk.

Cook broccoli in boiling salted water to which oregano has been added until tender. In top of double boiler, mix mayonnaise, cheese and milk; heat over hot, NOT boiling water, stirring until cheese melts and mixture is hot. Serve with broccoli. *Serves 6.*

Sweet 'N' Sour Red Cabbage

1 medium firm red cabbage
6 slices bacon
1 medium onion, chopped
1 tsp. salt
1/8 tsp. pepper
1/2 cup water
2 cups peeled and cored apples, thinly sliced
1/2 cup vinegar
1/4 cup brown sugar

Finely shred cabbage; cook bacon until crisp; remove bacon from drippings; crumble bacon; set aside. In bacon drippings saute onions for 2 minutes; add cabbage, salt, pepper, water, apples, vinegar and brown sugar. Add reserved crumbled bacon. Place mixture in a buttered casserole with lid. Bake in 325 degree F. oven for approximately 1 hour or until vegetabels are tender.

Whipped Onion Butter

A great topping for piping hot steaks or hamburgers.

1/4 cup butter or margarine
1 tsp. Worcestershire sauce
1/4 tsp. seasoned pepper
1/4 tsp. dry mustard
2 tbsp. minced onion
2 tbsp. chopped parsley

In small bowl, combine butter, Worcestershire sauce, seasoned pepper and dry mustard. Cream with wooden spoon until light and fluffly. Stir in onion and parsley. Spoon over piping hot steak or hamburgers. *Makes approximately 1/3 cup.*

Glazed Squash with Onions and Walnuts

3 acorn squash, cut in half lengthwise (seeds removed)	1/2 cup broken walnuts
salt	1/3 cup butter or margarine
2 cups cooked and drained small whole onions	1/3 cup light molasses
	1/4 tsp. cinnamon
	1/4 tsp. salt or to taste

Prepare squash. Place in shallow baking pan, cut side down in 350 degree F. oven for 35 to 40 minutes or until almost tender.

Turn cut side up. Season cavities lightly with salt. Fill with onions and walnuts. In small saucepan, melt butter; add molasses, cinnamon and salt. Spoon part of mixture over squash and filling. Return to oven and continue cooking 15 to 20 minutes longer or until squash is tender, brushing several times with remaining sauce to glaze. *Makes 6 servings.*

Baked Stuffed Onions

8 large sweet Spanish onions	2/3 cup canned well-drained whole kernel corn
salted water	
1/2 lb. pork sausage meat	dash pepper
1 cup soft bread crumbs	2 tbsp. butter or margarine
2 tbsp. chopped parsley	1/2 tsp. paprika

Peel onions; cut a slice from top of each onion, using a small knife; scoop out enough to leave a cavity approximately 1 to 1-1/2 inches deep. Reserve scooped-out onion. In large saucepan, place onions with just enough salted water to cover; bring to boiling. Reduce heat; simmer, covered, for 18 to 20 minutes or until **just** tender. Do **not** overcook. Drain well. Chop enough reserved onion to make 1/2 cup; set aside. In small skillet, brown sausage meat (crumbling meat with a fork); drain off excess fat.

Add reserved chopped onion and continue cooking until onion is tender. Remove skillet from heat; stir in bread crumbs, parsley, corn and a dash of pepper; set aside. Melt butter; add paprika; brush onions with mixture to coat well. Fill onion cavities with sausage mixture. Arrange stuffed onions in lightly greased shallow baking dish. Cover loosely with foil. Bake in a 400 degree F. oven for 15 minutes; remove foil cover and continue cooking 5 minutes longer or until onions and stuffing are piping hot and topping is lightly golden. *Makes 8 servings.*

Baked Spinach Topped Tomatoes

¼ cup butter or margarine,	1 cup fine dry bread crumbs,
1 medium onion, finely chopped,	2 eggs, beaten,
1 large clove garlic, minced,	2 tsp. salt or to taste,
2 packages (10 oz.) frozen chopped spinach,	pepper to taste,
¼ tsp. MSG,	4 large tomatoes, halved,
2 tsp. lemon juice,	grated Parmesan cheese.

In skillet, melt butter over medium heat; saute onion and garlic until tender but not browned. Add spinach, MSG, lemon juice and cook 7 to 8 minutes longer or until spinach is tender, breaking spinach up with spoon and stirring fairly frequently. Remove skillet from heat; add bread crumbs, eggs, salt and pepper. Stir to combine; set aside. Place tomato halves, cut side up in greased 13 x 9 x 2 baking dish (or similar size). If necessary, cut a thin slice from bottom of each tomato half so it stands upright. Divide spinach mixture into 8 portions and mound onto each tomato half. Cover and refrigerate. To serve: Preheat oven to 350 degrees F. Lightly sprinkle Parmesan cheese over spinach. Bake, uncovered, 35 minutes or until piping hot. *Makes 8 servings.*

Glazed Carrots and Onions

2 lbs. small carrots	1/4 cup brown sugar
2 tbsp. water	1 tbsp. lemon juice
1/2 tsp. salt or to taste	1 tsp. grated lemon rind
1/4 tsp. pepper	1 large onion, sliced and separated into rings
1/4 cup butter	chopped parsley

Wash and scrape carrots (if carrots are large, cut into julienne strips). In saucepan, place water, salt, pepper, butter, brown sugar, lemon juice and lemon rind. Heat until butter melts. Stir to combine. Add carrots and onions. Cook over low heat until vegetables are tender and nicely glazed. Sprinkle with chopped parsley. *Makes 4 to 6 servings.*

Onions Italiano

1 lb. small white onions	1 bay leaf
boiling, salted water	salt and pepper to taste
1 can (7-1/2 oz.) tomato sauce	coarsely chopped green pepper
1/2 tsp. Worcestershire sauce	for garnish if desired
1/2 tsp. oregano	

Peel onions; cook in lightly salted boiling water until almost tender. Drain well. Meanwhile, in saucepan, combine thoroughly tomato sauce, Worcestershire sauce, oregano and bay leaf. Season to taste with salt and pepper. Simmer for 10 minutes to blend flavours, stirring occasionally. Remove bay leaf. Add hot, cooked onions.

Cover and simmer gently until onions are tender. To serve, place in a heated serving dish and garnish with coarsely chopped green pepper. *Makes 4 servings.*

Vegetable Casserole

5 medium carrots, sliced (1½ cups), 1 medium onion, sliced, 1 (12 oz.) pkg. frozen leaf spinach, 3 tbsp. butter or margarine, 3 tbsp. all purpose flour, 1½ cups milk, 1 cup shredded Canadian cheese, ¼ tsp. salt, dash pepper, ½ cup buttered soft bread crumbs.

Cook carrots and onion in small amount salted boiling water, covered, until almost tender, about 8 minutes. Drain. Following package directions, cook spinach; drain. For sauce, melt butter; mix in flour; gradually blend in milk. Cook and stir until thick; remove from heat. Add cheese, salt and pepper, stirring until cheese melts. Place half the spinach in ungreased 1-quart casserole; cover with half the carrots and onions. Top with half the cheese sauce. Repeat layers. Sprinkle bread crumbs over top. Bake in 350 F. oven for 15 to 20 minutes. Serves 6.

Frypan Carrots

8 medium carrots, 3 tbsp. butter or margarine, ½ tsp. salt.

Coarsely shred the carrots. Melt butter in a skillet and add carrots. Sprinkle with salt. Cover and cook just tender, about 5 to 8 minutes. Top with snipped parsley.

Basque Potatoes

1 medium-size onion, chopped (1/2 cup); 1 small clove garlic, crushed; 2 tbsp olive oil; 3/4 cup chopped parsley; 1/4 cup chopped pimiento; 1 tsp salt; 1/8 tsp pepper; 1 envelope instant chicken broth (OR 1 tsp granulated chicken bouillon); 1 cup water; 6 medium-size potatoes.

In a medium-size skillet, saute onion and garlic in olive oil until soft; stir in parsley, pimiento, salt, pepper, chicken broth and water. Remove from heat; set aside. Peel potatoes and slice thinly (should have about 6 cups). Layer potato slices in the broth, in the skillet; heat to boiling. Reduce heat and simmer, covered, about 20 minutes, or until tender. Using a slotted spoon remove potatoes to a heated serving dish. Spoon remaining cooking liquid over potatoes. *Makes 8 servings.*

Lima beans

1/3 cup butter
  or margarine
2 packages (10 oz.)
  lima beans
1 tsp. sugar

1 tsp. salt
pepper to taste
1/4 cup chopped parsley
2 tsp. lemon juice

In medium-size, heavy saucepan, melt butter; add frozen lima beans, sugar, salt and pepper. Cover. Cook slowly 5 minutes; stir with fork to mix; cover. Cook gently 15 minutes longer or until tender. Sprinkle parsley and lemon juice over top. Toss gently. Serve immediately. *Makes 6 servings.*

Seasoned Vegetable Combo

1 tin (19 oz.) tomatoes, drained and coarsely chopped
1 tin (12 oz.) whole kernel corn, drained
1 medium green pepper, coarsely chopped
1 tbsp. butter

1/4 tsp. celery seed
dash oregano
1-1/2 tsp. salt or to taste
dash pepper

Combine all ingredients in saucepan. Cook, uncovered, over medium heat until green pepper is tender. Stir frequently. *Makes 6 servings.*

Lemon Turnips

2 cups turnip sticks
boiling, salted water
1-1/2 tbsp. butter or margarine
1 tsp. lemon juice

2 tsp. chopped parsley
1 tsp. very finely chopped onion
salt and pepper to taste

In saucepan, cook turnip sticks in boiling salted water just until tender - approximately 20 minutes; drain well. Keep hot. Meanwhile, in small saucepan, melt butter; add lemon juice, parsley and onion. Season with salt and pepper to taste. Stir to combine. Toss with hot drained turnip. *Makes 4 servings.*

Sweet'n'sour Soybeans

1 cup soybeans; water; 2 tbsp. salad oil; 1 large onion, cut in 1-inch squares; 2 large carrots, cut in 1/4-inch slices; 1 clove garlic, minced or mashed; 1 green pepper, seeded, cut in 1-inch squares; 3/4 cup canned pineapple chunks, drained; 2 small tomatoes, cut in 1-inch cubes; Sweet-Sour sauce.

Rinse soybeans; place in a large bowl. Add 3 cups water. Cover and soak for 6 to 8 hours or overnight. Drain beans, saving the liquid. Combine beans and reserved liquid in a 3-qt. saucepan, adding additional water, if necessary, to cover beans. Simmer, covered, for 3 hours, or until beans are tender. Stir several times; add a little additional water if needed to prevent sticking. Drain, reserving liquid for sauce; discard skins. Set beans aside. Prepare Sweet-Sour Sauce. In a large frypan or wok, heat oil over high heat.

Add in onion, carrots and garlic. Cook, stirring, for about 3 minutes or until slightly tender but still crisp. Add green pepper; cook 1 minute then add pineapple, tomato, soybeans and Sweet-Sour Sauce. Continue to cook, stirring, until mixture boils and all ingredients are covered with sauce, about 2 minutes. *Makes 4 to 6 servings.*

Sweet-Sour Sauce: Stir together 1 tbsp. cornstarch, 1/3 cup firmly packed brown sugar, 1/4 tsp. ground ginger, 1 tbsp. soy sauce, 1 tbsp. sherry, 5 tbsp. wine vinegar and 1/4 cup reserved cooking liquid or beef broth.

Beans Amandine

3 cups green beans
  [French cut]
1/2 cup almonds, slivered
2 tbsp. butter

1/2 tsp. salt
1/8 tsp. pepper
1/8 tsp. nutmeg

Cook beans until tender. Saute almonds in butter until golden. Drain beans. Pour almonds and butter over beans; add seasoning. Toss to mix. Serve.

Basic Ways to Prepare Beans and Beets

BEETS

There are two basic ways to prepare beets:
1. Cut off all of the greens to 1 inch of root. Wash and scrub thoroughly. Do not pare. Cook, covered, in boiling salted water for 35 to 60 minutes or until tender. Peel beets when cooked.
2. Pare and slice, cube or shred beet root. Cook covered in small amount of boiling salted water 10 minutes if shredded OR 15 to 20 minutes if sliced or cubed.

• Try seasoning beets with one or more of the following: a little lemon juice, a pinch of cloves or allspice, a little horseradish, a few sauteed onions.

• For an attractive garnish, marinate separated onion rings in beet juice for 30 minutes. Alternate marinated onion rings with white onion rings in a chain. Garnish a salad, open-face sandwiches or casserole most attractively this way.

BEANS

To prepare beans use either of the two following methods:
1. Wash beans well. Cut off ends and string. Cut into 1 inch pieces or cook whole in small amount of boiling salted water for 20 to 30 minutes or until tender-crisp.
2. Wash beans well. Cut off ends and string. Slit lengthwise. Cook in small amount of boiling salted water for approximately 10 to 12 minutes or until tender-crisp.

Note: To avoid making beans tough, add salt half way through cooking process.

• Beans lend themselves to a great variety of spices and combinations. Try one or more of the following suggestions: toasted almonds, chili sauce, dash curry powder, snipped parsley, lemon juice, Parmesan cheese, soy sauce, prepared mustard, sauteed mushrooms, slivered cooked carrots or chopped canned pimientos.

Orange Beets

1 tin (14 oz.) sliced beets,   1 tbsp. cider vinegar
   well drained   2 tbsp. butter or margarine
2 tbsp. orange marmalade   1/2 tsp. salt

In medium saucepan, combine all ingredients. Cook over low heat, stirring occasionally until beets are heated through. Turn into serving bowl. Serve immediately. *Makes 4 servings.*

The science of fishing can be had from books; the art is learned by the catching and the losing of fish. Brown Waters, 1915. W. H. Blake.

Mona says . . .

Before broiling fish, add bits of butter to bring out the flavour.

Season cod fillets, clams, oysters and prawns before dipping in batter.

Fry these luscious morsels a golden colour then garnish with one or more of the following: lemon wedges, strips of pimento, radish roses, parsley sprigs, tomato wedges.

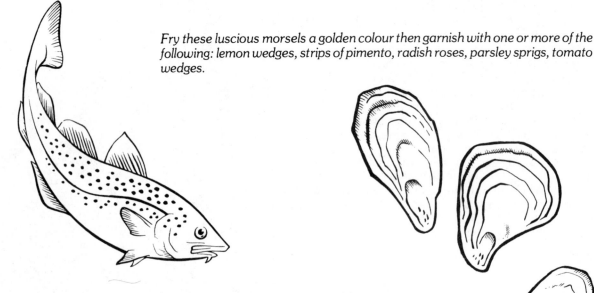

Broiled Salmon Steaks with Lemon-Parsley Butter

4 salmon steaks, cut 1/2 thick
1/4 cup butter or margarine

1 tsp. seasoned salt or to taste
dash pepper

Lemon-Parsley Butter

1/4 cup butter or margarine
2 tbsp. lemon juice

2 tbsp. chopped parsley
1/2 tsp. grated lemon rind (optional)

Wipe salmon steaks with a damp cloth; pat dry with paper towels. Place salmon steaks on rack of broiler pan. Melt butter; add seasoned salt and pepper. Brush top side of salmon with 2 tbsp. seasoned butter. Broil, 4 inches from heat, for 10 minutes. Turn steaks; brush with remaining seasoned butter. Broil approximately 8 minutes longer or until fish flakes easily when tested with a fork. Meanwhile, make Lemon-Parsley butter. In small saucepan, melt butter; add lemon juice, parsley and grated lemon rind. Stir to combine. Keep warm. When salmon is cooked, remove to a warm serving platter. Drizzle Lemon-Parsley Butter over top. *Makes 4 servings.*

Note: For a taste change, delete the 2 tbsp. parsley when making Lemon-Parsley Butter and substitute 2 tbsp. chopped chives.

Even the people who don't eat fish
May like the look of them on a dish — *W. Clark Sandercock,* A FISH STORY, 1937

SEAFOODS

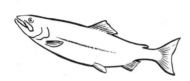

Fish and Shellfish

Fish can be baked, broiled, poached, fried, smoked, barbecued, pickled, and made into chowders. Fish are a good source of mineral salts and almost our only real source of iodine in the diet.

Whole baked, stuffed salmon has an aroma not soon forgotten. Oysters, clams, prawns, shrimp combine with raw vegetables and hot spicy sauces to whet our appetites, and lend elegance to our holiday dining. Seafoods are well worth that extra bit of work and attention.

Lemon Dill Butter

A super topping for your salmon steaks or sole fillets.

1/4 cup soft butter, 1/2 tbsp. lemon juice, 1/4 tsp. finely grated lemon rind, 1 tbsp. chopped parsley, 1/4 tsp. dillweed, dash white pepper.

In small bowl cream butter; gradually beat in lemon juice, lemon rind until all juice is absorbed. Stir in parsley, dillweed and pepper. Place in covered container and refrigerate. Remove from refrigerator 30 minutes before serving. *Makes 4 servings.*

Creamed Salmon on Muffin

1 can (7-3/4 oz.) salmon	1 cup liquid
3 tbsp. butter or margarine	(salmon juice plus milk)
3 tbsp. flour	2 green onions, chopped
1/2 tsp. salt	2 hard-cooked eggs, sliced
1/4 tsp. dry mustard	1/4 tsp. paprika
	2 English muffins

Drain salmon, reserving juice to combine with milk, and flake. Melt butter in saucepan. Combine flour, salt and mustard; blend into melted butter. Add salmon juice/milk liquid slowly, stirring constantly until thickened. Fold in flaked salmon and green onions. Split muffins and toast. Top muffin halves with creamed salmon. Garnish with egg slices and sprinkle with paprika. Serve hot immediately. *Makes 2 servings.*

Cheddar Cod Bake

2 tbsp. butter, ¼ c. flour, ½ tsp. salt, 1/8 tsp. pepper, 1 tsp. dry mustard, 1½ c. milk, 2 c. shredded Canadian Cheddar cheese, 1½ lbs. cod fillets, fresh or frozen, 3 tbsp. snipped parsley.

Butter a 9-inch square baking dish. Preheat oven to 400 F. Melt butter in saucepan, blend in flour and seasonings. Gradually stir in milk. Cook over medium heat, stirring constantly, until smoothly thickened. Add cheese and stir until melted. Wipe fillets with damp cloth and cut in serving pieces. Arrange fish in prepared baking dish, cover with cheese sauce and sprinkle with parsley. Bake in oven, 20 minutes. Makes 6 servings.

Crab Casserole

1 cup finely-chopped onion; 1 cup finely-chopped green pepper; 1 cup finely-chopped celery; 1/2 cup finely-chopped parsley; 6 tbsp butter or cooking oil; 1 can mushroom soup; 1 cup milk; 1½ tsp salt; 1 tsp dry mustard; 1½ tsp curry powder; 2 tsp Worcestershire sauce; 4 cups day-old bread crumbs; 2 lbs. crab meat; 1/2 cup bread crumbs, browned in butter; chopped parsley.

Saute the onion, green pepper, celery and parsley in butter or cooking oil for 30 minutes. Blend soup and milk in saucepan over medium heat. At simmering stage, add salt, mustard, curry powder and Worcestershire sauce. Blend well; add sauteed vegetables and stir in 4 cups bread crumbs. Add crab meat. Pour mixture into casserole dish. Sprinkle lightly with paprika and 1/2 cup buttered bread crumbs. Bake in 350°F oven until lightly browned, about 40 minutes. Garnish with chopped parsley before serving. *Makes 12 to 16 servings.*

Pacific Casserole

3 tbsp. butter or margarine, ¼ cup chopped onion, 2 tbsp. all-purpose flour, ¼ tsp. pepper, 1 pkg. (½ lb.) shell macaroni, cooked and drained, 2 (6¾ oz. each) cans pink salmon (or seafood of your choice), 1½ cups buttermilk, 1 cup (8 oz.) cottage cheese, 1 tbsp. melted butter or margarine, 3 tbsp. fine dry bread crumbs.

Melt butter or margarine in small frying pan; add onion and cook until tender and golden brown. Blend in flour and pepper, then stir into cooked macaroni. Add salmon, buttermilk and cottage cheese; toss lightly; turn into buttered 1 qt. baking dish. Mix together melted butter or margarine and bread crumbs; sprinkle over macaroni mixture. Bake in 350 F oven about 30 minutes, or until a golden brown on top. Serves 6.

Salmon Brunch

1 tin (7-3/4 oz.) salmon
3/4 cup grated Swiss cheese
2 tbsp. chopped green onion
3 tbsp. chopped stuffed olives
1/4 tsp. dill weed
1/8 tsp. pepper
2 tsp. lemon juice
1/4 cup mayonnaise
1 package (8 oz.)
  refrigerated crescent rolls.

Drain salmon, reserving the juice for Parsley Sauce. Flake salmon with a fork and combine with remaining ingredients, except crescent roll dough. Pinch sections of refrigerated rolls together to make one rectangle. Spread with salmon filling. Roll up from long side. Cut into 12 pinwheels. Place pinwheels cut-side down, in buttered baking dish. Bake in 375 degree F. oven for 20 to 25 minutes or until golden. Serve with Parsley Sauce. *Makes 4 to 6 servings.*

Pinwheels

hors d'oeuvre size:

Prepare salmon mixture as above. Divide dough into 4 rectangles, pinching seams together. Spread 1/4 of the salmon filling over each rectangle. Roll up from long sides. Cut each roll into 10 pinwheels. Place, cut-side down, on buttered baking sheet. Bake at 375 degrees F. for 12 to 15 minutes or until golden. *Makes 40 appetizers.*

Parsley Sauce

2 tbsp. butter
2 tbsp. flour
1/2 tsp. salt
1/8 tsp. pepper
1/4 tsp. dry mustard

Salmon Loaf

3 cans (7-3/4 oz. each) salmon
1 tbsp. lemon juice
3 cups toasted bread cubes
2 tbsp. wheat germ
1/2 cup grated Parmesan cheese
1/2 cup peeled, chopped cucumber
1 tbsp. chopped parsley
1 tbsp. chopped chives
2 tbsp. thinly sliced pimiento stuffed olives
2 tbsp. chili sauce
2 beaten eggs
1/2 cup unflavoured yogurt
salt and pepper to taste
extra Parmesan cheese (for topping)

In large bowl, place undrained salmon, flake salmon; sprinkle with lemon juice. Add remaining ingredients (except extra Parmesan cheese); combine thoroughly. Lightly pack mixture into a greased 9 x 5-inch loaf pan. Sprinkle extra grated Parmesan cheese over top of loaf. Bake in 400 degree F. oven for approximately 40 minutes or until done.

Serve with Mushroom Sauce. *Makes 6 to 8 servings.*

Mushroom Sauce

1 can (10 oz.) cream of mushroom soup
1/2 cup milk
1 tbsp. chopped chives
1 tbsp. lemon juice
dash Worcestershire sauce

In saucepan, blend all ingredients. Heat until piping hot (do not boil). Serve over Savory Salmon Loaf.

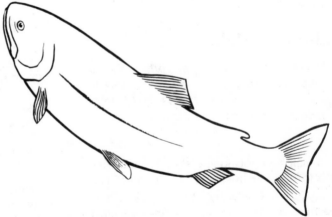

reserved salmon juice
1-1/2 cups milk
2 egg yolks, beaten
2 tbsp. snipped parsley

Melt butter. Blend in flour and seasonings. Add salmon juice and milk. Cook, stirring constantly, until thickened and smooth. Add a small amount of sauce to beaten egg yolks, then add egg yolks to remaining sauce. Cook, stirring constantly, until thickened. Add parsley and serve. *Makes about 2 cups sauce.*

Salmon Crunch, Whole Wheat Crust

2 tins (7-3/4 oz. each) Salmon
3 eggs, beaten
1 cup sour cream
1/2 cup shredded sharp cheddar cheese

1/4 cup mayonnaise
1 tbsp. grated onion
3 drops tabasco
1/4 tsp. dill weed
Whole Wheat Crust (recipe below)

Flake salmon including juice and mashed bones. Add eggs, sour cream, cheese, mayonnaise and seasonings to flaked salmon, mixing thoroughly. Turn into pie plate lined with whole wheat crust. Sprinkle with crumbs reserved from crust mixture. Bake in 400 degree F. oven for 45 minutes or until filling is set. *Makes 6 servings.*

Whole Wheat Crust

1-1/2 cups whole wheat flour
1 cup shredded sharp cheddar cheese
1/2 tsp. salt

1/2 tsp. paprika
1/2 cup butter
1/3 cup finely chopped almonds

Combine flour, cheese, salt and paprika. Cut in butter making crumbs. Add almonds and distribute evenly throughout mixture. Reserve 1 cup crumb mixture for topping. Press remaining crumb mixture into 9-inch pie plate.

Salmon Casserole

2 tins (7-3/4 oz. each) salmon
1 cup raw elbow macaroni
1-1/2 cups frozen kernel corn (or 1 tin (12 oz.) corn, drained)
1 large tomato, peeled, diced and drained
4 green onions, sliced
1/2 cup diced green pepper or celery

1 tin (10 oz.) cream of chicken soup
2 tbsp. lemon juice
1/2 tsp. grated lemon rind (optional)
1/2 tsp. salt
1/4 tsp. pepper
1 cup salad croutons
3 ounces cubed process cheese

Drain salmon and reserve juice. Mash bones and break salmon into chunks. Cook macaroni until tender and drain. Spread in a greased 2-1/2 to 3 quart casserole dish. Distribute salmon over macaroni. Add corn, tomato, onion and green pepper. Combine salmon juice, soup and remaining ingredients except croutons and cheese. Pour over contents of casserole and stir gently.

Spread evenly and bake, uncovered, in 375 degree F. oven for 20 to 25 minutes. Lightly stir again. Sprinkle salad croutons and cheese around the edge. Continue baking 10 to 15 minutes longer or until croutons and cheese are toasted. Garnish with crisp red apple wedges and sprigs of parsley. *Makes 5 to 6 servings.*

Note: To use leftover salmon casserole as a salad: - Moisten chilled leftovers with mayonnaise or salad dressing. Season to taste. Spoon into lettuce cups and garnish with egg slices, cucumber slices, crisp pickles or olives.

Seaside Salmon

2 tins (7-3/4 oz. each) salmon
1 cup frozen peas, uncooked
1/2 cup mayonnaise
1/3 cup finely chopped green onion
1 tsp. dillweed
1/2 package (approx. 6 oz.) jumbo seashell noodles, cooked and drained*

1 tin (10 oz.) condensed cream of mushroom soup
1/2 cup liquid (juice from salmon plus water to make up required amount)
1/4 cup chopped parsley

Drain salmon, reserving juice. Flake salmon into a bowl, including well mashed bones. Add peas, mayonnaise, onion and dillweed. Mix well. Stuff salmon mixture in cooked shells.

Arrange shells in single layer in greased baking dish. Stir liquid into condensed soup and pour over shells. Cover with foil. Bake in 325 degree F. oven for 25 minutes. Garnish with chopped parsley before serving. *Makes 8 servings.*

*Pasta will be further cooked in oven. Therefore, for initital cooking, reduce recommended cooking time on package by one-third.

Salmon Burgers

1 tin (7 3/4 oz.) salmon, drained, 2 tsp. lemon juice, 2 green onions, chopped, 2 tbsp. mayonnaise, dash pepper, 1/4 tsp. dill weed, 1/2 tsp. horseradish, 6 hamburger buns, prepared barbecue sauce, 3 slices processed cheddar cheese, halved, 1 tomato, cut in 6 slices.

Sprinkle salmon with lemon juice. In bowl combine thoroughly, salmon, green onions, mayonnaise, pepper, dill weed and horse radish. Split buns in half. Lightly spread barbecue sauce on cut sides of buns. Divide and spread salmon mixture on six halves.

Place 1/2 cheese slice and tomato slice on other 6 halves. Place top half of bun on bottom. Wrap each burger individually in foil. Place in 450 degree F. oven for 12 to 15 minutes or until cheese has melted and burger is piping hot. *Makes 6 salmon burgers.*

Salmon Steaks with Almond Sauce

2 lbs. salmon steaks, cut approximately 1-inch thick
2 tsp. minced green onions
1 tbsp. chopped parsley
1 tbsp. lemon juice

1/2 cup mayonnaise
1/3 cup unblanched almonds, minced finely
whole almonds for garnish, if desired

Wipe fish with damp cloth. If fish is frozen, do not thaw. Place salmon steaks on lightly greased steamer rack. Bring 2 inches of water to a rapid boil in steamer pot. Place salmon on rack in steamer and cover tightly. Steam fresh salmon 10 minutes per inch thickness; frozen salmon 20 minutes per inch thickness, or until fish flakes when fork tested. Remove from steamer to heated serving platter. In bowl, combine green onion, parsley, lemon juice, mayonnaise and unblanched minced almonds.

Spread mixture over hot steaks. Garnish with whole almonds if desired. Serve immediately. *Makes 6 servings.*

Halibut Steaks, Chinese Sauce

1-1/2 lbs. halibut steaks, cut approximately 1-inch thick	1 tsp. salt
2 tbsp. dry sherry	1/2 tsp. pepper
2 tbsp. lemon juice	1/2 tsp. ground ginger
2 tbsp. soya sauce	2 scallions, cut into pieces (or use 2 green onions)
2 tbsp. salad oil	

Fill steamer pot with water up to 1-1/2 inches below steamer rack. Bring to a rapid boil. Meanwhile wipe fresh halibut with a damp cloth. If frozen, do not thaw. Place halibut on large piece of double thickness heavy-duty foil. Turn edges of foil up all around fish to contain liquids to be added later. Lay fish on steamer rack over rapidly boiling water. Combine remaining ingredients. Pour over fish. Cover tightly. Steam fresh fish 15 minutes; frozen fish 25 minutes, or until fish flakes easily when fork-tested. Baste fish occasionally with sauce during cooking. *Makes 4 servings.*

Baked Halibut

2 lbs. halibut fillets, ¾ inch thick, fresh or frozen, 1½ tsp. salt, 1 tsp. paprika, 1 medium to large size lemon, peeled, seeded, finely chopped, ½ cup sliced ripe olives, ½ cup snipped fresh parsley, 1 large tomato, sliced, dairy sour cream, lemon wedges.

If frozen, thaw fillets. Cut into serving pieces and season with salt and paprika. Place in covered baking dish. Mix together chopped lemon and any juice from chopping, olives and parsley. Spread half of mixture over fillets; top each serving with a tomato slice and remaining lemon mixture. Cover and bake in 400 F. oven for 25 minutes; uncover and bake another 10 minutes. Garnish each serving with a topping of sour cream; serve with lemon wedges. Makes 4 to 6 servings.

Baked Halibut Royale

2 pounds halibut steak, cut 1 inch thick	1/2 cup chopped onion
1 tsp. salt	1 tbsp. butter or other fat
1/2 tsp. paprika	green pepper strips for garnish
few grains cayenne	
juice of one lemon	

Place halibut steaks in a shallow baking dish. Combine salt, paprika and cayenne with lemon juice and pour over the steaks.

Marinate in refrigerator for 1 hour, turning the steaks at half time so seasonings penetrate both sides. Cook onion in fat until tender. Spread steaks with onion. Top with green pepper strips and baste with marinade. Bake in hot oven (450 degrees F.) for 10 minutes or until fish flakes easily when tested with a fork. *Makes 8 servings.*

*Note: if cooking fish from the frozen state double the cooking time.

Mère's Salmon Potato Loaf

1 tin (15 1/2 oz.) OR 2 tins (7 3/4 oz.) pink salmon, undrained	2 eggs, well beaten
	2 tbsp. melted margarine
	3 tbsp. lemon juice
1 cup grated cooked potato, packed	2 to 3 tbsp. fine dry bread crumbs
1 cup grated raw carrot	3/4 tsp. salt
2 tbsp. finely chopped onion	dash pepper

Mash salmon and juice together. Discard dark skin, if desired. Add remaining ingredients and toss lightly together. Spread in greased loaf pan and set in pan of hot water. Bake in 350 degree F. oven for approximately 50 to 60 minutes, or until loaf is set.

Cool slightly and unmold. Serve in slices with tomato sauce or chopped egg-cream sauce. *Makes 5 to 6 servings.*

Salmon-Zucchini Wedges

A delicious appetizer or luncheon dish.

1-2/3 cups shredded zucchini (about 1/2 lb.)	4 tsp. lemon juice
1/3 cup finely chopped onion	3 tbsp. chopped parsley
water	1/4 tsp. dried dillweed
3 well beaten eggs	salt and pepper to taste
1/2 cup grated Parmesan cheese	1 tin (7-3/4 oz.) salmon, drained and flaked

In small saucepan, combine zucchini and onion; add water to cover. Bring mixture to boiling; reduce heat and simmer, covered, just until vegetables are tender (approximately 3 minutes). Drain well, squeezing out any excess liquid. In bowl, combine eggs, cheese and lemon juice. Stir in prepared vegetables, parsley and dillweed. Season to taste with salt and pepper. Fold in salmon. Turn mixture into an ungreased 8-inch pie plate. Bake in 350 degree F. oven until set - approximately 25 to 30 minutes. To serve as an appetizer, cut into 8 to 10 wedges and serve. If serving as a luncheon dish, cut into 4 wedges and serve with a crisp salad and hot crusty rolls.

Note: If making up in advance, cook; cool and refrigerate. To serve, reheat in a 300 degree F. oven for 10 to 12 minutes or until piping hot.

Fried Fish in Batter

2 lbs. fish fillets, 1 tsp. salt, 1 egg, 1 cup water, 1 cup all purpose flour, ¼ cup flour.

Season fish with ½ tsp. salt and cut in serving portions. If the pieces of fish are more than half an inch thick but not thick enough to slice conveniently, make 3 or 4 slits in the side. The fish will cook more evenly and quickly. To make batter, beat egg, add water. Stir in 1 cup flour and ½ tsp. salt, until just dampened; batter will be lumpy. Dip fish in ¼ cup flour then into batter. Fry fish in deep fat at 375 F. until golden brown, turning once. This will take about 7 minutes. Drain. <u>NOTE</u>: As a general rule a batter made with water will be crisp while a batter made with milk will be tender.

English Style Fish and Chips

Batter

1 cup flour; 1 egg yolk; 2 tablespoons beer; 1/4 teaspoon salt; 3 tablespoons milk; 3 tablespoons water; 1 egg white.

Pour the flour into a large mixing bowl, make a well in the centre and add the egg yolk, beer and salt. Stir the ingredients together until they are well mixed, then gradually pour in the combined milk and water, and continue to stir until the batter is smooth. Beat the egg white until stiff peaks form and then gently but thoroughly fold it into the batter. For a light texture, let the batter rest at room temperature for at least 30 minutes, although if necessary it may be used at once.

Chips

Vegetable oil or shortening for deep-fat frying; 8 medium-size potatoes, sliced lengthwise into strips 1/2 inch thick and 1/2 inch wide.

To cook the chips and fish, heat 4 to 5 inches of oil or shortening in a deep-fat fryer to a temperature of 375 degrees F. Preheat the oven to 250 degrees F. and line a large shallow roasting pan with paper towels. Dry the potatoes thoroughly and deep-fry them in 3 or 4 batches until they are crisp and light brown. Transfer them to the lined pan to drain and place them in the oven to keep warm.

Fish

1 pound white fish fillets (haddock, sole, flounder or cod) skinned and cut into 3 x 5 -inch serving pieces.

Wash the pieces of fish under cold running water and pat them completely dry with paper towels. Drop 2 or 3 pieces of fish at a time into the batter and, when they are well coated, plunge them into the hot fat. Fry for 4 or 5 minutes, or until golden brown, turning the pieces occasionally with a spoon to prevent them from sticking together or to the pan. To serve heap the fish in the centre of a large heated platter and arrange the chips around them. Traditionally, fish and chips are served sprinkled with malt vinegar and salt.

Tuna Biscuit Pot Pie

1 (10½ oz) can condensed cream of mushroom soup; 1 cup milk; 1 (10 oz) pkg frozen mixed vegetables; 2 (6½ oz) cans tuna in vegetable oil; 1 tsp instant minced onion; 1 (8 oz) can refrigerated biscuits; 1/2 cup shredded cheddar cheese.

Preheat oven to 400°F. Combine soup and milk in medium size saucepan; stirring until smooth. Place frozen vegetables into strainer and run under hot running water to separate into individual pieces; drain. Pour off oil from tuna and place in small bowl. Break into chunks, using a fork. Add vegetables, tuna and minced onion to mushroom sauce in saucepan. Stir over low heat for 5 minutes, until sauce starts to bubble around the side of the pan. Do not let it stick to the pan. Turn mixture into a 2-quart casserole dish. Separate biscuits apart; cut each into quarters. Place on top of tuna mixture and sprinkle with cheese. Bake in preheated oven for 15 minutes, until biscuits are golden brown and sauce is bubbly. *Makes 4 servings.*

Sole Thermidor

*5 tbsp. butter or margarine,
2 tsp. salt,
½ tsp. seasoned salt,
pepper to taste,
¼ cup chopped green onions,
4 medium sole fillets (approximately 1½ lbs.),
lemon juice,
1¼ cups milk,
3 tbsp. all-purpose flour,
½ tsp. dry mustard,
1 cup grated sharp cheddar cheese,
3 tbsp. dry sherry,
paprika,
chopped parsley.*

In small saucepan, over low heat, melt 2 tbsp. butter. Add salt, seasoned salt and pepper. Prepare green onions.

Sprinkle sole fillets with lemon juice. Brush fillets with butter mixture on both sides. Sprinkle one side of each fillet with 1 tbsp. chopped green onions. Roll up fillets from narrow end and place, seam side down in baking dish. Pour ½ cup milk over fillets and bake in 350 degree F. oven for 25 minutes or until fish flakes easily when tested with a fork. Meanwhile, in saucepan, melt remaining 3 tbsp. butter, stir in flour and dry mustard until well blended. Gradually stir in remaining ¾ cup milk and cook, stirring constantly, until mixture thickens. Reduce heat and stir in cheese until it melts; stir in sherry. When fish is done, remove from oven; pour off pan liquid, reserving ¼ cup; stir it into cheese sauce; stir to combine. Preheat broiler as manufacturer directs. Place sole fillets on oven-proof serving dish. Pour sauce over fish; sprinkle with paprika. Broil approximately 1 minute or until sauce is slightly golden. Sprinkle with chopped parsley. Serve immediately. *Makes 4 servings.*

Fillet of Sole Bonne Femme

*1/4 cup butter or margarine
3 green onions, chopped
6 fillets of sole, haddock or flounder (about 2-1/2 lbs.)
1/2 lb. mushrooms, sliced
1/2 tsp. salt or to taste
1/8 tsp. pepper or to taste
1 cup white wine
1 tbsp. chopped parsley
1-1/2 tbsp. flour
lemon wedges and parsley sprigs, for garnish, if desired*

In large skillet, melt 2 tbsp. butter. Add green onions; saute gently for 1 minute. Arrange fish over green onions. Placed sliced mushrooms over fish. Season over all with salt and pepper. Add wine. Bring to boiling; reduce heat and simmer, covered, for 10 minutes. Add parsley. Continue cooking until fish flakes easily with a fork - approximately 5 minutes. Drain fish well, reserving 1 cup liquid. Arrange fish, mushrooms and green onions in large shallow baking dish. In skillet, melt remaining 2 tbsp. butter; remove from heat. Stir in flour until mixture is smooth. Gradually stir in reserved liquid. Cook over medium heat, stirring constantly, until mixture is thickened. Pour sauce over fish and vegetables. Place under broiler for several minutes - just until top is golden brown. Serve immediately. Garnish with lemon wedges and parsley sprigs, if desired. *Makes 6 servings.*

Sole on Parmesan Spaghetti

6 fillets sole
  (approximately 2 lbs.)
salt and pepper
2 tbsp. chopped parsley
1 medium tomato,
  cut in 6 slices
6 slices Swiss cheese
2 tbsp. butter
6 tbsp. sherry

1 tin (4 1/2 oz.)
  sliced mushrooms,
  drained - reserving liquid
2 small onions, sliced
1 1/2 tbsp. flour
1/4 cup chopped parsley
1/4 tsp. chervil
1 cup light cream

Parmesan Spaghetti

1/2 of a package (16 oz.)
  spaghetti, cooked and drained
3 tbsp. butter or margarine
1/2 cup grated Parmesan cheese
1/4 cup chopped parsley

1/4 cup chopped walnuts
1/4 tsp. oregano
dash pepper
1/2 tsp. salt

Sprinkle fillets on both sides with salt, pepper and 2 tbsp. chopped parsley. Roll up each fillet. Arrange fillet rolls, seam-side down, tomato slices and cheese slices alternately down centre of 13 x 9 x 2 inch baking dish. In large skillet, melt butter, saute drained mushrooms and onions until golden brown. Stir in flour, parsley and chervil. Add cream, reserved mushroom liquid combined with enough water to make 1/2 cup and sherry. Stir well.

Correct seasonings. Bring to boil and pour over fish. Bake in 400 degree F. oven 20 minutes or until fillets are golden and easily flaked with fork but still moist. Meanwhile, prepare Parmesan Spaghetti, combining all ingredients and lightly mixing. Serve fillets with spaghetti. *Makes 6 servings.*

Tuna Chop Suey Style

1½ cups celery strips (about 1¼ inches long), 1 large onion, cut into 8 wedges, 1 medium green pepper, cut into strips, 1 large clove garlic, minced, 3 tbsp. salad oil, 2 tbsp. cornstarch, 1 cup cold water, 1 tbsp. soy sauce, 1 (7 oz.) can tuna, drained and flaked *, 1 tsp. salt, 1½ cups boiling water, 1½ cups packaged precooked rice, ½ tsp. salt, 1/3 cup sauteed almonds. * Or 1 cup cubed cooked chicken.

Sauté celery, onion, green pepper and garlic in salad oil in a skillet until vegetables are lightly browned, but still crisp. Blend cornstarch with 2 tbsp. of the cold water. Add remaining cold water and soy sauce to vegetables in skillet. Slowly stir in cornstarch mixture; then add in tuna and 1 tsp. salt. Cook and stir until liquid thickens and vegetables are glazed.

Make a space in centre of skillet by pushing vegetable mixture to the side of pan. Add 1 cup of the boiling water into centre, then sprinkle on rice and ½ tsp. salt. Add rest of boiling water over rice; stir to moisten rice. Cover, remove from heat and let stand 5 minutes. Fluff rice with fork. Spoon tuna mixture over rice and garnish with the sauteed almonds to serve. Makes 4 servings.

Oyster Scallop

1 pint fresh oysters,
1 tsp. lemon juice,
2 cups medium coarse
  saltine cracker crumbs,
½ cup butter or margarine,
2 cups sliced fresh
  mushrooms,
¾ cup light cream,

1 tsp. chopped parsley,
¼ tsp. Worcestershire
  sauce,
freshly cracked black
  pepper,
pimiento strips and green
  pepper rings for garnish,
  if desired.

Drain oysters; reserve ¼ cup oyster liquor. Sprinkle oysters with lemon juice. Prepare crumbs and combine with melted butter. Reserve ½ cup of crumbs for topping. In large bowl, combine drained oysters, remaining crumbs, mushrooms, cream, parsley, Worcestershire sauce and pepper.

Stir gently to combine. Place mixture into 8 inch round baking dish. Top with reserved crumbs. Bake in preheated 350 degree F. oven for 40 minutes or until done. Serve hot. Garnish with pimiento strips and green pepper rings, if desired. *Makes 8 servings.*

Sole With Oyster Sauce

1 lb. sole fillets
pepper
3/4 cup white wine
2 cups sliced mushrooms

4 tbsp. butter
1/2 cup whipping cream
1/2 pint fresh oysters
  (or canned equivalent)

Preheat oven to 350 degrees F. Arrange sole in single layer in casserole dish; sprinkle with pepper to taste. Pour wine over fish. Bake 10 minutes or until done. With large pancake turner, transfer fish to heated platter.

Keep warm. Reserve fish liquid. In medium skillet, over high heat, cook mushrooms in 2 tbsp. butter. Cook until golden. Arrange over fish. Pour fish liquid and cream into skillet; add remaining 2 tbsp. butter. Slowly cook for 5 minutes. Do NOT boil. Add oysters; heat through. Drizzle part of oyster sauce over cooked sole fillets and pass remaining separately. *Makes 4 servings.*

Pacific Oyster Stew

1-1/2 tbsp. flour, 1-1/2 tsp. salt, dash tabasco, 2 tbsp. cold water, 1 pint oysters and oyster liquor, 1/4 cup butter or margarine, 3 cups milk, 1 cup light cream, extra pats of butter, paprika and chopped parsley, if desired, for garnish.

In small bowl, combine flour, salt, tabasco and cold water; blend to a smooth paste. In saucepan, place oysters and oyster liquor.

Stir in flour paste; add butter and simmer oysters over low heat, stirring gently for approximately 5 minutes or until edges of oysters begin to curl. Meanwhile, in large saucepan, scald milk and light cream. Pour in oyster mixture. Remove from heat; cover. Allow to stand 20 minutes to blend flavours. Reheat stew to serving temperature. It is best to have soup tureen and soup dishes hot. Pour soup into tureen. If desired, garnish with butter pats, paprika and chopped parsley. *Makes 4 servings.*

Note: If oysters are small, prepare whole. If they are large, cut them accordingly.

Seafood Cocktail

1½ lbs. seafood
¼ cup thinly sliced celery
¼ cup chopped green pepper
2 green onions, chopped
1 tbsp. lemon juice

SAUCE:
¾ cup chili sauce
2 tbsp. horseradish

2 tbsp. lemon juice
2 tsp. Worcestershire sauce
¼ tsp. salt
1 tsp. grated onion
dash tabasco
shredded lettuce
6 lemon slices

Select seafood from any one or a combination of crab, shrimp, lobster, oyster or salmon. Combine with celery, green pepper, green onions, and lemon juice. Cover and chill. Combine all sauce ingredients in small bowl; mix well. Refrigerate covered at least 3 hours. To serve, arrange shredded lettuce in 6 sherbet glasses. Divide seafood mixture among dishes. Spoon some sauce over each. Garnish with lemon wedges. *Makes 6 servings.*

Saucy Oyster Cocktail

Sauce
3/4 cup chili sauce
2 tbsp. lemon juice
2 tbsp. horseradish
2 tsp. Worcestershire sauce
1 tsp. grated onion
salt [to taste]
dash tabasco

Combine well, chili sauce, lemon juice, horseradish, Worcestershire sauce, grated onion, salt and tabasco. Chill thoroughly. Makes approx. 1 cup sauce.

Cocktail
1 pt. oysters
lettuce
lemon twists
parsley sprigs

Oysters should be shucked (if in shell), washed, drained, and very well chilled; halve or quarter oysters if large. Line cocktail glasses with lettuce. Arrange oysters attractively on lettuce. Spoon prepared sauce over oysters. Garnish with lemon twists and parsley sprigs. Makes 6 servings.

Oyster and Spinach Delight

1 cup cooked spinach,
  well drained and
  chopped
1 pt. oysters, drained
  dash lemon juice
2 tbsp. chopped parsley
2 tbsp. chopped onion

dash paprika
dash tabasco
salt and pepper to taste
3 tbsp. very fine dry
  bread crumbs
1/4 cup butter
1 tbsp. butter, melted

Grease 1 1/2 qt. casserole dish. Place spinach on bottom. Drain oysters; sprinkle with lemon juice. Place oysters over spinach.

Combine parsley, onion, melted butter, paprika and tabasco. Sprinkle over oysters. Season with salt and pepper. Scatter bread crumbs over top; dot with 1/4 cup butter. Bake in 450 deg. F oven approximately 10 minutes or until dish is piping hot and top is browned. Makes 4 servings.

Garden Vegetable Stuffing

1 cup finely chopped onion, ¼ cup butter or margarine, 2 cups dry bread cubes, 1 cup shredded carrot, 1 cup cut-up fresh mushrooms, washed and trimmed, ½ cup snipped parsley, 1½ tbsp lemon juice, 1 egg, 1 clove garlic, crushed 2 tsp salt, ¼ tsp marjoram, ¼ tsp pepper.

Cook and stir onion in butter until onion is tender. Lightly mix remaining ingredients with onion and butter. If you have extra stuffing place in aluminum foil pan; cover and heat on grill 20 minutes before serving. Great for fish, especially salmon.

Tartar Sauce

1 cup mayonnaise, 1 tbsp. chopped capers (optional), 1 tbsp. chopped olives, 1 tbsp. chopped pickles, 1 tbsp. minced parsley

Mix together and serve with fish.

Seafood Sauce

1 cup tomato catsup, 1/3 cup lemon juice, 1 tbsp. minced onion, 1 tbsp. soy sauce, 1 tbsp. prepared horseradish, 1/2 tsp. anise seed, crushed.

Combine all ingredients and blend thoroughly. Cover and refrigerate several hours. Makes about 1½ cups.

Bearnaise Sauce

1/4 cup dry white wine
1/4 cup tarragon vinegar
2 tsp. dried tarragon
1 tbsp. chopped
  shallot OR green onion
1 tbsp. chopped parsley

1/8 tsp. freshly ground
  (coarse) black pepper
3 egg yolks
1/2 cup butter
  or regular margarine*
1 tbsp. chopped parsley
  or fresh tarragon

In saucepan, combine wine, vinegar, tarragon, shallot or green onion, 1 tbsp. chopped parsley and pepper. Bring mixture to boiling, stirring constantly. Reduce heat; simmer, uncovered, until mixture has reduced to 1/4 cup. This should take about 8 to 9 minutes. Strain mixture, squeezing herbs with back of a spoon to extract juices; discard herbs. Allow mixture to cool completely. In top of double boiler, beat egg yolks with 2 tbsp. of the prepared liquid with a wire whisk just until blended. Cook over HOT, NOT boiling water until mixture begins to thicken - approximately 1 minute. Add butter 1 tbsp. at a time (for convenience, have butter divided into 8 pieces in advance), beating constantly after each addition until butter is melted and mixture is a smooth consistency before adding next tablespoon butter.

This process should take approximately 5 minutes. As your sauce can curdle easily over high heat, do not allow water in bottom pan to boil - if it starts to, immediately add a small amount of cold water to cool it down. The water should not touch the bottom of the top pan. After all the butter has been added, remove double boiler top from hot water. Using a wire whisk, slowly beat in remaining 2 tbsp. prepared seasoned liquid, then 1 tbsp. chopped parsley or fresh tarragon. Beat until sauce is as thick as mayonnaise. Serve sauce either warm or cold. *Yields approximately 1 cup.*

*Do not use "soft" style margarine.

Mona says . . .

*I believe that the most important factor in Canada's conversion to the metric system is **NOT TO PANIC**. The next step is to purchase stainless steel or any durable type of measuring cups and spoons. This will enable you to continue using your old tried and true favourite recipes. Then purchase the new metric measures and gradually try out the new metric recipes. Don't try converting as you will be disappointed with the results.*

Home Makers will be able to work with both the Imperial and Metric units side by side without confusion in a gradual change over.

Trussing Chicken for the Barbecue

Remove the neck, but leave the skin from an eviscerated chicken. Pull the neck skin to the back; fold under. Fasten neck skin down with a skewer.

Season the cavity with a little poultry seasoning and salt. Place holding fork on spit rod, tines toward point of rod. Insert rod through centre of chicken pinching tines of holding fork and pushing securely into the breast meat.

With approximately 22 to 26 inches of cord (depending on size of chicken) tie wings. Start cord at back; loop cord around each wing tip making a slip knot so that wings won't straighten. Tie in the centre on breast bone leaving equal ends.

With a 17 to 19 inch cord, loop cord around chicken's tail, then around the crossed legs. Tie securely to hold chicken onto rod.

Pull wing cords and leg cords together and tie tightly, making sure that chicken is secure and compact bundle.

Place second holding fork on rod pinching tines and pushing firmly into dark meat. Tighten screws on holding forks so that the chicken is sure to turn with the rod.

Brush chicken with butter or oil and sprinkle with seasoning salt.

Luau Beans

½ lb. sliced bacon, 2 sliced onions, 8 c. Beans with Pork, 1 c. crushed pineapple, ¼ c. chili sauce, 2 tbsp. molasses, 1½ tsp. dry mustard, ½ tsp. salt.

Spicy Barbecue Butter

Cream together ½ cup butter, 3 tbsp vinegar, 3 tbsp Worcestershire sauce, 2 tbsp brown sugar, 1 tbsp chili powder, 2 tsp salt, 2 tsp dry mustard, ¼ tsp Tabasco sauce and ½ cup ketchup. Refrigerate for several hours. Brush on hamburgers and steaks while cooking.

Fry bacon until crisp. Remove from skillet and drain (save bacon dripping). Cook onions in drippings.

Crumble bacon and combine in Dutch oven with onions and remaining ingredients. Cover and bake on grill over *medium* hot coals for 1½ hours. Then remove cover and cook about 25 minutes. longer. Stir occasionally. Makes 10 to 12 servings.

BARBECUES

MICROWAVE

SLOW COOKERS

A TASTE OF METRICS

Barbecue Ribs

4 pounds meaty pork spareribs seasoned with seasoning salt
1/4 cup oil
1 large onion, chopped
1 (7-1/2-ounce) can tomato sauce
1/4 cup brown sugar
1/4 cup water
1/4 cup chili sauce
1/4 cup lemon juice
1/4 cup bottled steak sauce
1 tsp. salt

Lace ribs, accordion-style onto skewers approximately 14 to 16 inches long. In a medium-size saucepan heat oil; cook onion until tender but not brown. Add remaining ingredients and simmer uncovered for 20 to 25 minutes or until sauce is of a good basting consistency. Place skewered ribs on barbecue grill over hot coals. Cook ribs 15 to 20 minutes on each side. Brush ribs with sauce and cook an additional 15 to 20 minutes on each side brushing frequently with sauce. *Makes 4 to 5 servings.*

Barbecue Steak Roast

1 (2 to 2½ lb.) round steak, 1 to 1½ inches thick, ½ cup butter, 1 small onion (cut into rings), ¼ cup chili sauce, 1 tbsp vinegar, 1 tsp prepared mustard, 1 tbsp Worcestershire sauce, 1 tsp salt, 1 medium green pepper, cut in strips, 2 medium carrots, cut in sticks, 1 large tomato, cut in wedges.

Place steak on barbecue rack 4 to 6 inches above the hot coals; brown 4 to 5 minutes on each side. Meanwhile in a small saucepan combine butter, onion, chili sauce, vinegar, mustard, Worcestershire sauce and salt. Stir over low heat until butter is melted. Tear off about a 4-foot length of aluminum foil; fold in half lengthwise. Center steak on foil and cover with green pepper, carrots and tomato. Pour sauce over steak. Bring up sides of foil and fold down onto meat in tight double folds. Fold ends close to meat to seal. Place over slow coals about 1 hour, or until tender.

To Bake in Oven: Place meat under broiler 2 to 3 inches from heat; broil each side 4 to 5 minutes to brown. Preheat oven to 350F. Center steak on foil and cover with vegetables and sauce. Fold foil over meat and bake in preheated oven about 1 hour, or until tender. Makes 4 servings.

5-Minute Snowy White Frosting

1 cup sugar	dash salt
1/2 cup water	2 egg whites
1/4 tsp. cream of tartar	1 tsp. vanilla

Combine sugar, water, cream of tartar and salt in 2-cup glass measure. Microwave on ROAST (4) for 4 to 6 minutes or **until mixture boils.** Beat egg whites in small mixer bowl until soft peaks form. Gradually pour in hot syrup, beat about 5 minutes or until thick and fluffy. Blend in vanilla. *Frosts 13 x 9-inch cake or two 9-inch layers.*

*Recipe timing for Litton Moffat Microwave ovens. Time will vary with different microwave ovens.

Bananas Royale

6 tbsp. butter or margarine	1/4 cup light cream
6 tbsp. brown sugar, firmly packed	4 medium bananas, peeled
1/4 tsp. cinnamon	1/4 cup brandy, rum or flavoured liqueur
1/4 tsp. nutmeg	vanilla ice cream

Place butter or margarine in 9-inch round glass baking dish. Microwave on ROAST for 2 minutes or until melted. Stir in brown sugar, cinnamon, nutmeg, and cream. Slice bananas once lengthwise, then once crosswise, into buttered mixture. Stir to coat. Cover with plastic wrap or wax paper. Microwave on REHEAT for 4 minutes or until bubbly. Measure 1/4 to 1/2 cup brandy into 1-cup glass measure. Microwave on HIGH for 15 to 20 seconds or until warm. Pour over hot banana mixture and ignite. Serve immediately over ice cream. *Serves 6 - 8.*

Note: Recipe timing for Litton Moffat Microwave ovens. Time will vary with different microwave ovens.

Sausage and Potato Casserole

4 medium-size potatoes, peeled and sliced in 1/8-inch thick slices	1 lb. beef sausages cold water
1 medium-size onion, peeled and thinly sliced	1 recipe of white sauce 1 tsp. Mei Yen

Prepare potatoes and onions. Boil beef sausages in cold water 2 times to remove all fat from sausages. In a 2-quart casserole layer potatoes, onion and sausages until dish is 3/4 full. Cook on roast for 10 to 15 minutes or until potatoes are soft. Cover with plastic wrap or wax paper. Make a white sauce; add 1 tsp. Mei Yen. Pour seasoned sauce over sausages and vegetables. Reheat for 4 to 5 minutes. *Makes 4 servings.*

Note: Carrots can also be added to this casserole dish if desired.
*Recipe timing of Litton-Moffat Microwave ovens. Time will vary with different microwave ovens.

Honeyed Onions

8 medium whole onions, peeled	1/2 cup honey
2 tbsp. butter or margarine	

Place onions in 1-quart glass casserole. Cover with glass lid or plastic wrap. Microwave on HIGH (6) for 7 to 8 minutes or until onions are tender-crisp. Drain. Stir in butter and honey; re-cover, and continue cooking on HIGH (6) for 2 to 3 minutes or until onions are glazed. Let stand, covered, 3 minutes before serving. *Makes 3 to 4 servings.*

Note: Apple jelly may be substituted for honey, if desired.

*Recipe tested with Litton-Moffat Microwave oven. Times may vary with other microwave ovens.

Microwave

Mushroom Appetizers

2 lbs. large mushrooms	1 tsp. bread crumbs
1 small onion, finely chopped	2 tsp. cream
1 tbsp. butter, melted	parsley
1 hard-cooked egg, finely chopped	

Wash mushrooms; dry well. Remove stems from caps; finely chop stems. Mix prepared mushroom stems and onions with melted butter. Add chopped egg, bread crumbs and cream; mix well. Fill the insides of mushroom caps with 1 tsp. (approximately) of filling. Place stuffed mushrooms in an 8 x 14-inch pyrex dish (or similar size). Cook 2 to 4 minutes. Garnish with parsley.

*Recipe timing for Litton Moffat Microwave ovens. Times will vary with different microwave ovens.

Cherries Jubilee

1 can cherry pie filling (19 oz.)	1/4 cup rum
1/4 cup red currant jelly	1/4 cup brandy
1 tsp. grated orange rind	vanilla ice cream

Combine cherry pie filling with jelly, orange rind, and rum in a medium glass bowl; stir to blend. Microwave on REHEAT for 5 to 6 minutes or until heated in crentre; stir. Measure brandy into 1 cup glass measure. Microwave on HIGH for 15 to 20 seconds until warm. Pour brandy over cherry sauce and ignite. Immediately spoon over ice cream. *Yields approximately 3-3/4 cups sauce.*

Note: Recipe timing for Litton Moffat Microwave ovens. Times will vary with different microwave ovens.

Lemon Filling

1/2 cup sugar	1-1/2 tsp. grated lemon peel
2 tbsp. cornstarch	2 tbsp. lemon juice
1/8 tsp. salt	1 tbsp. butter or margarine
2/3 cup water	

Combine all ingredients in 2-cup glass measure; mix well. Microwave on HIGH (6) for 2 minutes. Stir and continue cooking on HIGH (6) for 2 to 2-1/2 minutes or until thickened; beat well. Cool and spread on cake. *Yields 1 cup filling.*

Note: Yellow food colouring may be added, if desired.

*Recipe timing for Litton Moffat Microwave ovens. Times will vary with different microwave ovens.

Fast and Slow Cookers

Note: *Cooking times may vary according to type of Slow Cooker used.*

Meatball Vegetable Stew

1 lb. lean ground beef	1 tbsp. sugar
salt and pepper to taste	1 tbsp. Worcestershire sauce
1 clove garlic, crushed	1/2 tsp. crushed basil
1 egg	3 medium potatoes, peeled
1 small onion, finely chopped	and finely diced
1/2 cup fine dry bread crumbs	4 small carrots, peeled and
1 tbsp. salad oil	thinly sliced on the bias
3 tbsp. flour	1 onion, coarsely chopped
1 tin (28 oz.) tomatoes,	2 celery stalks, thinly
undrained (break up tomatoes)	sliced on the bias
1/2 tsp. salt or to taste	2 tbsp. chopped parsley
pepper to taste	

In bowl, lightly combine beef, salt, pepper, garlic, egg, onion, and bread crumbs. Form mixture into meatballs. Heat oil in skillet. Brown meatballs on all sides. Remove meatballs from skillet; set aside. Blend flour into drippings in skillet; (add more salad oil if necessary to make up 3 tbsp.) When mixture is smooth, add remaining ingredients. Stir well to distribute seasonings. Pour mixture into Slow Cooking Pot. Add meatballs.

Cover. Set on medium heat and cook for 8 to 10 hours or until vegetables are tender. *Makes 4 to 6 servings.*

Pressure Cooker Stew

15 pounds pressure 25 minutes

2 tablespoons fat or drippings; 2 pounds stewing beef cut in 1-inch cubes; 2 teaspoons salt; 1/4 teaspoon pepper; 1 bay leaf; 1 tablespoon steak sauce or ketchup; 1/2 cup water; 6 small onions, peeled; 1 cup sliced celery; 4 medium potatoes, quartered; 4 medium carrots, sliced; 2 cups canned or fresh tomatoes; 3 tablespoons flour; 1/4 cup water; 1 beef bouillon cube.

Melt fat in cooker, brown meat on all sides. Place on rack in cooker. Add salt, pepper, bay leaf, steak sauce and 1/2 cup water. Cover and cook under pressure 20 minutes at 15 pounds pressure. Reduce pressure with cool water. Add vegetables, cover cooker, and cook under pressure again for 5 minutes at 15 pounds pressure. Reduce pressure with cool water and remove stew and rack, blend flour, water and bouillon cube, add to gravy, and cook uncovered, stirring constantly until thickened. Add stew, heat through and serve.

Stewed Tomatoes

4 or 5 large ripe tomatoes	1/2 tsp. dried sweet basil
2 tbsp. butter or margarine	1 small bay leaf
1 medium onion, thinly sliced	1 tsp. salt
1/2 cup chopped celery	1/8 tsp. pepper
1/4 cup chopped green pepper	2 tbsp. chopped parsley
1/2 tsp. sugar	

Quickly dip tomatoes in boiling water; remove skin. Quarter tomatoes; remove core and seeds. In slow-cooking pot, combine all ingredients except parsley. Cover and cook on low for 8 to 9 hours. Remove bay leaf. Sprinkle top with parsley. *Makes 4 to 5 servings.*

Mixed Vegetables en Pot

2 packages (10 oz. each)	1/2 tsp. seasoned salt
frozen mixed vegetables,	1 pkt. toasted onion dip mix OR
partially thawed	2 tbsp. onion soup mix
1/2 cup finely chopped celery	1/2 cup water
2 tins (10 oz. each) condensed	2 tbsp. melted butter or margarine
cream of celery soup	

In slow-cooking pot, combine mixed vegetables with celery. In medium bowl, mix soup with seasoned salt, dry dip mix, water and melted butter. Pour over vegetables in pot. Cover and cook on low for 4 to 5 hours or until vegetables are tender. *Makes 6 servings.*

Creole Zucchini

2 lb. zucchini	1/4 tsp. pepper
1 small green pepper,	4 tomatoes, peeled
chopped	and chopped
1 small onion, chopped	2 tbsp. butter or margarine
1 clove garlic, minced	2 tbsp. minced parsley
1 tsp. salt	

Cut zucchini into 1/4-inch slices. In slow-cooking pot, combine zucchini with green pepper, onion, garlic, salt and pepper. Top with chopped tomatoes, then butter. Cover and cook on high for about 2 hours or until tender. Sprinkle with chopped parsley. *Makes 6 to 7 servings.*

Note: This recipe is not suitable for Cornwall or Sears tray-type Crockery Cookers.

Metrics in the Kitchen

The metric system is based on multiples of 10. The basic metric units include:

LENGTH	= metre (m) or 100 cm
VOLUME	= litre (ℓ) or 1000 ml
MASS	= kilogram (kg) or 1000 g
TEMPERATURE	= degrees Celsius (°C)

METRICS IN THE GROCERY STORE

The changeover to the metric system in Canada should be completed by 1980. In 1977-78 many grocery items will change to new metric sizes. Items measured by volume such as milk and vinegar will be labelled in millilitres and litres. A litre is about 12% smaller than a quart. Items now sold by the pound will be sold by the gram or kilogram. A kilogram is equal to 2.2 pounds; 100 grams is slightly less than ¼ pound. Items like eggs that are packaged in dozens will continue to be sold by the dozen.

DRY MEASURES

For measuring dry ingredients, our Imperial four piece dry measures set (1 cup, ½ cup, 1/3 cup, ¼ cup) will be replaced by a three piece dry measures set:

250 ml (slightly more than 1 cup)
125 ml (slightly more than ½ cup)
50 ml (slightly less than ¼ cup)

LIQUID MEASURES

For measuring liquids, our Imperial 1 cup, 2 cup and 4 cup liquid measuring cups will be replaced by:

250 ml (slightly more than one 8 ounce cup)
500 ml (slightly less than 1 pint)
1000 ml or 1 ℓ (slightly less than 1 quart)

SMALL MEASURES

For measuring small amounts, the present set consisting of 1 tablespoon, 1 teaspoon, ½ teaspoon and ¼ teaspoon will be replaced by a five piece small measures set:

25 ml (about 1 coffee measure)
15 ml (about 1 tablespoon)
5 ml (about 1 teaspoon)
2 ml (slightly less than ½ teaspoon)
1 ml (slightly less than ¼ teaspoon)

BAKING DISHES

The capacity of baking dishes, now given in quarts, will be expressed in litres. Baking pan or pie pan sizes, now given in inches, will be given in centimetres. For example, a 1½ quart casserole dish will be replaced by a 1.5 ℓ dish and an 8 inch by 2 inch baking pan will be replaced by a 20 cm by 5 cm baking pan. As volume will be nearly the same, we can use present baking equipment for metric recipes.

TEMPERATURE

Cooking temperatures are affected by the change from the Fahrenheit to the Celsius scale. Water freezes at 0° C and boils at 100° C. The following scale is a comparison of °F and °C.

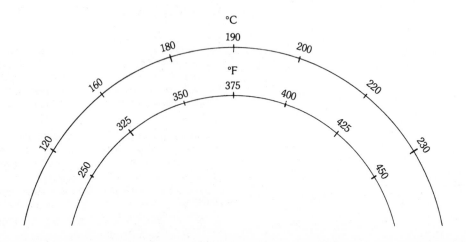

A Taste of Metrics

Cheese Stuffed Mushrooms

20 large mushrooms
225 ml grated sharp
    cheddar cheese
30 ml softened butter
30 ml minced green
    onion
1/2 clove garlic, crushed
    dash pepper

Wash mushrooms; dry well; remove stems (use stems in soups, gravies, sauces or stews). Blend cheese, butter, green onions, garlic, and pepper. Place mushroom caps on broiler pan; spoon mixture into caps. Place low under broiler; broil until cheese is melted and bubbly. Makes 20 stuffed mushrooms.

Cheddar Cheese Sauce

125 ml shredded sharp
    cheddar cheese
60 ml mayonnaise
125 ml sour cream
    paprika

Combine cheese and mayonnaise. Cook over low heat, stirring constantly until cheese melts. Beat with wire whisk until smooth. Blend in sour cream; heat through. Sprinkle lightly with paprika. Serve over hot vegetables (cauliflower, broccoli, or asparagus).

Appetizer Tray with Cheesey Dip

225g 2% creamed-style
    cottage cheese
2 green onions, chopped
30 ml milk
15 ml. chopped pimiento
3 ml seasoned salt
    ]or to taste]
    dash freshly ground
    black pepper

Dippers: raw cauliflower flowerets, celery sticks, carrot sticks, cucumber sticks, green pepper sticks, raw mushrooms, small tomatoes, sliced radishes

Combine well cottage cheese, green onions, milk, pimiento, salt and pepper. Cover. Refrigerate until well chilled. To serve, pour dip into small bowl. Place on tray surrounded with selection of preferred dippers. **Note:** For a smoother consistency use your blender to mix dip ingredients. For variation, add on top of baked potatoes.

Potatoes Anna

5 medium potatoes
2 medium onions
10 ml seasoning salt
100 ml grated Parmesan cheese
50 ml butter
2 ml pepper

Peel and thinly slice potatoes and onions. Lightly grease a shallow casserole dish. Toss potato and onion slices with seasoning salt, pepper and Parmesan cheese. Arrange a third of potato and onion slices on bottom of casserole. Dot with a third of the butter. Repeat layers twice, dotting with butter each time. Bake, covered, at 100 degrees C for 45 minutes. Remove cover and bake 5 minutes longer until vegetables are tender and lightly browned. Makes 6 servings.

Beef Stew

700 g stewing beef
50 ml fat
125 ml chopped onion
1 clove garlic, crushed
75 ml flour
10 ml salt
1 ml pepper
25 ml chopped parsley
2 ml savory
2 ml thyme
750 ml water
250 ml chopped carrot
3 small onions, quartered
250 ml chopped turnip

Cut beef in 2-cm pieces. Brown in fat. Remove from pan. Add onion and garlic and saute until onion is transparent. Return meat to pan; sprinkle with flour and brown again. Add seasonings and water. Cover and simmer 1-1/4 hours. Add vegetables and continue cooking until vegetables are tender (about 30 minutes longer). *Makes 6 servings.*

Piquant Sauce for Fish Sticks

450 ml mayonnaise
    or salad dressing
15 ml chopped parsley
10 ml prepared mustard
10 ml minced onion
60 ml crumbled bleu cheese
    chopped chives or
    green onions for garnish
    hot fish sticks

In bowl, combine mayonnaise, chopped parsley, prepared mustard, minced onion and bleu cheese. Allow to chill. To serve, sprinkle with chopped chives or green onions. Serve over hot fish sticks.

Cucumbers in Sour Cream

1 good-sized cucumber,
    thinly sliced
5 ml salt
125 ml sour cream
15 ml vinegar
    dash tabasco
30 ml chopped chives
5 ml dill seed
    dash pepper

Thinly slice cucumber; sprinkle with salt. Allow to stand for 30 minutes. Drain well. In bowl, thoroughly combine sour cream, vinegar, tabasco, chives, dill seed and pepper. Pour mixture over drained cucumbers. Chill, covered, for approximately 30 minutes. *Makes 4 to 5 servings.*

There is nothing like feeding a man if you want to put him in a good humour.
Francis W. Grey, THE CURE OF ST. PHILIPPE, 1899

YEAST DOUGHS

Nothing so commands respect for the cook as freshly baked bread. Nothing so captures the imagination as its aroma and no culinary achievement gives greater satisfaction.

Using a pair of flat stones, the early settlers ground their own wheat into flour. Sourdough served in place of yeast and doughpans were wrapped in woolen coats and blankets to protect them from the cold. Today, skillfully milled and blended flour, fast rising yeast and thermo-statically controlled temperatures in the home have taken the guesswork out of breadmaking. The challenge becomes not so much how the thing is done as how to create family favorites by putting to use good basic recipes.

Mona says . . .

Yeast doughs lend themselves to experiment. A careful look through the rules and you'll be in command of the magic.

Flour — It is essential to use an all-purpose flour. Pastry flour does not contain sufficient gluten to produce an elastic dough. Use only enough flour to keep dough from sticking to hands.
For best nutrition, use enriched flours.

Yeast — is a living thing and responds to gentle treatment. Too much will hasten the rising of the dough but detract from the bread's flavour. Too little will lengthen the time required for yeast activity. To ensure good yeast activity and lessen time elapse between mixing and finished product begin with utensils and ingredients at room temperature. Any closed space with a bowl of hot water inside makes an ideal place to set dough to rise.

Salt — is not only necessary for flavour but controls fermentation.

Sugar — not only sweetens but encourages yeast activity.

Potato water, shortening, milk and **butter** improve the flavour and keeping quality of the loaf.

Rising — grease doughs before putting to rise to prevent crust forming on surface.

Texture — thorough kneading will ensure a fine even texture. Knead on floured board using three motions: fold, press and turn. Repeat.

If tops brown too quickly, cover loaves with foil for last 20 minutes of cooking time.

When done brush with butter. For a crisp crust leave the loaf uncovered. Cool on a rack. Store in a ventilated box.

The finished dough products, such as bread and buns, freeze well and may be stored for months. Frozen doughs should not generally be stored longer than two weeks.

Every recipe in the book tested in the Mona Brun Kitchen Centre.

95

GUIDE TO MAKING

Never Fail White Bread

2 tbsp. sugar
¼ cup warm water (about 110°F)
1 package active dry yeast
2 cups milk, scalded
2 tsp. salt
1 tbsp. shortening
6 to 6¼ cups sifted all-purpose flour

Dissolve sugar in warm water. Sprinkle yeast over top. Set aside until frothy. In large bowl, combine scalded milk, salt and shortening. Cool to lukewarm. Add softened yeast. **Gradually beat in flour.** Add sufficient flour to make a moderately stiff dough.

Turn dough out on a lightly floured surface. Knead until smooth and satiny — about 8 to 10 minutes. Shape into a ball.

Place dough in roomy greased bowl. Grease dough surface. Cover and set in a warm place. Allow dough to rise and double in bulk — approximately 1½ hours.

YOUR OWN BREAD

Photos: Courtesy Studio '75

Punch down and allow to rise again — about 45 minutes. **Cut into two equal portions.** Form into balls. Rest 10 minutes.

Shape into loaves by rolling ball of dough into a 7" x 15" rectangle on a lightly floured board. Then roll up dough jelly roll fashion, starting at narrow end. Tuck ends under as you roll. Place seam side down in greased bread pan 8½"x4½"x2¾". Repeat for second loaf. Grease tops of loaves, cover with greased waxed paper and let rise till dough reaches 1½ inches above top of pan in centre, and corners are filled (1 to 1½ hours).

Bake at 400°F for 35 to 40 minutes. Remove from pans at once. Brush tops with butter or margarine. Cool on wire rack. To slice fresh bread use a serrated knife.

Oatmeal Loaf

1 1/2 cups boiling water
1 tbsp. butter or margarine
1 1/2 tsp. salt
1/3 cup brown sugar
1 1/2 cups rolled oats

1 envelope (1 tbsp.)
  active dry yeast
1/4 cup warm water
3 cups all-purpose flour

Pour boiling water into a large bowl. Add butter, salt, sugar and oats; mix well; cool to lukewarm. Dissolve yeast in warm water. Add dissolved yeast mixture to oat mixture; stir in flour; mix well. Knead dough about 20 times. Shape into a round loaf (1 large or 2 small) and place on a greased cookie sheet. Let rise for 1 1/2 hours in warm place. Bake in a 375 degree F. oven for 30 to 50 minutes depending on size of loaf or until bread tests done.

Potato Bread

2 envelopes active
  dry yeast
2 cups warm water
  [105-115 deg. f.]
1/4 cup sugar
1 tbsp. salt

1 cup mashed potatoes,
  unseasoned, unbuttered
1/2 cup butter, softened
6 1/2 to 6 3/4 cups unsifted
  all-purpose flour
2 tbsp. melted butter

In large bowl sprinkle yeast over warm water. Stir until dissolved. Stir in sugar and salt; stir until dissolved. Add mashed potatoes, softened butter, 3 cups flour. With electric mixer at medium speed beat until smooth (approx. 2 minutes). Clean dough from beaters with spatula if mixer does not have dough attachment. Mix dough with hand, gradually add balance of flour, as needed, to make smooth dough stiff enough to leave side of bowl.

Turn dough out on lightly floured surface. Knead until dough is smooth and elastic and small blisters appear on the surface, about 10 minutes. Place in lightly greased large bowl. Turn dough to bring greased surface side up. Cover with damp cloth. Let rise in warm place free from any drafts (85 deg. f.) until double in bulk (approx. 1 hour). Turn dough out onto lightly floured surface.

Divide in half. Roll out one half into 16-inch by 8-inch rectangle. Roll up, starting one end. Press ends even and pinch to seal. Place seam side down in greased 9 x 5 x 3-inch loaf pans. Brush surface lightly with some melted butter. Repeat with other half of dough.

Let loaves rise in warm place (85 deg. F.); away from drafts until sides come to top of pan and tops are rounded. **Important** : Set oven rack on lowest level (may look done, but bottom may not be baked). Preheat oven 400 deg. F. Bake 35 to 45 minutes or until crust is deep golden brown and loaves sound hollow when tapped. **Note**: If crust becomes too brown during cooking protect by covering with piece of brown paper. Turn out of pans onto wire racks. Brush tops with remaining melted butter. Let cool completely. Makes two loaves.

Bacon and Cheese Bread

1/2 cup milk; 1 (10 oz.) can condensed Cheddar Cheese soup, undiluted; 1/4 cup butter or margarine; 3½ cups un-sifted flour; 1 pkg. active dry yeast; 1 tsp. salt; 1 large egg; 6 slices bacon, cooked and crumbled.

Stir milk into soup gradually in medium-size saucepan. Add butter or margarine. Heat over low heat until warm (120°F to 130°F). Combine 2 cups of flour, undissolved yeast and salt in large bowl of mixer. Add soup mixture. Beat on low speed until dry ingredients are moistened. Add egg and 1/2 cup flour. Beat 2 minutes at medium speed, scraping bowl with rubber spatual. Remove from mixer. Stir in 1 cup of flour and crumbled bacon with spoon to make a firm but sticky dough. Cover bowl with plastic wrap; refrigerate 1 hour or until dough is doubled in bulk. Grease 2 qt. casserole. Shape dough into ball with well-greased hands. Place in prepared casserole. Cover with towel. Let rise in warm place (85°F), free from draft, 1 hour or until doubled in bulk. Heat oven to 350°F. Bake bread 50 minutes, or until golden brown. Remove from casserole immediately. Cool completely on a wire rack; wrap. *Makes 1 loaf.*

Whole Wheat Bread

1 packet active dry yeast
1/4 cup water
2 1/2 cups hot water
1/2 cup brown sugar
3 tsps. salt

1/4 cup shortening
3 cups whole-wheat
  flour
5 cups sifted all-purpose
  white flour

Soften yeast in 1/4 cup warm water (110 degrees). Combine hot water, sugar, salt and shortening; cool to lukewarm.

Stir in the whole wheat flour and 1 cup of the white flour; beat well. Stir in the softened yeast. Add enough of the remaining flour to make a moderately stiff dough. Turn out on a lightly floured surface; knead until smooth and satiny (10 to 12 minutes).

Shape dough in a ball, place in lightly greased bowl, turning once to grease surface thus preventing a hard crust forming. Cover; let rise in warm place until double in bulk (approx. 1 1/2 hrs). Punch down. Cut in 2 portions; shape each in smooth ball. Cover and let rest 10 minutes.

Shape in loaves; place in greased 8 1/2 x 4 1/2 x 2 1/2 inch loaf dishes. Let rise until double (approx. 1 1/4 hours). Bake in 375 degree F. oven approximately 45 minutes. Cover with foil last 20 minutes if necessary to prevent too much browning. Makes 2 loaves.

Sweet Dough

2 tsp. sugar; 1/2 cup warm water; 2 pkgs. active dry yeast; 7 - 7½ cups all-purpose flour; 1 cup milk; 1/2 cup sugar; 2 tsp. salt; 3/4 cup cold water; 1/4 cup soft butter, margarine or shortening; 2 eggs.

Dissolve 2 tsp. sugar in warm water in large, warm bowl; sprinkle yeast into water mixture and let stand 10 minutes, then stir well. Scald milk; mix in sugar and salt. Add cold water and cool to lukewarm. Add milk mixture, butter, eggs and 2 cups flour to dissolved yeast mixture. Beat with rotary beater until smooth. Add 5 cups of remaining flour gradually, adding more if necessary to make a soft dough which leaves sides of bowl. Turn out on floured board.

Round up into a ball. Knead 5 to 10 minutes or until dough is smooth, elastic and no longer sticky. Place in lightly greased bowl; grease top of dough and cover with greased waxed paper. Set in warm place (75°-85°F) until double in size (about 1½ hrs.). Punch down and turn out on board. Cut into 4 equal portions; gather up each portion. Cover and let rest 10 minutes. Shape each portion into rolls or coffee cake as desired. Cover with greased waxed paper.

Let rise in warm place until doubled (30 - 60 minutes). Bake in 375°F oven for 25 to 30 minutes for coffee cakes or 12 to 15 minutes for rolls. Brush with butter if desired. Rolls and coffee cakes can be brushed with a glaze of 1 tbsp. sugar dissolved in 1 tbsp. water 5 minutes before end of baking time.

Pan Buns

1/4 Sweet Dough Recipe

Roll dough with palms of hands into a cylinder about 12 inches long. Cut dough into 16 equal portions; roll each into balls. Place evenly in well-greased 8-inch square pan. Brush with melted butter or shortening.

Parkerhouse Rolls

1/4 Sweet Dough Recipe

Roll dough to 1/4" thickness; cut into circles using floured 2½" round cookie cutter. Make off-center crease; fold so top overlaps slightly; seal end edges of each roll. Place on well-greased baking sheet; brush with melted butter. (Leftover dough can be used for Cloverleaf Rolls.)

Fan Tans

1/4 Sweet Dough Recipe

Roll dough into 9"x14" rectangle; spread with soft butter. Cut into 6 strips lengthwise. Stack strips and cut into 9 pieces. Place cut-side down in well-greased muffin cups.

Cloverleaf Rolls

1/4 Sweet Dough Recipe

Form dough into 1" balls. Place 3 balls in each well-greased muffin cup. Brush with melted butter.

Crescent Rolls

1/4 Sweet Dough Recipe

Roll dough into 12" circle; cut into 12 wedge-shape pieces. Beginning at rounded edge, roll up each piece. Place point down on greased baking sheet. Curve into crescents.

Streusel Coffee Cake

1/4 Sweet Dough Recipe; 1/3 cup all-purpose flour; 1/3 cup brown sugar, packed; 1/2 tsp. cinnamon; 3 tbsp. butter; 1 egg yolk; 2 tsp. milk.

Depending on type of pan used (8" or 9" square or round), roll dough into a square or circular shape, with dough just fitting pan. Place in greased pan; grease top of dough and cover with greased waxed paper. Set in warm place (75° - 85°F) until double in size (45-60 minutes). In small bowl, combine flour, brown sugar and cinnamon; mix well. Cut in butter until mixture is crumbly; set aside. With fork prick top of risen dough; brush over with mixture of egg yolk and milk. Sprinkle crumb mixture over top. Bake in 375°F oven for 25 to 30 minutes. Loosen edges with spatula; lift out onto wire rack. Serve warm or cold. Makes 1 coffee cake.

Air Buns   (overnight method)

1 envelope active dry yeast, 2 teaspoons sugar, 1 cup lukewarm water, 6 eggs, 1 cup sugar, 4 cups warm water, 1 cup cooking oil, 2 tablespoons salt, 16 to 18 cups flour, pre-sifted.

Dissolve sugar and yeast in 1 cup of lukewarm water. Let stand 10 minutes. Beat eggs in a **very** large bowl (punch bowl is excellent) and slowly add 1 cup sugar. Beat well and add yeast mixture. Add warm water, oil and salt. Mix in flour (start with 16 cups adding more flour as needed).

Turn out on floured surface and knead 10 minutes or until dough is smooth and elastic. Place in a very large greased bowl turning once to grease surface. Make dough mixture up at 4 o'clock, then let rise in warm, draught-free place until 7 o'clock. Punch down and let rise to 10 o'clock. Make into buns or loaves and let rise overnight (rising area need not be warm for overnight rising but not too cold either). Bake loaves or buns in the morning. Bake loaves at 350 degrees F. for 30 to 35 minutes. Bake buns at 400 degrees F. for 15 to 20 minutes depending on size. Bread is done when you hear a hollow sound when tapped.

Sourdough Bread

1 envelope active dry yeast, 1 cup very warm water, 1½ cups Sourdough Starter, 2 tbsp. sugar, 2 tsp. salt, 5½ cups sifted all purpose flour, 1 egg white, 2 tbsp. cold water.

Sprinkle yeast into very warm water in a large bowl. (Very warm water will feel comfortably warm when dropped on wrist.) Then stir in starter, sugar and salt. Beat in 2 cups flour until smooth. Beat in enough of the remaining flour to make a soft dough.

Turn out onto lightly floured board. Knead about 10 minutes, until smooth and elastic, using only as much flour as needed to keep dough from sticking. Place in a greased large bowl, turn to coat all over with shortening. Cover with a clean towel and let rise in a warm place (away from draft) until double in bulk, about 1 hour. Punch dough down; turn out onto board, invert bowl over dough and let rest 20 minutes.

Grease two large cookie sheets; sprinkle with cornmeal. Divide dough in half and knead each a few times. Roll up tightly in jelly roll fashion from long side. Pinch long seam tightly to seal. Taper ends by gently rolling loaf back and forth with hands. Place loaf diagonally on greased cookie sheet. Roll out second half of dough to a 28 inch strip and roll up, jelly roll fashion, starting from a long side. Shape roll into a ring on second cookie sheet. Place in warm place, away from draft and let rise until double in bulk, about 45 minutes. Make slits 2 inches apart on top of breads with a very sharp knife or razor blade. Beat egg white and cold water together in a small cup; brush mixture onto loaves. Bake in 400 F. oven for 40 minutes, or until golden. Loaves should have hollow sound when tapped. Remove from cookie sheets to wire racks. Let cool. Makes two 17 oz. loaves.

Although a commercial yeast has been added to quicken the process of raising the bread the special flavour of Sourdough Bread is retained.

Sourdough Bread Starter

2 cups milk, 2 cups sifted all purpose flour.

Pour milk into a glass or ceramic bowl; cover bowl with cheesecloth and let stand outdoors for 1 day. Stir in flour and recover bowl with cheesecloth; place outdoors again for 2 days. Place bowl in a sunny spot indoors and allow to stand until mixture bubbles and starts to sour (about 2 days). Spoon into a quart jar with a screw-type cap and store in refrigerator at least 1 day before using. Should top of starter start to dry out at any time during process, stir in a little lukewarm water. (If using 1½ cups sourdough starter, simply replace with ¾ cup milk and ¾ cup flour and stir into jar. Cover jar with cheesecloth and place in sunny spot for 1 day. Remove cheesecloth; cover jar and return to refrigerator.) Makes 4 cups of starter.

Air Buns

2 tsp. sugar; 1/2 cup warm water; 2 pkgs. active dry yeast; 4 - 4½ cups all-purpose flour; 2 cups raisins; 3/4 cup milk; 1/4 cup sugar; 2 tsp. salt; 1/4 cup shortening; 2 eggs.

Dissolve 2 tsp. sugar in 1/2 cup warm water in large, warm bowl; sprinkle yeast into water mixture and let stand 10 minutes, then stir well. Scald milk; mix in sugar and salt; cool to lukewarm. Add milk mixture, shortening, eggs and 1 cup flour to dissolved yeast mixture. Beat with rotary beater until smooth. Stir in raisins (that have been lightly coated with flour called for in recipe). Add 3 cups of remaining flour gradually, adding more if necessary to make a soft dough which leaves sides of bowl. Turn out on floured board. Round up into a ball, knead 5 to 10 minutes or until dough becomes smooth, elastic and no longer sticky. Place in lightly greased bowl; grease top of dough and cover with greased waxed paper. Set in warm place (75°-85°F) until double in size (1½ - 2 hrs.). Punch down. Turn out on board and divide dough into 2 equal portions. Gather up each portion; cover and let set 10 minutes. Shape each portion into a loaf; place in two greased 8½"x4½" bread pans. Grease top of loaves; cover with greased waxed paper.

Let rise in warm place until doubled (1 - 1½ hrs.). Bake at 400°F for 35 to 40 minutes. Remove from pans. Brush top crust with margarine or butter for soft shiny crust. Cool on wire racks. Makes 2 loaves.

Overnight Buns

1 pkge. active dry yeast
1/2 tsp. sugar
Dissolve yeast and sugar in 1/2 cup warm water; let stand 5-10 minutes.

In a large bowl combine:
11-12 cups all-purpose flour
4 cups cold water
3/4 cup salad oil
1 cup berry sugar
1 1/2 tsp. salt

Blend well. Add yeast mixture. Mix until completely moistened. Turn out on lightly floured board and knead well (approximately 10 mins.) Place in greased bowl. Prepare this dough around 4 p.m. Do **NOT** set bowl in a warm place. When dough is doubled (around 10 p.m.) shape into buns and place on lightly greased cookie sheet. Cover with a cloth and leave overnight in a very cool place. While breakfast is cooking, place buns in 375-400 degree F. oven for 15 minutes or until done. *Yield approximately 6 dozen.* They are just like balls of fluff.

Easter Bread with Almond Filling

EASTER BREAD

1 envelope active dry yeast; 1 teaspoon sugar; 1/4 cup luke-warm water (100 to 115 degrees F.); 1/4 cup milk, at room temperature; 1 teaspoon vanilla extract; 1/2 teaspoon grated lemon peel; 1/4 cup sugar; 1/2 teaspoon salt; 3 egg yolks; 2 cups all-purpose flour; 4 tablespoons butter, softened; 1 egg, lightly beaten with 1 tablespoon of milk.

Dissolve the sugar in the warm water. Sprinkle in the yeast. Let stand for 2 to 3 minutes until the yeast dissolves. Set in a warm draft-free place for about 5 minutes or until the yeast has begun to bubble and has almost doubled in volume. Combine the yeast solution, milk, vanilla, lemon peel, sugar and salt. Stir in the egg yolks 1 at a time and then beat in the flour 1/2 cup at a time. Beat the soft butter into the dough a tablespoon at a time. Knead the dough on a floured surface for about 10 minutes or until the dough is smooth and elastic, sprinkling more flour on the dough or working surface if either becomes sticky. Place in a greased bowl turning once to grease the top and let rise in a warm draft-free area for about 1 hour or until double in bulk.

ALMOND FILLING

4 tablespoons butter, softened; 1/4 cup sugar; 1 egg yolk, lightly beaten; 1/2 cup finely grated almonds; 1 teaspoon grated orange peel; 1/2 cup raisins; 1/2 teaspoon vanilla extract.

Cream the butter and sugar. Beat in the egg yolk and gradually stir in the almonds, peel, raisins and vanilla. Blend thoroughly. Set aside.

Turn the dough out on a floured surface, knead it again for a minute. Roll the dough into a rectangle about 9 inches wide and 13 inches long; it should then be about 1/4 inch thick. With a metal spatula spread the almond filling over the rectangle of dough leaving an unspread border of 3/4 inches on each side. Starting with the 13 inch side, roll the dough up like a jelly roll. (Do not close the ends). Place the roll seam side down on a lightly greased baking sheet. Brush the top and sides of the roll with the egg-milk mixture. Let it rise in a warm draft-free place until doubled in bulk, (about 45 minutes to 1 hour). Brush it again with the egg-milk mixture. Bake in a 350 degree F. oven 40 to 45 minutes or until it is a light golden brown.

Greek Easter Bread

½ c. milk, ¼ c. granulated sugar, ¾ tsp. salt, 2 tbsp. soft butter, 1/3 c. warm water, 1 tsp. granulated sugar, 1 envelope dry granular yeast, 1 egg, well beaten, 2½ to 3 c. sifted all-purpose flour, ¼ c. currants, ½ c. chopped almonds, melted butter, ¾ c. sifted icing sugar, 1 tbsp. milk, whole blanched almonds, candied cherries.

Scald the ½ c. milk; stir in the ¼ c. granulated sugar, salt and butter. Cool to lukewarm. Meanwhile measure water into a large warm bowl; stir in the 1 tsp. sugar. Sprinkle with yeast. Let stand 10 minutes then stir well. Stir in lukewarm milk mixture and egg. Add 1½ c. of the flour and beat for 2 to 3 minutes with electric mixer, at medium speed, or until smooth. Add and mix in currants and almonds. Gradually stir in sufficient additional flour to make a soft dough, 1 to 2 c. more. Turn out dough onto lightly floured board or canvas and knead until smooth and elastic (5 to 10 minutes). Place dough in a buttered bowl. Cover with plastic wrap and towel and let rest in a warm place 30 minutes. Punch down dough.

Turn out onto lightly floured board or canvas. Divide dough into 3 equal portions. Shape into 3 round loaves. Place loaves on a buttered cookie sheet in the shape of a 3-petaled flower. Brush top with melted butter. Cover dough loosely with plastic wrap. Place bread in refrigerator set at moderately cold setting for 2 to 24 hours. Remove dough 20 minutes before baking, uncover and let rise in a warm place. Meanwhile, preheat oven to 375 F. Bake in preheated oven 35 to 40 minutes.

Remove from cookie sheet and cool on cake rack. Combine the ¾ c. icing sugar and the 1 tbsp. milk and pour over each of the three loaves. Arrange almonds and cherries in flower shapes on frosting Cut into thin slices and serve with butter.

(Makes One 3-Leaf Flower Shaped Bread)

"Substantial foods is like hugs, but fancies might come under the 'ead of kisses."
Mazo de la Roche, EXPLORERS OF THE DAWN, 1922

QUICK BREADS
AND BASIC MIXES

Muffin Variations

2 cups sifted, all-purpose flour; 4 teaspoons baking powder; 1/2 teaspoon salt; 1/4 cup sugar; 1 egg, beaten; 1/4 cup melted shortening; 1 cup milk.

Sift dry ingredients together. Mix egg, shortening and milk together thoroughly. Combine mixtures, stirring just enough to dampen flour. Fill greased muffin pans 2/3 full. Bake in hot oven (400 degrees F.) for 25 minutes. *Makes 12 to 15.*

Bacon or Ham Muffins
Reduce sugar to 2 tablespoons and add 1/2 cup coarsely chopped, crisp bacon or fine-cut, boiled ham to dry ingredients.

Blueberry Muffins
Add 1 cup blueberries to dry ingredients. Drain frozen or canned berries.

Cheese Muffins
Add 1/2 cup grated cheese and 1/8 teaspoon paprika to dry ingredients.

Cherry Muffins
Add 2/3 cup drained, chopped cherries to dry ingredients.

Corn-Meal Muffins
Use 1 cup corn meal and 1 cup flour instead of 2 cups flour.

Cranberry Muffins
Add 2/3 cup chopped cranberries mixed with 2 tablespoons sugar to dry ingredients.

Fruited Muffins
Add to dry ingredients 1/2 cup of one of the following dried fruits, chopped, sliced, or whole; apricots, currants, dates, figs, peaches, prunes, or a combination of two or more.

Nut Muffins
Add 1/3 cup chopped nuts of your choice to dry ingredients.

Pineapple Muffins
Add 1 cup crushed pineapple, drained to dry ingredients.

Raisin Muffins
Add 1/3 cup raisins to dry ingredients.

Whole-Wheat Muffins
Use 1 cup whole-wheat flour and 1 cup white flour instead of 2 cups flour. Add bacon bits or cracklings, if desired.

Boston Brown Bread

1 cup yellow corn meal; 1 teaspoon baking soda; 1 teaspoon salt; 2 cups whole-wheat flour; 3/4 cup molasses; 1½ cups sour milk or buttermilk.

Sift corn meal, baking soda and salt together. Stir in whole-wheat flour. Add molasses and buttermilk (or sour milk) and mix well. Place rounds of greased paper in bottom of 1-pound baking powder cans (or use 4 14-ounce cans).

Grease sides of cans and fill 1/2 to 2/3 full. Place cans on rack in large pot. Add hot water to half the height of the cans. Cover the pot and heat water to boiling. Boil gently for 3 hours. More boiling water may have to be added from time to time. Remove from water, uncover and place in hot oven (400 degrees F.) for a few minutes to dry the top. Remove from cans immediately. Serve hot .

Raisin Brown Bread

Add 1 cup raisins dredged with flour to the above recipe.

Apricot Nut Bread

3/4 cup brown sugar, firmly packed; 1 cup cut-sup soft dried apricots; 3 cups teabiscuit mix; 3/4 cup chopped nutmeats; 1 egg, slightly beaten; 1/2 cup orange juice.

Combine sugar, nutmeats and apricots. Stir in egg and orange juice. Add in biscuit mix; beat with wooden spoon, about half a minute. Turn into a buttered 9x5 loaf pan (for smaller slices, use 2 small 5x7 loaf pans). Bake in 350°F oven for 45 minutes, or until a toothpick inserted in the middle comes out clean.

Apple Oat Bread

1 beaten egg	1 tsp. baking powder
1 cup shredded,	1 tsp. salt
raw peeled apple,	1 tsp. baking soda
firmly packed	1/2 cup brown sugar
3/4 cup sour milk	1/2 cup quick cooking oats
2 tbsp. molasses	1/3 cup raisins
1/4 cup margarine, melted	1/3 cup chopped walnuts
1 3/4 cups sifted	
all-purpose flour	

In bowl, combine beaten egg, shredded apple, sour milk, molasses and melted margarine. In separate bowl, sift together flour, baking powder, salt and baking soda; then stir in sugar, oats, raisins and walnuts. Add liquid ingredients to dry ingredients all at once and stir until mixture is blended. Turn batter into greased loaf pan and bake in 350 degree F. oven for 50 to 60 minutes, or until done. Cool, then wrap to slice the next day. *Makes 1 loaf.*

Pecan Bread

3 cups sifted all-purpose flour; 1 cup sugar; 4 tsp baking powder; 1 tsp salt; 1 cup very finely chopped pecans (or walnuts); 2 tsp grated lemon rind; 2 eggs; 1 cup milk; 1/4 cup vegetable oil; pecan halves (or walnuts)

Sift flour, sugar, baking powder and salt together into a large bowl. Stir in chopped pecans and lemon rind. In a small bowl, beat eggs well with milk; mix in oil. Add to flour mixture, stirring until evenly moist. Turn into a greased 8x4x2-inch loaf pan; spread top even. To decorate, press pecan halves down center of batter. Bake in 325°F oven for 1 hour and 20 minutes, or until a wooden toothpick inserted in center comes out clean. Let cool in pan on a wire rack for 10 minutes. Loosen around edges with knife; turn out onto rack. Place right side up. Let cool completely. Store overnight to mellow flavours and for easier slicing (wrap in foil, transparent wrap or waxed paper).

Molasses Nut Bread

3 cups sifted all-purpose flour; 3 tsp. double-acting baking powder; 1½ tsp. salt; 1/2 tsp. baking soda; 1/2 cup firmly packed light brown sugar; 1/2 cup molasses; 1 egg, well beaten; 1 cup milk; 1/4 shortening, melted; 1/2 cup finely chopped nuts; 1 cup raisins.

Sift together flour, baking powder, salt and baking soda. Add brown sugar. In separate bowl combine molasses, egg and milk. Add milk mixture and shortening to flour mixture, mixing only to dampen flour. Fold in nuts and raisins. Turn into a 9" x 5" loaf pan and bake at 350 degrees F. for 65 - 70 minutes or until done. Allow to cool. Wrap in wax paper or saran and store overnight.

Ginger Bread

1/2 cup white sugar	1 tsp. soda
1/2 cup molasses	1 tsp. ginger
1/2 cup bacon drippings	1/2 tsp. cinnamon
1/2 cup boiling water	1/2 tsp. nutmeg
1 egg	1/2 tsp. cloves
1 1/2 cups flour	pinch salt

Place sugar in 1 cup measure; fill cup with molasses. Pour mixture into large bowl. Place bacon drippings into 1 cup measure; fill cup with boiling water. Pour over molasses mixture. Add egg. Stir to combine ingredients. In separate bowl, mix together flour, soda, ginger, cinnamon, nutmeg, cloves and salt. Add dry ingredients to molasses mixture. Mix well. Pour batter into greased and floured 8 inch or 9 inch square pan. Bake in 375 degree F. oven for 25 minutes or until done. Delicious served with whipped cream.

Graham Bread

5 cups graham flour; 2½ cups all-purpose flour; 3/4 cup sugar; 4½ tsp. baking soda; 5 tsp. salt; 1 quart buttermilk.

Blend together dry ingredients; add buttermilk. Mix until just blended. Place in greased loaf pans; set aside for at least 30 minutes. Bake in 350°F oven for 1 hour and 15 minutes. *Makes 2 small loaves or 1 large loaf.*

Baking Powder Biscuits

2 cups all-purpose flour; 1 tbsp baking powder; 1/2 tsp salt; 1/3 cup shortening; 3/4 cup milk.

Combine flour, baking powder and salt; stir well. Cut in shortening until mixture resembles coarse crumbs. Make a well in dry mixture; add milk all at once. Stir just until dough clings together. Gently knead on lightly floured surface (10 to 12 strokes); roll to 1/2-inch thickness. Cut with 2½-inch cutter; dip cutter in flour between cuts. Place on ungreased baking sheet. Bake in 450°F oven 10 to 12 minutes, until golden. *Makes 10 biscuits.*

Drop: Follow Baking Powder Biscuits Recipe, except increase milk to 1 cup. Do not knead; drop from tbsp onto greased baking sheet. Brush with milk. *Makes 16.*

Buttermilk; Follow Baking Powder Biscuits, except add 1/4 tsp baking soda to flour mixture. Use buttermilk in place of regular milk. *Makes 12.*

Whole Wheat: Follow Baking Powder Biscuits Recipe, except decrease flour to 1½ cup and add in 1/2 cup whole wheat flour. *Makes 12.*

Potato Scones

1 cup sifted	*1 cup well-mashed*
all-purpose flour	*potatoes (unseasoned)*
4 tsp. baking powder	*2 tbsp. butter or margarine*
1/4 tsp. salt	*1/2 cup milk (approximately)*

Sift flour, baking powder and salt twice; then add potatoes. Work in butter lightly. Add milk gradually (the amount may vary according to the amount of moisture in potatoes). Dough should be soft. Turn out on lightly floured board. Roll out to 1/2-inch thickness. Cut with biscuit cutter. Bake on greased baking sheet in 400 degree F. oven for about 15 minutes or until done.

Pumpkin Loaf

3 cups all purpose flour	*1/2 tsp. salt*
2 cups sugar	*2 tsp. cinnamon*
1 1/2 cups salad oil	*1 tin (14 oz.) pumpkin*
4 eggs	*1 cup raisins*
2 tsp. baking powder	*1/2 cup chopped walnuts*
2 tsp. baking soda	

In large bowl, place all ingredients. Mix with electric beaters or rotary beater until all is combined. Grease and flour 2 loaf pans. Place batter in prepared pans. Bake in 350 degree F. oven for 50 to 60 minutes or until cooked and knife inserted in loaf comes out clean. *Makes 2 loaves.*

Note: This recipe can be halved if desired.

Carrot-Date Loaf

2 cups sifted all-purpose flour	*1/2 cup salad oil*
1 cup sugar	*3/4 cup lemon-lime*
1 tsp. baking soda	*carbonated beverage*
3/4 tsp. salt	*1 cup finely grated carrots*
1/2 tsp. cinnamon	*1 cup chopped dates*
2 eggs, slightly beaten	

In bowl, mix together flour, sugar, baking soda, salt and cinnamon. In large bowl, combine slightly beaten eggs, salad oil, lemon-lime carbonated beverage, carrots and dates. Mix in dry ingredients. Turn mixture into greased and floured 9 x 5-inch loaf pan. Bake in 350 degree F. oven for 50 to 55 minutes or until cake tester inserted into centre, comes out clean. Remove from pan immediately. Cool on wire rack. *Makes 1 loaf.*

Note: This loaf freezes well. To serve - thaw the wrapped loaf at room temperature.

Basic Mixes

Pudding Mix

2/3 cup cornstarch; 1 cup sugar; 3/4 tsp. salt; 4 cups skim milk powder.

Blend together all ingredients; sift 3 times. Store in air-tight container. Makes 5 cups.

Vanilla Pudding: To 1 cup Basic Pudding Mix add 1½ cups water. Cook in double boiler, stirring constantly, until thick (about 10 minutes). Blend in 2 tbsp. butter. Cool slightly; add 1½ tsp. vanilla. Makes 3 servings.

Chocolate Pudding: To 1 cup Basic Pudding Mix add 3 tbsp. cocoa. Prepare as Vanilla Pudding.

Coconut Pudding: To 1 cup Basic Pudding Mix add 1/4 cup coconut. Prepare as Vanilla Pudding.

Pie Filling: Use any of the above puddings. When pudding is thick, gradually add a little hot mixture to 2 beaten egg yolks. Return to remaining hot mixture. Cook 1 to 2 minutes. Fills one baked 9–inch pie shell.

Tea Biscuits

1¾ cups all-purpose flour, 3 tsp. baking powder, 1 tsp. salt, ¼ cup shortening, ¾ cup milk.

Measure flour into measuring cup and level off; pour into mixing bowl. Blend in baking powder and salt, stirring well. Cut in shortening until mixture is like coarse meal. Add milk all at once. Stir with fork until all ingredients are moistened. Turn mixture out on lightly floured surface; gather up and knead gently about 20 times. Roll dough out with a floured rolling pin to ½ inch thickness. With a floured 2 inch biscuit cutter cut dough with one sharp cut for each.

Place on ungreased baking sheet (¾ inch apart for crusty biscuits, or close together for soft sides. Gather up leftover dough, pat together and cut with cutter. Do not re-roll. Bake in 450 F. oven for 8 to 10 minutes. Makes 1 dozen.

Drop Biscuits: Use Basic Tea Biscuit except increase flour to 2 cups and milk to 1 cup. Omit kneading; drop mixture by tablespoonfuls onto ungreased baking sheet. Bake in 450 F. oven for 12 to 15 minutes.

Buttermilk Biscuits: Use Basic Tea Biscuit except add ¼ tsp. soda to dry ingredients. Replace buttermilk or sour milk for sweet milk.

Extra Rich Biscuits: Use Basic Tea Biscuit except increase shortening to ½ cup (part butter) and add 2 tbsp. sugar to dry ingredients.

Cheese Biscuits: Use Basic Tea Biscuit except cut in ¾ cup grated sharp cheese into dry ingredients after shortening.

Make-It-Yourself Mix

10 c. all purpose flour, 1/3 c. baking powder, 1 tbsp. salt, 2 1/3 c. (1 lb.) shortening.

Pour or spoon flour into dry measuring cup. Level off and pour into a large mixing bowl. Add baking powder and salt; stir well to blend. Cut in shortening with pastry blender until mixture resembles coarse meal. Yields about 16½ cups.

Store mix in closed cannister, at room temperature. Use when desired in any of the following recipes. (NOTE: When measuring mix, spoon into dry measuring cup. Do not pack.)

Muffins

2½ c. 'Make-It-Yourself-Mix', 3 tbsp. sugar, ¾ c. milk, 1 egg, beaten.

Stir sugar into mix, then add milk and beaten egg. Stir just until all ingredients are moistened. Batter will look lumpy. Fill well-greased muffin tin two-thirds full. Bake at 400 F. for 20 to 25 minutes. Loosen edges and turn out on wire rack. Serve warm. Variation: Fruit Muffins: *Stir ¾ c. raisins, cut-up date or candied fruit into the dry mix.*

(Yields 1 dozen)

Pancakes

1½ c. 'Make-It-Yourself-Mix', 1 tbsp. sugar, 1 c. milk, 1 egg, beaten.

Stir sugar into mix, then add milk and beaten egg. Stir until blended. Pour batter by ¼ cupfuls onto lightly greased hot griddle. Bake until puffy and bubbly. Turn and bake other side. Serve hot with butter and syrup. Makes about 12 fluffy 4 inch pancakes.

Cinnamon Ring

¼ c. halved maraschino cherries, 1 c. sugar, 1/3 c. chopped nuts, 4 tsp. cinnamon, 6¾ c. 'Make-It-Yourself-Mix', ½ c. sugar, 1¾ c. milk, 2/3 c. melted butter, ¼ c. raisins.

Place cherries over bottom of well-greased 9-inch tube pan. Combine 1 c. sugar, nuts and cinnamon in small bowl. Stir in ½ c. sugar into mix in a large bowl. Add milk to mix. Stir with fork just until all ingredients are moistened. Drop heaping tablespoons of dough in melted butter, then in cinnamon-sugar mixture. Place balls slightly apart in a single layer in bottom of pan; sprinkle with raisins. Repeat for second layer. Press lightly in place to give an even surface. Bake at 350 F. for 50 to 60 minutes. Invert immediately onto serving plate. Serve warm or cold.

Breakfast and Dessert Ideas

Blintz Pancakes

1 cup sifted all-purpose flour; 1 tbsp sugar; 1/2 tsp salt; 1 cup dairy sour cream; 1 cup small-curd cottage cheese; 4 eggs, well beaten.

Sift together flour, sugar and salt. Add in dairy sour cream, cottage cheese and well beaten eggs. Stir just until mixed. Bake on hot, greased griddle. Stack pancakes and top with Blueberry Sauce. *Makes about 24.*

Blueberry Sauce: In saucepan, combine 1 (14 oz) can blueberries and 2 tsp cornstarch. Cook, stirring, until mixture thickens and bubbles. Blend in 1 tsp lemon juice.

Crepes

4 ounces flour	*3 eggs*
1/2 ounce sugar	*10 ounces milk*
salt	

Mix above ingredients together and make thin crepes.

Crepes Soufflees

Add a spoonful of your favourite souffle mixture to the centre of a crepe and fold crepe over; place on a buttered oven dish and bake for 8 minutes 375 Degrees F.

Sauce

Mix together juice of 3 oranges, 1 lemon and 1 ounce sugar; cook until reduced to half original quantity; add orange flavoured liqueur and pour over crepes at time of serving.

Crepes Flambees

Melt 1 ounce of butter with 1 ounce of sugar and cook until slightly caramelized; place crepes in pan and heat; fold; add orange flavoured liqueur; flame and serve. As prepared by the Chef of Marnier Lapostolle, Mr. J. Delaunay.

Scottish Tea Pancakes

1 cup flour	*1/2 tsp. salt*
1/4 cup sugar	*2/3 cup milk*
2 tsp. baking powder	*1 egg*
1/2 tsp. soda	*2 tbsp. melted butter*

In large bowl, sift together flour, sugar, baking powder, soda and salt. Add milk, egg and melted butter. Mix well. Fry in skillet in 2 inch rounds. Serve cold, buttered and spread with honey or jam.

Note: If not using non-stick type of skillet, lightly butter skillet as needed.

Apple Pancakes

In a skillet melt 2 tbsp. butter. Combine 1 tsp. cinnamon with 2 tbsp. sugar and sprinkle evenly over the melted butter. Peel, core and slice 2 small apples and arrange slices over sugar and cinnamon mixture. Simmer 5 minutes. Combine 3 tbsp. flour with 1/4 tsp. baking powder and a pinch of salt. Separate 2 eggs - add the yolks to the dry ingredients with 3 tbsp. milk. Beat egg whites until foamy, gradually adding 3 tbsp. sugar, beat until soft peaks form. Fold into flour mixture. Pour over apple slices, spreading to the edge of pan. Bake 10 minutes at 400 degrees F. or until golden and puffy. DO NOT OPEN THE OVEN DOOR THE FIRST 8 MINUTES! *Invert onto a serving plate.*

For breakfast or brunch, serve with bacon, sausage or ham. For dessert, top with sour cream, ice cream or whipped cream.

Note: It is important that the sides of your skillet are not greased, otherwise the pancake will not rise very high. Also make sure you carefully spread the batter over the apples right to the edges.

Pancakes With Orange Sauce

Orange Sauce

3/4 cup sugar	*1/8 tsp. salt*
4 tsp. cornstarch	*2 tbsp. butter or margarine*
1 1/2 cups orange juice	*1 tsp. vanilla*
(juice from approximately 4 medium oranges)	

Pancakes

1 1/4 cups all-purpose flour	*3 tbsp. salad oil*
2 tbsp. sugar	*1 1/3 cups milk*
3/4 tsp. salt	*1 egg*
2 tsp. baking powder	*salad oil for brushing skillet or griddle*

Orange Sauce

In saucepan, mix sugar and cornstarch. Stir in orange juice and salt until well blended. Heat mixture to boiling, over medium heat, stirring constantly; remove from heat. Stir in butter and vanilla until blended. Keep warm.

Pancakes

In large bowl, mix flour, sugar, salt and baking powder. In small bowl, mix 3 tbsp. salad oil, milk and egg. Stir egg mixture into flour mixture just until flour is moistened. Lightly brush skillet or griddle with salad oil. Pour batter by scant 1/4 cupfuls onto hot griddle, making a few pancakes at a time; cook until bubbly and bubbles burst. Turn pancakes and cook until undersides are golden; place on heated platter; keep warm. Repeat until all the batter is used. Brush griddle with more salad oil if necessary. Serve pancakes with Orange Sauce. *Makes approximately 12 4-inch pancakes.*

Note: For thicker pancakes, reduce milk to 1 cup. Makes 8 4-inch pancakes.

Buttermilk Pancakes

2 cups sifted
  all-purpose flour
1 tbsp. sugar
1 tsp. salt

1 tsp. baking soda
2 eggs, well beaten
2 cups buttermilk
2 tbsp. salad oil

Sift together flour, sugar, salt and baking soda. In large bowl, combine beaten eggs and buttermilk. Add sifted dry ingredients all at once to egg-mixture. Beat until smooth. Stir in salad oil. Cook pancakes on a medium-hot griddle. Serve immediately. *Makes 4 to 6 servings.*

Pancake Toppin's

Maple Syrup: Blend together 1 cup light corn syrup, 1/2 cup brown sugar and 1/2 cup water; cook, stirring, until dissolved. Add dash maple flavouring and 1 tbsp butter.

Whipped Butter: Beat 1/2 cup butter with electric mixer until fluffy.

Orange Butter: Add in 1 tbsp sugar and 1/4 cup grated orange peel to Whipped Butter.

Honey Butter: Gradually add in 1/4 cup honey to Whipped Butter; beat smooth. Add 2 tsp grated orange peel.

Cinnamon-Maple Syrup

Heat 1 cup maple-flavoured syrup with 1 tablespoon butter or margarine and 1/2 teaspoon cinnamon. Serve warm.

Maple Whip

Cream 1/2 cup soft butter or margarine. Add 1 cup maple-flavoured syrup gradually. Beat until smooth and spreading consistency.

Lemon Syrup

Mix 1/2 cup sugar, 1 tablespoon cornstarch and 1/8 teaspoon salt in saucepan. Gradually stir in 1-1/2 cups hot water. Bring mixture to a boil, stirring constantly. Simmer 5 minutes. Remove from heat. Blend in 3 tablespoons butter or margarine, 2 tablespoons lemon juice, 1 teaspoon grated lemon rind and 1/2 teaspoon nutmeg. Serve warm.

Sausage Ball Syrup

1/2 pound pork sausage in bulk; 1-1/3 cups maple-flavoured syrup.

Form pork sausage in small balls, 1/2 inch in diameter. Cook thoroughly about 10 minutes. Drain sausage balls; add to syrup. Heat slowly 5 minutes. Serve hot over pancakes. No need to cook another breakfast meat.

French Toast

9 slices dry white bread, ¾ c. pancake mix, ½ tsp. vanilla, 2 eggs, ¾ c. milk, ½ c. honey, ½ c. softened butter or margarine.

Cut bread in half diagonally. Into a bowl add pancake mix, vanilla, eggs and milk and beat with beater until smooth. Dip bread slices into batter; then fry in butter in skillet until golden brown. Serve with honey-butter (made by beating honey and butter together). Makes 6 servings.

Orange Doughnuts

3 tbsp. shortening, 1 c. sugar, 2 eggs, well beaten, 2 tbsp. grated orange rind, 1 c. orange juice, 3½ c. sifted all purpose flour, 4½ tsp. baking powder, 1 tsp. cinnamon, ¾ tsp. salt.

Blend soft shortening and sugar thoroughly. Add eggs and mix well, then orange rind. Alternately add sifted dry ingredients and orange juice. The dough should be soft but still easily handled. Chill for at least an hour. Roll or pat dough on floured board to ½ inch thickness. Cut with floured doughnut cutter.

Fry in deep fat, heat to 370 F. (a cube of day-old bread will brown in it in 60 sec.). Cook only as many doughnuts at one time as will easily float on top of fat. As soon as doughnuts rise to surface, turn, then turn again, if necessary, to ensure even browning. Remove doughnuts from fat with long-handled fork and drain on paper towel. Ice with orange frosting.

ORANGE FROSTING

3 oz. cream cheese, 1 lb. (3½ c.) icing sugar, 3 tbsp. orange juice, 1 tsp. grated orange rind.

Beat cheese until soft and smooth; add sugar and orange juice, mixing well; fold in orange rind . Red and yellow food colouring may be added for a deeper orange colour.

Doughnuts

3 cups all-purpose flour; 4 tsp. baking powder; 1/2 tsp. salt, 1/4 tsp. nutmeg or mace; 1 cup sugar; 3 tbsp. butter; 1 tsp. vanilla; 2 eggs; 2/3 cup milk.

Spoon flour into dry measuring cup. Pour onto wax paper. Add baking powder, salt and nutmeg; stir well to blend.

Cream sugar, butter and vanilla thoroughly. Beat in eggs, one at a time, mixing well after each addition. Stir in dry ingredients alternately with milk starting and ending with dry ingredients. Chill dough for at least 35 minutes for easier handling. Turn out dough onto lightly floured surface. Round up into a ball. Roll out dough with floured rolling pin to about 1/2 inch thickness. Cut with floured doughnut cutter. Fry in deep hot fat (375 degrees F.). Turn doughnuts as they rise to the surface. Fry until golden brown on both sides. Fry only 3 or 4 at a time. Drain on absorbent paper. Cool and dust with granulated sugar or icing sugar. *Yield approximately 1-1/2 dozen doughnuts.*

Hints:
Fry dough from centre cut-out . . . makes tasty nibbling. Watch cooking time as over-cooking will cause doughnuts to become hard after a few hours.

Doughnuts may be freshened by heating in a moderate oven in a paper bag. Close bag securely and sprinkle with cold water before placing in the oven.

For quick dusting of doughnuts, place several doughnuts in a paper bag with granulated or icing sugar and shake gently. Doughnuts will be lightly coated with the sugar.

POTPOURRI OF CAKES

Mona says . . .

Store fruitcakes and shortbreads in airtight tins. For drop cookies, fill a pastry bag with dough (without using a metal tip), then press out just the right amount of dough onto cookie sheet and flatten.

To split cake layers, measure halfway up the side of cake and mark with toothpicks. Using a serrated knife, cut across and through, using picks as a guide.

Basic rule for baking cakes and cookies . . . sponge and loaf cakes on the lowest shelf of the oven; cookies on the top shelf. Thick to the bottom, thin to the top.

Roll jelly rolls using a towel. When roll is filled and ready, place on towel, start first tight turn with hand, then lift towel higher and higher. Jelly roll will roll by itself.

Before frosting a cake always allow it to cool thoroughly and brush all loose crumbs away. To leave the cake plate clean when icing, place strips of wax paper under bottom edge of cake — after frosting, remove.

To keep cookies soft, store in tightly covered container with a slice of fresh bread or an apple wedge if they become dry. Keep crisp cookies in a jar with a loose-fitting lid. To freeze cookies, wrap in moisture-vaporproof material; place in sturdy container; overwrap with moisture-vaporproof material; seal, label, and freeze. Thaw, unopened, in the container.

Cake slices best when it is chilled but tastes best at room temperature.

To keep mixing bowls steady when mixing or whipping, place them on a wet folded cloth.

Strawberry Angel Delight

[See photo opposite page]

Cake:
1 1/4 cups sugar
1/2 cup water
8 fresh eggs, separated
1 cup sifted cake flour
1/2 tsp. salt
1 tsp. cream of tartar
1 tsp. almond flavouring

Combine sugar and water. Boil over high heat until it spins a thread (230 degree F. on candy thermometer). Beat egg yolks until light and lemon-coloured. While continuing to beat, pour hot syrup over yolks in a thin stream. The mixture should thicken noticeably. Sift the flour and salt 7 or 8 times; measure. After egg mixture has cooled to room teamperature, fold in flour. Beat egg whites until frothy, add cream of tartar. Continue beating until whites are stiff but not dry. Fold egg whites into flour mixture; add almond flavouring. Pour into ungreased tube pan. Bake in 300 degree F. oven for approximately 1 1/2 hours. Invert pan while cooling.

Filling:
1 1/4 cups whipping cream
1/4 cup sugar

3 cups strawberries, [or raspberries) washed & hulled

Whip and sweeten cream with sugar. Split cake in half. On bottom layer place half the berries and half the whipped cream. Place other layer on top; add remaining berries, decorating with remaining whipped cream.

CAKES
FROSTINGS
FILLINGS

Conventional Type Cakes

Cakes — *It is most important to follow recipe suggestions exactly. Use the ingredients suggested in the recipe and have them at room temperature. **Never** double a cake recipe as you will not get proper beating and blending of ingredients.*

You may "sift" or "blend" together the dry ingredients. If blending be sure to do it thoroughly.

Use the size of pan recommended in the recipe. The batter should about ½ fill the pan and should be evenly spread.

For best results add the dry ingredients 1/3 at a time, the liquid ½ at a time. Start and end with the dry ingredients and simply stir to combine the batter. DO NOT BEAT as this may result in a coarse, tough cake.

Grease cake pans on bottoms only, using unsalted shortening or vegetable oil. Line with waxed paper cut to fit; or add about 1 tsp. flour and shake to coat the bottom. Discard excess flour. Sprinkle berry sugar lightly over flour.

A cake is baked if the top springs back when pressed with the finger tips or when a cake tester, inserted in the centre, comes out clean.

Let a cake stand in the pan for about 10 minutes and then remove from the pan and cool on a rack.

Cake-Batter Basic

½ cup shortening, ¾ cup sugar, 2 well beaten eggs, 1 tsp vanilla, 1¾ cups all purpose flour sifted, 2 tsp baking powder, ¼ tsp cream of tartar, ½ tsp salt, ⅔ cup milk.

Cream shortening. Gradually blend in sugar; beat until light and fluffy. Add eggs and vanilla and beat until well combined. Sift together flour, baking powder, cream of tartar and salt. Add dry ingredients to the creamed mixture, alternately with milk, mixing well. Pour into 8 or 9-inch square cake pan or two 8-inch round layer pans, which have been greased and the bottom lined with waxed paper or dusted lightly with flour. Bake in preheated 350F oven for 45 to 50 minutes for a square cake, or 30 to 35 minutes for layer cake.

Spice: Prepare Basic White Cake (as above) and add 1 tsp cinnamon, ½ tsp. ginger, ½ tsp nutmeg and ¼ tsp allspice to the dry ingredients.

Marble: Prepare Basic White Cake. Divide the batter into two portions. To one half add a mixture of 1 square unsweetened chocolate, melted, 2 tsp sugar, ⅛ tsp baking soda and 2 tsp hot water. The other half of mixture is left plain. Alternately drop spoonfuls of the two batters into greased floured pan. Swirl for a marbled effect. Bake as directed.

Maple Nut: Prepare Basic White Cake, substituting the vanilla with 1 tsp maple flavouring. Add ½ cup finely chopped walnuts into the batter. Bake as directed.

110

Chocolate Zucchini Cake

2-1/2 cups all-purpose flour, unsifted	3 eggs
1/2 cup cocoa	2 tsp. vanilla
2-1/2 tsp. baking powder	2 tsp. grated orange peel
1-1/2 tsp. soda	2 cups coarsely shredded zucchini
1 tsp. salt	(not to be peeled -
1 tsp. cinnamon	grate on coarse grater)
3/4 cup soft butter or margarine	1/2 cup milk
2 cups sugar	1 cup chopped pecans or walnuts
	Glaze (recipe below)

Combine flour, cocoa, baking powder, soda, salt and cinnamon; set aside. With a rotary mixer, beat together butter and sugar until smoothly blended. Add eggs, one at a time, beating well after each addition. With a spoon, stir in vanilla, orange peel and zucchini. Alternately stir the dry ingredients and the milk into zucchini mixture, including the nuts with last addition. Pour batter into a greased and floured 10-inch tube pan or bundt pan. Bake in a 350 degree F. oven for about 1 hour or until a toothpick inserted in centre comes out clean. Cool in pan for 15 minutes; turn out cake on wire rack to cool thoroughly.

Glaze
Mix together 2 cups icing sugar, 3 tbsp. milk and 1 tsp. vanilla; beat until smooth. Drizzle glaze over cake. Cut cake in thin slices to serve. *Makes 10 to 12 servings.*

Spicy Chocolate Cake

2 egg whites, ¼ cup sugar, 1½ cups all-purpose flour, 1 cup sugar, ½ cup cocoa, 1¼ tsp soda, 1¼ tsp salt, 1 tsp cinnamon, ½ tsp cloves, 2 egg yolks, ⅔ cup salad oil, 1 cup sour milk or buttermilk.

Beat egg whites until foamy; gradually add ¼ cup sugar, 1 tbsp at a time and beat to soft peaks. Set aside. Pour flour into dry measuring cup and level off. Pour into large mixing bowl and add 1 cup sugar, cocoa, soda, salt and spices. Stir well to blend. Add egg yolks, oil and sour milk to dry ingredients in bowl. Blend with mixer until smooth. Fold egg white mixture into batter. Pour batter evenly into two greased and floured 8-inch round layer pans. Bake in 350F oven for 25 to 30 minutes or until knife inserted in centre comes out clean. Let cake cool 10 minutes in pan before turning out on wire rack.

Chocolate Wacky Cake

1-1/2 cups flour	1 tbsp. vinegar
1 cup sugar	1 tsp. vanilla
4 tbsp. cocoa	6 tbsp. vegetable oil
1/2 tsp. salt	1 cup water
1 tsp. soda	

Into an 8-inch or 9-inch square pan, stir flour, sugar, cocoa, salt and soda. Make 3 holes in dry ingredients. Into 1 hole pour vinegar; into second hole pour vanilla and in third hole the vegetable oil. Pour water over all. Stir until dry ingredients are well blended. Bake in a 350 degree F. oven for approximately 30 minutes or until done. Allow to cool before icing.

Note: This is a lovely moist cake that can be doubled.

Mocha Icing

3 to 4 tbsp. butter	1 tsp. instant coffee dissolved
sifted icing sugar	in 1 tbsp. hot water

Combine butter, icing sugar, (use enough to obtain desired consistency) and coffee. Spread over cooled cake.

Applesauce Cake

1/3 cup shortening, ½ cup brown sugar, ½ cup granulated sugar, 1 egg, 1 cup applesauce, 1 2/3 cups sifted all-purpose flour, 1 tsp. salt, 1 tsp. soda, ¼ tsp. cloves, ½ tsp. cinnamon, ¼ tsp. nutmeg, 1/3 cup water, 1/3 cup chopped nuts, 2/3 cup raisins.

Cream shortening, add sugars; cream together until light and fluffy. Add egg, beat well. Stir in applesauce. Sift together flour, soda, salt and spices. Add the dry ingredients to the creamed mixture alternately with the water. Stir in nuts and fruit when adding the last portion of flour. Spread in greased 9" square pan. Bake at 350 F. for about 40 — 45 minutes.

Chocolate Cream Roll

3/4 cup sifted cake flour; 1/2 cup cocoa; 1 tsp. baking powder; 1/4 tsp. salt; 3 eggs; 1-1/3 cups sugar; 5 tbsp. water; 1 tsp. vanilla; 2 cups whipping cream.

Preheat oven to 375°F. Grease a 10x15x3/4-inch jelly roll pan and line with waxed paper. Sift together flour, 1/4 cup of cocoa, baking powder and salt. Beat eggs until thick. Gradually beat in 1 cup sugar. Stir in water and vanilla. Add flour mixture all at once. Beat just until smooth.

Spread batter in prepared pan. Bake in preheated oven 12 to 15 minutes. Remove from oven and immediately invert cake on tea towel sprinkled with icing sugar. Peel off paper. Roll up loosely in tea towel. Cool completely on wire rack.
Frosting: Combine remaining 1/4 cup cocoa and cream. Refrigerate at least 1 hour. Whip until softly stiff. Beat in remaining 1/3 cup sugar. Unroll cake and spread with half the chocolate whipped cream. Re-roll cake and frost with remaining chocolate whipped cream. Chill until serving time. *Makes about 10 servings.*

Hints for Chiffon Type Cakes

Have all ingredients assembled and accurately measured before you start mixing your cake.

Do not grease pans. Use size of pan indicated in recipe.

*Sift Dry ingredients into bowl — then add **in order** oil, yolks, liquid and flavouring — then beat until batter is very smooth.*

Egg whites should be very stiff — do not underbeat.

Pour egg-yolk batter over the entire surface of egg whites in a thin stream — then fold just until ingredients are blended. Cake is cooked when it springs back after being lightly touched with fingertips.

After removing cake from oven invert it over a bottle until it cools to room temperature — then remove from pan by loosening cake around sides and tube with a knife or spatula. Turn cake upside down over wire rack or plate; then remove pan.

Sponge, Chiffon and Angel Type Cakes

Mocha Chiffon Cake

4 level tsp. instant coffee	5 egg yolks
3/4 cup boiling water	1 tsp. vanilla
2-1/4 cups sifted **cake** flour	3 squares (1 oz. each) semi-
1-1/2 cups sugar	sweet chocolate, thinly shaved
3 tsp. baking powder	1 cup egg whites
1 tsp. salt	(approximately 8)
1/2 cup salad oil	1/2 tsp. cream of tartar

Dissolve coffee in boiling water; allow to cool. Into bowl, sift cake flour, sugar, baking powder and salt. Make a well in centre. Add salad oil, egg yolks, cooled coffee and vanilla **in order given**. Beat until smooth. Stir in shaved chocolate. In large clean mixing bowl, place egg whites and cream of tartar. Beat until stiff peaks form. Pour egg yolk-mixture over whites in a thin stream; gently fold to blend. Bake cake in an **ungreased** 10-inch tube pan in 325 degree F. oven for 55 minutes - then at 350 degrees F. for 10 to 15 minutes longer or until done. Invert pan and allow to cool before removing from pan.

Hot Milk Lemon Sponge Cake

1 cup flour (all-purpose); 1 teaspoon baking powder; 1/2 teaspoon salt; 3 eggs; 1 cup sugar; 1 tablespoon lemon juice; 6 tablespoons hot milk; 1 tablespoon lemon rind.

Mix flour, baking powder and salt together. Beat eggs at high speed until thick and lemon coloured (about 5 minutes) in a separate bowl. Gradually add sugar and beat until light and fluffy. Add lemon juice and rind. With electric mixer at low speed add dry ingredients to egg mixture. Add hot milk all at once and mix quickly. Spread batter in an ungreased tube pan or angel cake pan. Bake at 375 degrees F. for 25 to 30 minutes. Invert cake and let hang until cool. Glaze.

Lemon Glaze

2 tablespoons lemon juice; 1/4 cup sugar.

In a heavy saucepan combine lemon juice and sugar and bring to a boil. Simmer for 3 to 5 minutes and drizzle over cooled sponge cake.

Rocky Road Angel Cake

1 package Chocolate	1/2 cup chopped pecans
Angel Food Cake Mix	1/4 cup chopped chocolate chips
3 cups whipping cream	1 tbsp. butter
1/4 cup icing sugar	2 squares unsweetened
2/3 cup miniature marshmallows	cooking chocolate

Prepare and bake cake mix as directed. Cool; break into small pieces. Beat whipping cream and icing sugar. Set aside about half of the whipping cream. Into remaining cream fold in marshmallows, nuts and chocolate chips. Line bottom of 13 x 9-inch glass baking pan with half of the angel food cake pieces. Spread with whipped cream mixture; then lay the remainder of Angel Food cake on the mixture. Top with the reserved whipped cream. Melt butter and squares of unsweetened baking chocolate over heat. Drizzle chocolate on top of cake (use a tsp.). Chill.

Angel Cake

1 cup sifted cake flour; 3/4 cup sugar; 12 egg whites (1½ cups); 1½ tsp cream of tartar; 1/4 tsp salt; 1½ tsp vanilla; 3/4 cup sugar.

Sift 4 times flour with 3/4 cup sugar; set aside. Beat egg whites, cream of tartar, salt and vanilla until soft peaks form, but still moist and glossy. Add in remaining 3/4 cup sugar, 2 tbsp at a time, continuing to beat until egg whites hold stiff peaks. Sift about 1/4 of flour mixture over whites; fold in. Repeat, folding in remaining flour, a quarter at a time. Bake in ungreased 10-inch tube pan in 375°F oven for 35 to 40 minutes, or until done. Invert cake in pan; cool. Remove from pan.

Heavenly Berry Cake

Thaw 1 (10 oz) pkg frozen strawberries or raspberries. In top of 10-inch angel cake, between center and edge, cut slits 1 inch apart in a circle around the cake. Cut slits through to bottom. With knife in slit, pull cake away slightly and spoon some berries and juice into each slit.

Whip 2 cups whipping cream with 1/4 cup sugar, 1 tsp vanilla and 6 drops red food colouring, Frost cake; chill. Trim with additional berries. *Serves 10 to 12.*

delectable cakes and toppings from here and there

Lazy Daisy Cake

2 eggs
1 tsp. vanilla
1 cup sugar
1 cup flour

1 tsp. baking powder
1 tsp. salt
1/2 cup milk
2 tbsp. butter or margarine

Icing

2 tbsp. butter, softened
3 tbsp. cream

1/2 cup brown sugar
1/2 cup coconut

In bowl, beat eggs; add vanilla and sugar, and beat. Add flour, baking powder, and salt. Heat milk with butter (until butter melts). Add to egg-flour mixture and combine well. Bake in 350 degree F. oven for 30 minutes or until done.

Icing

Combine softened butter, cream, brown sugar and coconut. Spread over hot, cooked cake. Return cake to oven until topping is bubbly.

Glazed German Apple Cake

Cake

2/3 cup margarine, 2 cups sugar, 2 eggs, well beaten, 2 tsp. vanilla, 2 cups flour, 2 tsp. soda, 1 tsp. salt, 2 tsp. cinnamon, 6 medium-size apples, peeled and chopped, 1/2 cup chopped walnuts.

Glaze Topping

1/2 cup evaporated milk, 1/2 cup sugar, 1 egg yolk, 1 1/2 tsp. butter, 1 tsp. vanilla 1/2 cup coconut, 1/2 cup chopped walnuts.

In large bowl cream margarine and sugar. In small bowl beat eggs; add vanilla. Combine and mix thoroughly egg mixture and butter mixture. In medium bowl sift together flour, soda, salt and cinnamon. Prepare apples. Add dry ingredients to the creamed mixture alternately with apples. Stir well after each addition. Add walnuts. Pour batter in a greased and floured 10'' x 13'' pan and bake at 375 degrees F. for 40 to 45 minutes or until cooked. Allow to cool.

Topping

In saucepan combine evaporated milk, sugar, egg yolk, butter and vanilla. Cook until thickened, stirring constantly. Remove from heat. Beat until cool. Stir in walnuts and coconut. Spread over cake.

Mocha Torte

1 pkg (2-layer size) white cake mix; 1 (6 oz) pkg semisweet chocolate chips; 3 cups miniature marshmallows; 1/2 cup milk; 2 tsp instant coffee powder; 1 cup whipping cream, whipped.

Prepare cake mix according to label directions. Bake in greased 13x9x2 inch pan. Cool; remove from pan and let cool completely.

Mocha Frosting: Combine chocolate chips, marshmallows, milk and coffee powder in top of double boiler. Heat, stirring, over hot water until marshmallows melt. Remove from heat; cover and chill. Fold in whipped cream.

Cut cake in half lengthwise, then split each half of cake into 2 layers (use toothpicks to guide knife). Spread chilled Mocha Frosting between layers; frost top and sides. Cover and let chill for several hours.

Apple Torte

Crust

1 1/4 cups flour, 1 egg yolk, 1 tbsp. sugar, grated rind of 1 large lemon, 1/2 cup softened butter.

Sift flour into large bowl. Make well in middle. Place egg yolk, sugar, lemon rind and butter in well. Stir with fork. Work dough till all ingredients are well blended and dough is smooth. Pat dough in bottom and on sides of 9 inch flan pan or 9 inch pie plate. Chill 2 hours.

Filling

6 cups apples, peeled, cored and sliced, 1/2 cup sugar, 1/2 tsp. nutmeg, 1/2 cup whipping cream, 1 egg yolk, 1/2 cup blanched almonds, slivered.

Place apple slices in attractive fashion over pastry. Sprinkle with sugar and nutmeg. Bake in 350 degree F. oven 15 minutes. Remove from oven. Beat whipping cream, egg yolk and almonds slightly to combine; cover apples with whipping cream mixture. Return torte to oven and bake for 20 to 25 minutes longer or until golden brown. Garnish with extra whipped whipping cream if desired. Makes 8 servings.

Lemon Cake Pudding

3 tbsps. butter or margarine
1 cup sugar
4 eggs, separated
3 tbsps. flour
1/4 tsp. salt

6 tbsps. freshly squeezed lemon juice
1 cup milk
1 tsp. freshly grated lemon rind

In a small bowl, cream butter and sugar; add well beaten egg yolks, mix well. Stir in flour, salt and lemon juice; blend in milk and lemon peel. Beat egg whites until stiff but not dry; fold into batter. Pour mixture into a buttered 1 1/2 quart casserole. Place casserole into a shallow pan of water (about 1 inch deep). Bake in a 325 degree F. oven for 50 to 60 minutes. Serve hot or cold.

Apple Coffee-Cake

½ c. chopped almonds, ¼ c. lightly-packed brown sugar, ½ tsp. cinnamon, 2 c. sifted all-purpose flour, 2 tsp. baking powder, 1 1/3 c. granulated sugar, 2 eggs, 2/3 c. milk, ½ c. butter, melted, 2 tsp. grated orange rind, 2¼ c. coarsely chopped, apples..

Topping

Combine almonds, brown sugar and cinnamon.

Cake

Butter a 9-inch square cake pan. Preheat oven to 350 F. Sift together the flour, baking powder and sugar. Beat eggs well; stir in milk, melted butter and orange rind. Make a well in dry ingredients and add liquid all at once, mixing lightly until just combined; do not over mix. Turn into prepared pan; spread evenly. Bake in preheated oven 20 minutes. Top with apples and sprinkle with topping; continue baking 45 to 50 minutes. Cut into 9 squares and serve warm. Makes 9 servings.

Apricot Coffee Cake

2 cups Make-It-Yourself-Mix, ¼ cup sugar, 2/3 cup milk, 1 egg, beaten ½ cup apricot jam, or jam of your choice.

Stir sugar into mix, then add milk and beaten egg. Stir just until all ingredients are moistened. Spread batter into greased 8 inch square pan. Spread jam over top. Sprinkle Streusel Topping over jam. Bake at 400 F. for 30 to 35 minutes. Serve warm.

Make-it-yourself mix - turn to p. 105

Streusel Topping

½ cup all purpose flour, ¼ cup brown sugar, ¼ cup butter.

Combine flour and sugar in small bowl. Cut or rub in butter until mixture is mealy.

Cheesecake Deluxe

Line a 9-inch spring form pan with the crust of your choice. Cream 1 lb. cream cheese, add ¾ cup sugar, 3 egg yolks and 1 tsp vanilla. Beat 3 egg whites and fold in carefully. Spread on base. Bake at 350F for 25 minutes. While baking, mix ½ pint sour cream, 14 oz. tin crushed pineapple, drained, ½ tsp vanilla, and 10 to 12 maraschino cherries. Remove cake from oven, cool 10 minutes; spread on sour cream mixture and bake 5 minutes more. Sprinkle crushed wafers on top.

Low Calorie Cheesecake

7 Zwieback biscuits, crushed; 4 tbsp sugar; 1/2 tsp cinnamon; 2 tbsp butter or margarine; 1 envelope unflavoured gelatin; 1/2 cup milk; 2 egg yolks; 1½ cup milk; 2 tbsp sugar; 1½ tbsp liquid non-caloric sweetener; 1/2 tsp salt; 2 cup cottage cheese; 2 tsp lemon juice; 1/2 tsp grated lemon rind.

Mix crushed biscuits with 4 tbsp sugar, cinnamon and butter; press firmly into 7½-inch spring form pan. Chill until firm. Soften gelatin in 1/2 cup milk for 5 minutes. Beat egg yolks; add in 1½ cup milk, 2 tbsp sugar, sweetener and salt. Cook over boiling water, stirring constantly until slightly thick. Add gelatin, stir until dissolved. Cool slightly. Rub cottage cheese through a sieve; stir in cooled custard, lemon juice and rind. Pour into crust. Chill for 4 hours.

Pineapple Cheesecake

2½ cup crushed pineapple; 2 tbsp PLUS 1 tsp. gelatin; 1/2 cup pineapple syrup; 4 egg yolks, slightly beaten; 1 cup sugar; crumb base mixture; 2 tsp grated lemon peel; 1/4 tsp salt; 2 tbsp pineapple syrup; 3 cups cottage cheese; 1 tbsp vanilla; 2 cups heavy cream, whipped.

Line a 9-inch spring form pan with crumb base. Drain pineapple, reserving syrup. Measure 1/2 cup syrup and soften gelatin in this. Combine egg yolks, sugar, lemon peel, salt and 2 tbsp pineapple syrup. Cook, stirring constantly, until a smooth custard mixture is formed (this will be thin). Remove from heat. Add softened gelatin, crushed pineapple, cottage cheese and vanilla. Fold in whipped heavy cream. Chill until firm, about 5 hours. Loosen sides from pan with spatula before removing. Garnish with pineapple slices and maraschino cherries.

[*See page 128 — Basic Crumb Crust*]

Chocolate Cheesecake

1-1/4 cups finely crushed chocolate wafer crumbs	1 cup sugar
	2 tsp. vanilla
1/4 cup butter or margarine, melted	3 eggs, separated
	6 ounces semi-sweet cooking chocolate, melted and cooled
1 envelope unflavoured gelatin	
1/4 cup cold water	1/4 cup sugar
4 oz. cream cheese, softened	1/2 pint whipping cream
1 cup cottage cheese, sieved	

In bowl, combine crumbs and melted butter thoroughly; press mixture into bottom of a buttered 9-inch spring form pan. Chill.

Sprinkle gelatin over water; allow to stand and soften for 5 minutes. Dissolve over hot water; allow to cool. In bowl, beat softened cream cheese, sieved cottage cheese, 1 cup sugar and vanilla until mixture is smooth. Add egg yolks, one at a time, beating well after each addition. Stir in melted and cooled chocolate and gelatin. Beat whites until soft peaks form; gradually beat in 1/4 cup sugar until stiff peaks form. Whip cream until softly stiff. Fold egg whites and whipped cream into chocolate mixture. Pour over crumb layer in prepared pan. Chill until firm.

Basic Cake Batter

1 1/3 cups all-purpose flour; 3/4 cup sugar; 3 tsp baking powder; 1/2 tsp salt; 1/4 cup shortening; 3/4 cup milk; 1 egg.

Combine flour, sugar, baking powder, and salt in mixing bowl; stir well. Cut in shortening until mixture resembles coarse meal. In a separate bowl combine milk and egg, beat slightly with beater. Add liquid ingredients, all at once, to dry ingredients, mixing just until all the mixture is moistened. Use batter for the following Dutch Apple Cake or Lemon Sauce Pudding.

Dutch Apple

1 'Cake Batter' recipe; 4 medium size apples, peeled and sliced; 1/3 cup brown sugar, packed; 1/2 tsp cinnamon.

Blend together apples, brown sugar and cinnamon, mixing well. Spread half the 'Cake Batter' in bottom of greased 8-inch square baking dish. Place half the apple mixture on top, then spread remaining cake batter over fruit. Arrange the other half of the apple mixture on top in a pattern. Bake in a 350°F oven for 45 to 50 minutes. Serve warm with Brown Sugar Sauce. *Makes 8 servings.*

Brown Sugar Sauce: Combine 1/2 cup packed brown sugar, 1 tbsp cornstarch, and 1/8 tsp salt in a small pan. Blend in 1 cup warm water gradually; cook over medium heat until mixture thickens and is clear, about 3 to 5 minutes; stir constantly. Remove from heat. Mix in 1 tbsp butter and 1 tsp vanilla. Serve hot. *Makes 1 cup.*

Lemon Sauce Pudding

1 'Cake Batter' recipe; 1 cup sugar; 1 cup hot water; 1/3 cup lemon juice; 2 tsp grated lemon rind.

Spread 'Cake Batter' in a greased 8-inch square pan. Mix together the sugar, boiling water, lemon juice and rind. Pour carefully over top of batter; do not stir. Bake in 350°F oven for 40 to 45 minutes. When serving, spoon into dishes with cake side down, top with whipped cream, if desired. *Makes 6 to 8 servings.*

Pineapple Upside-Down Cake

3 tbsp butter or margarine, 2½ cups Pineapple (crushed or tidbits), maraschino cherries, walnut halves, ⅔ cup brown sugar, 1/3 cup shortening, 1/2 cup sugar, 1 egg, 1 tsp vanilla, 1¼ cups sifted cake flour, 1½ tsp baking powder, ½ tsp salt.

Topping: Melt butter in 9x1½ inch round pan. Drain pineapple, saving ½ cup syrup. Arrange cherries and nuts in bottom of pan. Cover with brown sugar, then add pineapple.

Cake: Cream together shortening and sugar; add egg and vanilla; beat until fluffy. Sift together flour, baking powder, and salt; add dry ingredients alternately with reserved syrup to mixture, beating well after each addition. Spread over pineapple. Bake in 350F oven for 45 to 50 minutes. Let stand 5 minutes before removing from pan. Serve warm.

Banana Bread

1 cup white sugar; 1/2 cup shortening; 2 eggs, well beaten; 3 ripe, medium-size bananas, mashed; 1-1/4 cups cake flour; 1/2 tsp. salt; 1 tsp. soda.

Cream sugar and shortening. Add eggs and bananas. Sift dry ingredients. Blend wet and dry mixtures. Do not over mix. Bake in loaf pan at 350 degrees F. for approximately 45 minutes. *This recipe makes a 20-ounce loaf.*

Applesauce Cake

1¼ c. sifted flour, ½ tsp. salt, 1 tsp. baking powder, 1 tsp. baking soda, 1 tsp. nutmeg, 1 tsp. cinnamon, ½ tsp. allspice, ½ c. shortening, ¾ c. brown sugar, 1 egg, 1 c. applesauce, 1 c. raisins.

Coat raisins with 1 tbsp. flour; set aside. Mix dry ingredients together. Cream shortening, add sugar gradually and cream well until light and fluffy. Add egg and beat well. Add dry ingredients alternately with applesauce, a little at a time, beating after each addition until smooth. Fold in floured raisins. Bake in a greased and lined 8-inch square pan in a 350 F. oven for 40 to 50 minutes. Cool 10 minutes before removing from pan. Frost with butter icing, if desired.

Water Cake

1 cup water	2 cups flour
1 cup sugar	1 tsp. baking powder
1 cup raisins	1 tsp. allspice
6 oz. margarine	1/2 tsp. baking soda

In saucepan, combine water, sugar, raisins and margarine. Bring mixture to boiling. Reduce heat. Simmer for 5 minutes. Allow mixture to cool slightly. In mixing bowl, stir together flour, baking powder, allspice and baking soda. Add cooled water mixture and mix thoroughly. Line an 8-inch square baking pan with waxed paper. Pour batter into pan. Bake in 350 degree F. oven for 35 to 40 minutes or until done. Ice cake when it is cooled, if desired. This cake is better when left 12 hours before cutting.

Walnut Loaf

2 1/2 cups sifted all-purpose flour (sift before measuring)	3/4 cup sugar
3 tsp. baking powder	1/4 cup butter or margarine, melted
1/2 tsp. salt	1 1/4 cups milk
1 egg, beaten	1 1/4 cups chopped walnuts
1 tsp. vanilla	1 tsp. grated lemon rind

Sift flour with baking powder and salt. Set aside. In large bowl, combine egg, vanilla, sugar and melted butter. Beat until well blended. Add milk and blend well. Add flour mixture; beat until smooth. Stir in walnuts and lemon rind. Pour batter into greased and floured 9 x 5 x 3 inch loaf pan. Bake in 350 degree F. oven 60 to 65 minutes or until done. Allow to cool in loaf pan 10 minutes. Remove from pan and cool completely.

Coco-Chocolate Cake

2 egg whites; 1/4 cup sugar; 1-1/2 cups all-purpose flour; 1 cup sugar; 1/2 cup cocoa; 1-1/4 tsp. baking soda; 1-1/4 tsp. salt; 2 egg yolks; 2/3 cup salad oil; 1 cup sour milk or buttermilk.

Beat egg whites until foamy; gradually add in 1/4 cup sugar, 1 tbsp. at a time, and beat to soft peaks. Set aside. Into a large mixing bowl, combine flour, 1 cup sugar, cocoa, baking soda, and salt. Stir well to blend.

Add egg yolks, oil and sour milk to dry ingredients. Blend with mixer until smooth. Fold egg white mixture into batter. Pour batter evenly into two greased and floured 8-inch round layer pans. Bake in 350°F. oven for 25 to 30 minutes, or until knife inserted in centre comes out clean. Let cake cool 10 minutes in pan before turning out on wire rack.

Banana Spice With Seafoam Frosting

2-1/2 cups sifted cake flour	*3/4 tsp. nutmeg*
1-2/3 cups sugar	*1/2 tsp. ground cloves*
1-1/4 tsp. baking powder	*2/3 cup liquid shortening*
1-1/4 tsp. baking soda	*2/3 cup buttermilk*
1 tsp. salt	*1-1/4 cups mashed bananas*
1-1/2 tsp. cinnamon	*2 eggs, unbeaten*

Sift dry ingredients into large mixing bowl. Add shortening, buttermilk and mashed bananas and mix until all flour is dampened. Beat at fast speed for 2 minutes. Add eggs - beat 1 minute longer. Turn batter into three 8 or 9-inch greased and floured layer cake pans. Bake cakes in 350 degree F. oven for 30 to 35 minutes or until done. When cooked, allow to cool completely before frosting.

Seafoam Frosting
Combine 2 egg whites, 1-1/2 cups brown sugar, 5 tbsp. water and dash of salt in top of large double boiler. Mix. Place over boiling water, beat with mixer at high speed until frosting stands in peaks - about 7 minutes. Remove from heat - add 1 tsp. vanilla. Beat 1 to 2 minutes until frosting is thick enough to spread. Spread between cooled layers of cake. Slice 1 large banana and put in frosting between layers. Stack layers and frost cake as one.

Seed Cake

3/4 cup butter	*1 tbsp. baking powder*
1 1/2 cups sugar	*1/4 tsp. salt*
3 eggs separated	*1 tbsp. caraway seed*
3 cups flour	*1 cup milk*

Cream butter and sugar until light. Add egg yolks one at a time. Alternately add sifted dry ingredients and milk. Add Caraway seed. Fold in well-beaten egg whites. Pour batter into well-greased and floured loaf pan.

Bake in slow oven (300 to 325 °F.). Baking time: 50 to 60 minutes.

Rhubarb-Mallow Upside Down Cake

2 1/2 cups frozen rhubarb, thawed	*1 package 1 layer white or golden cake mix*
3/4 cup quartered large white marshmallows	*sweetened, whipped whipping cream, if desired*
1/2 cup sugar	

Place rhubarb in greased 8 inch square pan. Sprinkle evenly with marshmallows and sugar. Prepare cake mix according to package directions. Pour batter over rhubarb mixture. Bake in 350 degree F. oven for 55 to 60 minutes, or until cake is done. Cool in pan 10 minutes. Invert cake gently onto serving plate. Serve warm with sweetened, whipped whipping cream.

Lemony Sunshine Cake

6 eggs, separated, 1½ cups sifted cake flour, ½ tsp. salt, ½ tsp. cream of tartar, 1½ cups sugar, 3 tbsp. freshly squeezed lemon juice, 5 tbsp. water, 1 tbsp. grated lemon peel, fresh lemon glaze.*

Place egg whites in large mixer bowl and yolks in small mixer bowl; let stand until they reach room temperature. Measure sifted flour, then sift again with salt onto piece of waxed paper. Beat whites until frothy; add cream of tartar and beat at high speed until moist peaks form. Gradually add ½ cup sugar, 2 tbsp. at a time; continue beating until stiff, but not dry. Set aside. Beat yolks a full 2 minutes until very thick and light. Add remaining sugar very gradually; continue beating at high speed until thick.

Beat in lemon juice and water, blending until smooth; stir in lemon peel. Add flour all at once; gently fold, then partially stir until well blended. Add to egg whites and fold in quickly, but gently. Pour into ungreased 10 inch tube pan; cut through batter with table knife to remove large air bubbles. Bake at 325 F. about 1 hour, or until cake springs back when lightly touched. Immediately invert on wire rack; leave in pan until completely cool. Loosen around tube and sides with narrow spatula turn onto cake plate. Glaze top with Fresh Lemon Glaze, allowing some to drizzle over edges.

* Lemon Glaze

1½ cups sifted confectioners' sugar, 1½ to 2 tbsp. squeezed lemon juice.

Blend together sugar and juice until smooth.

Peach Parfait Torte

1 cup sifted regular flour; 1/4 cup sugar; 6 tbsp. butter or margarine; 1 egg yolk; 1-3 oz. package strawberry-flavour gelatin, (jelly powder); 1½ cups hot water; 1/2 pt. vanilla ice cream, softened; 1 can (14 oz.) cling peach slices, well drained.

Sift flour and sugar into a medium-size bowl; cut in butter or margarine with pastry blender until mixture is crumbly. Stir in egg yolk; mix thoroughly with a fork until pastry holds together and leaves side of bowl clean. Press into bottom and 1 inch up side of an 8 inch spring-form pan, (Do not prick). Bake in a moderate oven, 375 degrees F. for 20 minutes, or until golden. Cool shell completely in pan on a wire rack.

Dissolve gelatin in hot water in a medium-size bowl. Measure 1/2 cup for glazing top and set aside. Stir ice cream, a tablespoon at a time, into remaining gelatin in bowl. The mixture will start to thicken. Pour into cooked shell; chill 45 minutes or until firm. Chill saved 1/2 cup gelatin mixture 5 minutes, or just until as thick as unbeaten egg white. Arrange drained peach slices in an attractive pattern on top of filling in shell; spoon the 1/2 cup gelatin over and around peaches.

Chill several hours, or until firm. When ready to serve, loosen pastry around edge of pan with knife; release spring and carefully lift off side of pan; place torte, still on metal base, on serving plate. Cut into thin wedges with a sharp thin-bladed knife. If desired decorate around base and on top with whipped cream.

Glazed Orange Loaf

1 2/3 c. sifted all-purpose flour, 1½ tsp. baking powder, ½ tsp. salt, 2/3 c. chopped pecans, ½ c. soft butter, 1¼ c. sugar, 2 eggs, 2 tsp. orange rind, ½ tsp. vanilla, 2/3 c. milk, 2 tbsp. frozen orange juice concentrate, thawed.

Butter a 9 x 5-inch loaf pan. Preheat oven to 350 F. Sift together the flour, baking powder and salt; add and mix in pecans. Cream butter, gradually beat in 1 c. of the sugar. Add eggs, one at a time, beating in well after each addition.

Add and mix in orange rind and vanilla. Add sifted dry ingredients to creamed mixture alternately with milk, combining lightly after each addition. Turn batter into prepared pan. Bake in preheated oven 50 to 55 minutes. Meanwhile combine orange juice and the remaining ¼ c. sugar. As soon as loaf is removed from oven, drizzle with the orange juice mixture. Cool completely in pan on cake rack. Remove from pan. Store wrapped in foil for 24 hours. Slice and serve with butter. Makes one 9 x 5-inch loaf.

Cherry Pound Cake

3/4 lb. butter; 1½ cups berry sugar; 6 eggs, separated; 3 cups sifted all-purpose flour; 1/2 tsp. salt; 1 tsp. baking powder; 1 tsp. vanilla; 1 cup candied cherries, halved.

Cream butter with sugar until light and fluffy. Add well-beaten egg yolks, blend well. Sift dry ingredients and add half to batter. Combine the other half with cherries to coat well, then add to batter. Stir in vanilla. Gently fold in stiffly-beaten egg whites. Turn into tube pan lined with 3 thicknesses brown paper (or 2 thicknesses of foil wrap) greased on side next to cake. Bake in 325°F oven 1 hour and 45 minutes or until done.

Budget Pound Cake

3 cups sifted cake flour, 1½ tsp. baking powder, ¼ tsp. mace, 1/8 tsp. salt, 1 cup butter, 1½ cups sugar, 1 tsp. vanilla, 3 eggs, beaten, ½ cup milk.

Sift flour, baking powder, mace and salt together three times. Cream butter with sugar and vanilla until fluffy. Add eggs, and beat thoroughly. Add sifted dry ingredients and milk alternately in small amounts, beating well after each addition. Pour into greased tube pan and bake in moderate oven (350 F.) about 60 minutes. Makes 1 (10 inch) cake.

Sultana Loaf

Great for the lunch box!

2 lbs. sultana raisins	1 tsp. vanilla
boiling water	1 tsp. almond extract
1 cup softened butter	1/2 cup glace
1-1/2 cups sugar	cherries, coarsely chopped
6 eggs	3 cups flour
1 tsp. lemon extract	1 tsp. baking powder

Place raisins in large bowl; cover with boiling water; allow to stand 5 minutes; drain and dry thoroughly. In large bowl, cream butter and sugar until light and fluffy. Add eggs, one at a time, beating well after each addition. Stir in lemon extract, vanilla and almond extract. Place prepared raisins and cherries in bowl. Sift flour and baking powder over top. Stir until fruit is well coated with flour. Add fruit mixture to egg mixture one-third at a time, beating well after each addition. Pour batter into 2 greased loaf pans. Bake in 300 degree F. oven for 1-1/2 hours or until cake tester or toothpick inserted in centre comes out clean. *Makes 2 loaves.*

Note: This recipe can be halved if desired.

Hints on Fruit Cake Baking

When making a light fruit cake watch that your fruit and nut mix is all light coloured.

Chop or slice nuts for best results; electric blenders will grind the nuts too fine, releasing some of their natural oils. Set a pan of water on the bottom of the oven to keep the top of the cake moist and give it a shiny look.

Lay a sheet of foil over cake during the last part of baking to prevent overbrowning.

It is best to work with no more than double a recipe and to use your mixer only for creaming the butter or margarine with the sugar and beating in the eggs.

Last-Minute Fruit Cake (eggless)

3 cups thick unsweetened applesauce; 1 cup shortening; 2 cups white sugar; 1 lb. dates, pitted and chopped; 1 lb. light or dark raisins; 1 lb. chopped nuts; 1/4 lb. glace cherries; 1/4 lb. glace pineapple; 1/4 lb. citron, chopped; 4½ cups sifted all-purpose flour; 4 tsp. baking soda; 1 tsp. nutmeg; 2½ tsp. cinnamon; 1/2 tsp. cloves; 1 tsp. salt.

In a saucepan, combine applesauce, shortening, and sugar; bring to a boil. Boil 5 minutes. Let stand until cool. Mix nuts and fruits in a large mixing bowl. Sift dry ingredients over all; mix well with hands to coat fruits and nuts with flour. Stir in cooled applesauce mixture. Mix well. Spoon into 2 large sized loaf pans lined with 3 layers of brown paper greased on side next to batter. Bake in 250°F oven for 2 hrs. or until done. This cake should stand 7 to 10 days to mellow.

Rich Fruit Cake

4 cups seedless raisins; 2 cups currants; 1 cup cut-up pitted dried prunes; 1 cup cut-up dried apricots; 1½ cups slivered mixed candied peels and citron; 1 cup red and green candied or maraschino (well-drained) cherries, halved; 1/2 cup slivered blanched almonds; 1/4 cup coarsely-chopped pecans; 2-2/3 cups sifted all-purpose flour; 1 tsp. salt; 2 tsp. cinnamon; 1 tsp. nutmeg; 1 tsp. allspice; 1/4 tsp. ground cloves; 1¼ cups soft butter; 1½ cups lightly-packed brown sugar; 8 eggs; 1/3 cup grape juice; 1/3 cup cold strong coffee.

Pick over, wash and dry raisins and currants. Cut up prunes, apricots, candied peel and citron; halve cherries. Chop almonds and pecans. Sift together twice the flour, salt, cinnamon, nutmeg, allspice and cloves. Add prepared fruit and nuts, toss lightly until all are coated with flour. Line a deep 9-inch round cake pan or 2 deep 6-inch round cake pans with 2 layers of foil. Preheat oven to 300°F. Cream butter; gradually beat in sugar. Add eggs, one at a time, beating well after each addition. Combine grape juice and coffee. Add to creamed mixture alternately with floured

fruit, combining lightly after each addition. Turn batter into prepared pan or pans; spread evenly. Bake in preheated oven about 2½ hrs. for the large cake or 1¾ hrs. for smaller cakes. (Let cake mellow for about 1 month.) *Makes 1 deep 9-inch round cake or 2 deep 6-inch round cakes.*

Miniature Fruit Cakes

2½ cups sifted flour; 1/2 tsp. salt; 1 tsp. baking soda; 2 eggs, slightly beaten; 3 cups (24 oz. jar) mincemeat; 1-1/3 cup (15 oz tin) sweetened condensed milk; 2 tbsp. sherry (optional); 1 cup walnuts, coarsely chopped; 2 cups fruit cake fruit mix.

Preheat oven to 300°F. Sift flour, salt and baking soda. Combine eggs, mincemeat, milk, sherry, fruit and nuts. Fold in dry ingredients. Place small size paper baking cups in 2x1-inch muffin tins. Spoon mixture into paper cups with a teaspoon. Fill cups about 2/3 full. Bake about 1 hour or until the cakes are done. Do not remove paper cups. Cool on cake rack. If desired, decorate each with glazed cherry or walnut half. *Makes 6 dozen.*

For 9-inch Fruit Cake: Butter 9-inch tube, spring form pan or loaf pan. Line with brown paper (2 thicknesses). Butter paper; Pour batter into pan. Bake about 2 hrs. until the centre springs back and top is golden. Cool; turn out and remove paper. Wrap in waxed paper or foil. Store in refrigerator. May be frozen.

Golden Fruit Cake

3 cups light seedless raisins; 2 cups cut-up candied pineapple; 1½ cups red and green candied or maraschino (well-drained) cherries, halved; 1 cup coarsely-chopped pecans; 5¾ cups sifted all-purpose flour; 1 tsp. baking powder; 1/2 tsp. salt; 1/4 tsp. mace; 1/4 tsp. nutmeg; 1 cup shredded coconut; 2 cups soft butter; 2¼ cups fruit or fine granulated sugar; 9 eggs; 1 tbsp. grated lemon rind; 1/4 cup lemon juice.

Pick over, wash and dry raisins. Cut up pineapple; halve cherries and chop pecans. Sift together the flour, baking powder, salt, mace and nutmeg. Add prepared fruit, nuts and coconut; toss lightly until all are coated with flour. Line a deep 8-inch square cake pan and a deep 6-inch square cake pan with 2 layers of foil. Preheat oven to 300°F.

Cream butter; gradually beat in sugar. Add eggs, one at a time, beating in well after each addition. Add and mix in lemon rind and juice. Add floured fruit, part at a time, mixing well after each addition. Turn batter into prepared pans; spread evenly. Bake in preheated oven 2 to 2¼ hours. (Let cakes mellow for 2 to 3 weeks.) *Makes 1 deep 8-inch square and 1 deep 6-inch square cakes.*

Unbaked Christmas Cake

1 lb. graham wafers, finely ground; 1 lb. seedless raisins; 1 cup diced candied fruit & peel; 1 lb. marshmallows, cut in 1/4's; 3/4 cup orange juice; 1 tbsp. orange peel; 1/4 tsp. nutmeg; 1/8 tsp. ginger; 3 cups shelled whole brazil nuts; 1 (6 oz) jar cherries, drained; 1/4 cup dates; 1 tsp. vanilla; 1/4 tsp. cinnamon; 1/4 tsp. ground cloves; 1/8 tsp. allspice.

Line loaf pan (9x5x3) with 2 strips of foil. Extend about 3 inches above side of pan. Place nuts in large mixing bowl; add graham cracker crumbs with raisins, dates, candied fruits and cherries. In top of double boiler combine marshmallows and remaining ingredients. Stir until marshmallows are melted. Add to fruit mixture, blending thoroughly. Turn into pan; pack down. Drugstore wrap. Chill in refrigerator.

Clever Judy Frosting

3 1/2 squares unsweetened chocolate, 3 cups sifted icing sugar, 4 1/2 tablespoons hot water, 1 egg, 1/2 cup soft butter or margerine, 1 1/2 teaspoons vanilla.

Melt chocolate in bowl over hot water. Remove from heat. Beat in sugar and water with electric mixer. Beat in egg, then butter and vanilla. Place bowl in a larger pan of ice water and beat until frosting is of spreading consistency. Frosts tops and sides of 2 - 9 inch layer cakes.

Snowy White Frosting

1-1/2 cups sugar; 1/2 cup water; 3 egg whites; 1/8 tsp. cream of tartar; pinch of salt; 1 tsp. vanilla.

In small saucepan, combine sugar and water. Cook over medium heat, stirring, until sugar is dissolved. Cover and bring to a boil. Remove cover and cook mixture until soft ball stage, or 236-238°F. on candy thermometer. Beat egg whites, cream of tartar and salt in large mixing bowl until moist stiff peaks form.

Pour hot syrup over egg whites in a thin stream. Beat constantly with mixer at high speed until frosting holds stiff peaks. Add in vanilla. Tint frosting with food colouring if desired. Makes enough frosting and filling for 8-inch or 9-inch double layer cake.

Blender Frosting

1 cup sugar, 3 (1 oz.) squares unsweetened chocolate, 3/4 cup evaporated milk, dash of salt, 1/4 tsp. peppermint extract (optional).

Put sugar in blender, cover, and blend at high speed about 1 minute. Cut chocolate squares into small pieces; add into blender along with milk, salt, and peppermint, if desired. Blend at high speed for about 3 minutes or until thick; scrape sides with rubber spatula if necessary. Makes enough to cover tops of two 8-inch layers. (Chill frosted cake for firmer frosting, if desired.)

Fluffy Frosting

2 egg whites, 1/4 tsp cream of tartar, 2 tbsp light corn syrup, 2 1/2 tbsp water, 1 1/2 tsp vanilla, 1/2 tsp lemon extract, 3 1/2 cups icing sugar, sifted.

Mix together egg whites and cream of tartar in medium-size bowl; beat until firm peaks form. Set aside. Combine corn syrup, water, vanilla, and lemon extract in a cup. Add alternately with icing sugar to egg-white mixture, beating well after each addition. Beat until frosting is creamy-stiff and easy to spread. Makes enough to frost top and side of one 9-inch triple layer cake.

Broiled Frosting

1/4 cup soft butter or margarine, 1/2 cup lightly-packed brown sugar, 3 tbsp evaporated milk or cream, 1/2 cup coconut or coarsely chopped nuts.

Combine all ingredients together. Spread mixture over a warm 8 or 9-inch square cake. Place about 6 inches from heat and broil for 2 or 3 minutes, or until the topping bubbles and browns.

Cream Cheese Frostings

4 oz. cream cheese	*2-1/2 cups sifted icing*
1 tbsp. milk (approximately)	*sugar (approximately)*
	1/2 tsp. vanilla

Blend thoroughly, cream cheese and milk; gradually beat in icing sugar. Add vanilla. (Add a small amount of extra milk or icing sugar if necessary until frosting is a good spreading consistency).

Yields enough frosting for top and sides of an 8-inch or 9-inch square cake. Double the recipe to frost and fill an 8-inch or 9-inch layer cake.

Variations

Chocolate-Cream Frosting

Add 1 square melted unsweetened chocolate and a dash of salt to above ingredients.

Almond Frosting

Delete vanilla and add 1/2 tsp. almond flavouring.

Orange-Cream Frosting

Delete milk and vanilla. Substitute 1 tbsp. orange juice for milk and add 1/2 tsp. grated orange rind.

COOKIES, BARS AND SQUARES

Anyone who has followed Mona on television will be familiar with the many superb concoctions that come out of her oven. Some of the recipes in this section are fairly time consuming but the extra time and effort bring rewards.

Sugar Cookies

2/3 cup shortening; 3/4 cup sugar; 1 tsp. vanilla; 1 egg; 4 tsp. milk; 2 cups sifted all-purpose flour; 1½ tsp. baking powder; 1/4 tsp. salt.

Cream shortening, sugar and vanilla thoroughly. Add in egg and beat until light and fluffy. Stir in milk, Sift flour, baking powder and salt together; blend into creamed mixture. Divide dough in half; chill 1 hr. Using half of dough (keep other half chilled), roll out on lightly floured surface to 1/8-inch thickness; cut in desired shapes with cutters. Bake on greased cookie sheet in 375°F oven for 6 to 8 minutes. Cool slightly; remove from pan. Cool on rack. *Makes about 2 dozen.*

To Decorate: Before baking, sprinkle cookies with candy decorettes, crushed hard peppermint stick candy, gumdrops (whole or sliced), coloured sugar.

To Frost: Let cookies cool before frosting. Make icing by adding enough light cream to sifted icing sugar to make spreading consistency. If various colours are desired, divide icing into portions and tint with food colouring. Pipe on different coloured designs with an icing tube or add colourful candies.

Gingerbread Cookies

1 cup shortening; 1 cup sugar; 1 egg; 1 cup molasses; 2 tbsp. vinegar; 5 cups sifted all-purpose flour; 1½ tsp. baking soda; 1/2 tsp. salt; 2 to 3 tsp. ginger; 1 tsp. cinnamon; 1 tsp. cloves.

Cream shortening with sugar thoroughly. Stir in egg, molasses and vinegar; beat well. Sift together dry ingredients; stir into molasses mixture. Chill about 3 hours. Roll dough to 1/8-inch thickness on lightly floured surface. Cut with cutter. Place on greased cookie sheet 1 inch apart. Bake in 375°F oven for 5 to 6 minutes. Cool slightly; then remove to rack and cool. *Makes about 5 dozen 4-inch cookies.*

Gingerbread Boys: For cookies that will stand up, bake gingerbread boys with 'built-in' skewers: Place wooden skewers on cookie sheet; then place cut-out dough on top with skewer 1/3 the way up back of cookies; then bake. Cool thoroughly. To decorate, use Icing Sugar frosting in icing tube.

Basic Drop Cookies

3½ cups flour; 1 teaspoon baking powder; 1 teaspoon baking soda; 1/2 teaspoon salt; 2 cups brown sugar, packed; 1 cup butter or margerine; 2 eggs; 1 teaspoon vanilla; 1/2 cup sour milk (to make milk sour mix with 2 teaspoons lemon juice or vinegar).

Mix together flour, baking powder, soda, and salt. Cream sugar, butter, eggs and vanilla. Add flour mixture alternately with sour milk to creamed mixture. Mix well. Drop by teaspoonfuls onto greased baking sheets. Bake at 375 degrees F. for 12 to 15 minutes.

Variations

Chocolate Nut Drops
to the basic recipe add 1 cup chocolate pieces and 1/2 cup chopped walnuts.

Almond Date Drops
to the basic recipe add 1 cup cut-up dates and 1/2 cup chopped almonds. Substitute 1 teaspoon almond flavouring for vanilla. Before baking sprinkle cookies with a mixture of 1 tablespoon grated orange rind, 2 tablespoons sugar and 1/4 teaspoon cinnamon.

Hermits
to the basic recipe add 2 teaspoons cinnamon, and 1 teaspoon nutmeg to the flour mixture. Add 1 cup cut-up dates, 1 cup raisins and 1 cup chopped nuts.

Cherry Coconut Drops
to the basic recipe add 1 cup coconut and 1 cup cut-up maraschino cherries (drained). Drop dough by teaspoonfuls into crushed cornflakes and toss lightly to coat. Shape into balls and top with half a maraschino cherry.

Fruitcake Cookies

1-1/4 cups sifted all-purpose flour (sift before measuring)	1 egg
1/2 tsp. baking soda	1 package (1 lb.) pitted dates, coarsely chopped
1/2 tsp. salt	4 oz. cut orange peel
1/2 tsp. cinnamon	4 oz. cut lemon peel
1/2 cup butter or margarine	1/2 cup glace cherries, chopped
3/4 cup sugar	3/4 cup walnuts

Preheat oven to 375 degrees F. Sift flour, baking soda, salt and cinnamon together; set aside. In large bowl, with wooden spoon or portable electric mixer at medium speed, beat butter, sugar and egg until light and fluffy. Stir in flour mixture until well combined. Add fruits and nuts; mix well. Drop by level tablespoonfuls, 2 inches apart, on ungreased cookie sheet. Bake 8 to 10 minutes or until lightly browned. Let stand 1 minute. Remove to wire rack or waxed paper; cool. *Makes about 4 dozen.*

Basic Refrigerator Dough

2/3 cup butter or margarine; 1 cup light brown sugar; 1 egg; 1 tsp. vanilla; 2 cups sifted all-purpose flour; 1/4 tsp. salt; 1/2 tsp. baking soda.

Cream butter; then gradually add in sugar, beating well. Add egg and vanilla; mix well. Blend together flour, salt and baking soda; stir into butter batter. Use dough as it is or 1/3 of dough in any of the suggested variations. Shape finished dough into long rolls, about 2 inches in diameter. Cover with waxed paper; chill until firm (about 1 to 2 hours). Slice thinly and place on ungreased cookie sheet. Bake in 350°F oven for 8 to 10 minutes. *Makes about 5 dozen.*

Variations

Nut & Fruit: Follow Basic Recipe. Mix 2 tbsp. red and green chopped maraschino cherries (well drained) and 2 tbsp. chopped nuts to dough.

Chocolate: Follow Basic Recipe, blending in 1 square unsweetened chocolate, melted and cooled into butter mixture. For Chocolate Nut Variation, mix 4 tbsp. chopped nuts into dough.

Black & White: Prepare plain chocolate dough. Top each cookie with miniature marshmallow for last 3 minutes of baking time.

Turtles: Prepare plain chocolate dough; chill. Cut rolls into thin slices. Between 2 slices of dough, place whole walnut or pecan for head, and 4 pieces chopped walnut or pecan for legs.

Additional Variations

Orange: Follow Basic Recipe, omitting vanilla. Mix in 1½ tbsp grated orange rind to butter mixture.

Lemony Coconut: Follow Basic Recipe, omitting vanilla. Add in 1/2 tsp. lemon extract to butter mixture. Mix 2 tbsp. shredded coconut into dough.

Almond: Follow Basic Recipe, omitting vanilla. Stir in 1/2 tsp. almond extract to butter mixture. Top each cookie with blanched almond half before baking.

Sandies: Follow Basic Recipe for plain cookies. While baked cookies are still warm, dredge with coloured berry sugar.

Pinwheels: Roll out rectangle of Basic Dough and Plain Chocolate Dough 1/8-inch thickness. Place one on top of the other; roll in jelly-roll fashion.

Raisin Drops

1 cup light or dark raisins, ½ cup shortening, 1 cup sugar, 2 eggs, ¼ cup milk, 1 2/3 cup quick-cooking rolled oats, 1½ cup sifted flour, 1 tsp. soda, ½ tsp. salt, 1 tsp. cinnamon.

Rinse raisins in boiling water; drain. Cream shortening and sugar. Add eggs and milk; beat well. Stir in rolled oats and raisins. Add dry ingredients; stir well. Drop by teaspoons onto greased cookie sheet. Bake at 350 F. for 15 – 18 minutes. This recipe may be doubled.

Refrigerator Oatmeal Cookies

Great for packed lunches:
1 cup shortening, 1 cup brown sugar, 1 cup white sugar, 2 eggs, 1 tsp. vanilla, 1-1/2 cups sifted flour, 1 tsp. salt, 1 tsp. soda, 3 cups quick-cooking oatmeal, 1/2 cup chopped walnuts.

Thoroughly cream shortening and sugars. Add eggs and vanilla; beat well. Sift together flour, salt and soda; combine with creamed mixture. Add oatmeal and walnuts. Mix thoroughly. Form dough into rolls 1'' to 1-1/2'' thick. Wrap well in waxed paper. Allow to chill thoroughly. To cook, slice cookie dough approximately 1/4'' thick and bake on an ungreased cookie sheet at 350 degrees F. for approximately 10 minutes or until lightly browned. *Yields approximately 5 dozen cookies.*

Orange Drop Cookies

2 cups all-purpose flour	2 eggs, well beaten
2 tsp. baking powder	1/4 cup orange juice
1 tsp. salt	1 tbsp. grated orange rind
1 cup butter or shortening	2 cups bran flakes
1 cup sugar	

Mix together flour, baking powder and salt. Cream butter. Gradually blend in sugar, creaming well after each addition. Thoroughly mix in eggs. Alternately add flour and orange juice, mixing well after each addition. Add orange rind and cereal; mix thoroughly. Drop by rounded tablespoonfuls onto greased baking sheets. Bake at 350 degrees F. for about 13 minutes or until lightly browned. *Makes about 4 dozen cookies.*

When decorating cookies, etc. with small amounts of chocolate, place chocolate in a custard cup and stand in a pan of simmering water. (Do not allow any water into chocolate in custard cup.)

Peanut Butter Cookies

1 1/4 cups sifted all-purpose flour	1 cup brown sugar
1/2 tsp. baking soda	1 egg, beaten
1/4 tsp. salt	1 cup chocolate or butterscotch chips
2/3 cup peanut butter	1/2 cup chopped walnuts, optional
1/2 cup butter or margarine	

Sift together flour, baking soda and salt. Cream peanut butter, butter and sugar. Beat in egg until mixture is light and fluffy. Add sifted ingredients, mixing well. Stir in chips and nuts if desired. Shape into 1-inch balls and place on a cookie sheet. Flatten with a water-dampened fork to a 1/4-inch thickness. Bake in a 350 degree F. oven 8 to 10 minutes or until lightly browned.

Butterscotch Brownies

1/2 cup butter or margarine; 1 cup firmly packed brown sugar; 3/4 cup sifted all-purpose flour; 1/4 tsp. salt; 1 beaten egg; 1 tsp. baking powder; 1 tbsp. milk; 1/2 cup chopped pecans(or walnuts); 1 tsp. vanilla.

Place butter and brown sugar in a heavy skillet over low heat; stir until butter melts and mixture is smooth. Cool in a mixing bowl. Beat in egg. Combine dry ingredients and sift together; add to sugar-egg mixture. Blend in milk, pecans and vanilla. Pour into a buttered 8-inch square pan. Bake in 350°F oven for 25 minutes or until firm on top. Cool in pan; remove and cool completely. Spread with Chocolate Ripple Frosting.

Chocolate Ripple Frosting: Prepare a butter icing and spread over cake. Melt one square semi-sweet chocolate over hot water. (Thin with butter, if necessary.) Drizzle in parallel lines about 1 inch apart over entire cake. Then draw a knife crosswise through the chocolate lines.

122

Lemon Squares

Cookie Layer

2 cups sifted flour	1/2 cup icing sugar
1 cup butter	

Mix all ingredients and pack into bottom of a greased 13 x 9-inch pan. Bake in 350 degree F. oven for 20 minutes.

Filling

4 eggs	1/4 tsp. baking powder
2 cups sugar	1/4 tsp. salt
6 tbsp. lemon juice	sifted icing sugar for topping
1 tsp. lemon rind	
1/4 cup flour	

Beat eggs slightly; add sugar, lemon juice and lemon rind. Sift together flour, baking powder and salt. Mix with egg-lemon mixture and beat **only** until smooth. Pour over baked cookie layer as soon as it is removed from the oven. Return to oven and continue cooking at 350 degree F. for approximately 25 minutes or until done. Sift extra icing sugar over top while cake is still warm. Cut into squares when cool.

Note: For a decorative touch, place a paper doily with open design on square (or any unfrosted cake). Sprinkle with sifted icing sugar; lift doily straight up to remove. Design will remain on square or cake.

Sunflower Seed Cookies

1 cup margarine or butter; 1 cup firmly packed brown sugar; 1 cup granulated sugar; 2 eggs; 1 tsp vanilla; 1½ cup all-purpose flour (unsifted); 3/4 tsp salt; 1 tsp baking soda; 3 cups quick cooking rolled oats; 1 cup sunflower seeds.

Cream butter, brown sugar and granulated sugar together thoroughly. Add in eggs, and vanilla; beat to blend well. Add in flour, salt, baking soda and rolled oats; mix well. Gently blend in sunflower seeds. Roll into long rolls (1½ inches in diameter); wrap in transparent food wrap. Chill thoroughly. Cut into 1/4-inch slices; place on ungreased cookie sheet. Bake in 350°F oven for 10 minutes or until lightly browned. Cool on wire racks. Store in air-tight containers. Makes approx. 9 dozen. (Dough can be kept in refrigerator for several days before baking.)

Peanut Whirls

1/2 cup shortening; 1/2 cup peanut butter; 1 cup sugar; 1 egg; 1 tsp. vanilla; 1¼ cups sifted flour; 1/2 tsp. baking soda; 1/2 tsp. salt; 2 tbsp. milk; 1 (6 oz) pkg. semi-sweet chocolate chips.

Cream shortening, peanut butter and sugar together. Add egg and vanilla. Beat well. Sift flour, baking soda and salt together; add to peanut butter mixture, alternating with milk. Turn onto lightly floured surface. Roll into rectangle 1/4-inch thick. Melt chocolate pieces over hot water and cool slightly. Spread onto rolled cookie dough. Roll as for jelly roll. Chill 1/2 hour. Cut into 1/4-inch slices. Place on baking sheet. Bake in 350°F oven about 10 minutes. *Makes 3 dozen.*

O'Henry Cake (squares)

whole graham wafers (enough to line pan and to top slice)	1 cup crushed graham wafers
	1 cup chopped walnuts
	1 cup coconut
1 cup brown sugar	1 tsp. vanilla
1/2 cup milk	1 recipe of your
1/2 cup butter	favourite butter icing

Lightly grease an 8-inch or 9-inch square pan; line with whole graham wafers. In saucepan, place sugar, milk and butter; boil for 1 minute. Remove from heat and immediately add crushed wafers, walnuts, coconut and vanilla. Mix thoroughly. Place mixture over wafers in pan and cover with whole wafers. Spread with butter icing immediately. Place in refrigerator to cool before serving.

Nanaimo Bars

1/2 cup margarine or butter; 1/4 cup white sugar; 1 egg; 5 tbsp. cocoa; 1 tsp. vanilla; 2 cups graham wafer crumbs; 1 cup coconut; 1/2 cup chopped nuts; 1/4 cup butter; 3 tbsp. canned milk; 2 tbsp. vanilla custard or instant pudding powder; 2 cups sifted icing sugar; 4 squares semi-sweet chocolate; 1 tbsp. butter.

Mix together 1/2 cup butter, white sugar, egg, vanilla, and cocoa, in top of double boiler. Set over boiling water and stir until mixture resembles a custard. Combine crumbs, coconut and nuts. Add to custard mixture, blending well.

Spread and press tightly into 9-inch square pan. Refrigerate; Cream 1/4 cup butter, milk, custard powder and icing sugar. Spread over mixture in pan. Allow to stand 15 minutes. Melt the chocolate over hot water. Add butter and blend well. Spread over top. Refrigerate.

Chinese Chews

3/4 cup sifted flour	1 cup chopped dates
1 cup sugar	3/4 cup chopped walnuts
1 tsp. baking powder	2 eggs
1/4 tsp. salt	fine granulated sugar or sifted icing sugar

Sift together, flour, sugar, baking powder and salt. Add dates and nuts. Beat eggs until light. Add eggs to flour mixture and mix well. Spread the batter into a greased 9-inch square pan. Bake in 350 degree F. oven for approximately 30 minutes or until done. While warm, cut into fingers - then roll in fine granulated sugar or sifted icing sugar.

Melting Moments

1 cup butter; 1/2 cup sifted icing sugar; 1 tsp. lemon extract; 2 cups sifted all-purpose flour; 1/4 tsp. salt; lemon filling.

Cream butter to thickness of mayonnaise; add sugar gradually, creaming constantly. Add lemon extract, flour, and salt and blend well. Using a level teaspoon of dough, shape into balls and flatten slightly. Place on ungreased cookie sheet 1-inch apart; bake in 400°F oven for 8 to 10 minutes or until very lightly browned. Sandwich together with lemon filling. *Makes about 5 dozen double cookies.*

Lemon Filling

1 slightly beaten egg; grated peel of 1 lemon; 2/3 cup sugar; 3 tbsp. lemon juice; 1½ tbsp. softened butter.

In top of double boiler, blend together all ingredients. Cook over hot water, stirring constantly, until thick. Chill until firm.

Creme De Menthe Balls

2½ cups (about 60) finely crushed vanilla wafers; 1 cup sifted icing sugar; 2 tbsp. cocoa powder; 1 cup finely chopped walnuts; 1/4 cup light corn syrup; 1/4 cup white creme de menthe; granulated sugar.

Combine crushed wafers, icing sugar, cocoa and walnuts. Stir in corn syrup and creme de menthe. Add a few drops of water to form mixture into 1-inch balls, if necessary. Roll in granulated sugar. Store in tightly covered container. *Makes 3½ dozen.*

Butter Tart Bars

Base: 3/4 cup sifted all-purpose flour; 1/4 cup brown sugar; 1/3 cup butter.

Topping: 1 cup seedless raisins; 2 eggs; 1/2 cup granulated sugar; 1/2 cup dark corn syrup; 1/8 tsp. salt; 1 tsp. vanilla; 1/4 cup all-purpose flour.

Combine base ingredients until crumbly; press into bottom of ungreased 8-inch pan. Bake in 350°F oven, for 12 to 15 minutes. Rinse and drain raisins. Beat eggs; gradually beat in sugar. Add corn syrup, salt, vanilla and flour. Pour over baked base. Return to oven (350°F) and bake for 25 to 30 minutes, until topping is golden. Cool; cut into bars. (This topping makes an excellent filling for Butter Tarts.)

Surprise Bars

Pastry
1 cup flour
1/2 cup butter
1/4 cup icing sugar

Mix until crumbly. Press into an 8-inch square pan. Bake in a 350 degree F. oven for 10 to 15 minutes or until lightly golden.

Topping
2 eggs	2 tbsp. flour
1 cup brown sugar	1/2 tsp. salt
1 tsp. vanilla	1/2 cup coconut
1 tsp. baking powder	1 cup walnuts

Beat eggs until light. Add brown sugar and vanilla. Add baking powder, flour and salt. Stir to combine ingredients thoroughly. Stir in coconut and walnuts. Spread over baked pastry. Bake in a moderate oven (350 degrees F.) for 25 minutes or until done.

Coconut Raspberry Bars

1 cup all-purpose flour; 1 tsp. baking powder; pinch of salt; 2 beaten eggs; raspberry jam; 2 cups coconut; 1/2 cup sugar; 2 tbsp. butter; 2 tbsp. hot milk.

Sift together flour, baking powder, salt. Add 1 beaten egg. Mix well. Spread in a shallow pan. Spread with a layer of raspberry jam. Mix coconut, sugar, 1 beaten egg, butter, hot milk together. Spread over raspberry layer. Bake in 375°F oven for 15 minutes.

Dollie Bars

1 cup graham wafer crumbs	1 cup fine coconut
1/4 cup butter or margarine, melted	1/3 cup chopped maraschino cherries
1 cup chocolate chips	1 tin (14 oz.) sweetened condensed milk
1 cup chopped walnuts or chopped pecans	

Mix graham wafer crumbs and melted butter; press mixture into greased 8 x 8 inch pan. Over this sprinkle in layers, chocolate chips, walnuts, coconut, and cherries. Pour condensed milk over all. Spread lightly. Bake in 350 degree F. oven for approximately 30 minutes or until done. Cool and cut into bars or fingers.

Cherry Rounds

1/2 cup butter or margarine	1 1/4 cups sifted flour
1/4 cup brown sugar	1 slightly beaten egg white
1 egg yolk	3/4 cup finely chopped walnuts
1/2 tsp. vanilla	1/3 cup cherry preserves
1/4 tsp. salt	

Cream together butter, sugar, egg yolk, vanilla and salt until light and fluffy. Stir in flour. Chill approximately 30 minutes.

Shape into 1 inch balls; dip in slightly beaten egg white and roll in nuts. Place 2 1/2 inches apart on greased cookie sheet; press centres with thumb. Fill centres with small amount of cherry preserves (approximately 1/2 tsp. in each). Bake in 350 degree F. oven 12 to 15 minutes or until done. Cool slightly. Remove from pan. Makes approximately 3 dozen.

Note: For attractive tea-table cookies, press centres of cookies before baking, but do not fill with preserves until serving time.

Danish Apple Bars

2-1/2 cups flour	1 cup crushed corn flakes
1 tsp. salt	4 apples
1 cup shortening	1 cup sugar
1 egg yolk plus enough milk to make 2/3 cup liquid	1 tsp. cinnamon
	1 egg white

Sift flour and salt. Add shortening. Cut until mixture is crumbly. Slowly add egg-milk mixture to flour mixture. Lightly stir to moisten. Divide in half. Roll one half into 12-inch by 17-inch rectangle or size of jelly roll pan (or cookie sheet with sides). Place pastry on greased cookie sheet. Sprinkle with crushed cornflakes. Slice thinly, over crumbs, the apples; sprinkle apples with sugar and cinnamon. Cover with another 12-inch by 17-inch sheet of pastry. Pinch edges closed all around. Beat egg white until stiff; brush top crust with beaten white. Bake in 400 degree F. oven for 35 to 40 minutes or until done.

When baked and still warm, drizzle over the top a light glazing made from 1 cup icing sugar, 1 tbsp. water and 1/2 tsp. vanilla. Serve Danish Apple Bar either warm or cold.

Rice Krispie Bars and Variations

1/4 cup butter or margarine	1/2 tsp. vanilla
approximately 40 regular unflavoured marshmallows or 4 cups unflavoured miniature marshmallows	approximately 5 cups Rice Krispies

In large saucepan, melt butter. Add marshmallows; cook, stirring constantly, over low heat until marshmallows are melted. Remove from heat. Add vanilla. Stir in rice krispies. Press warm mixture into well buttered 13 x 9 x 2-inch pan. Cut into squares when cool. Makes about 24 squares (2 x 2-inches).

Note: Mixture may more easily be pressed into pan with a buttered spatula or knife, or use a piece of waxed paper and press into shape with hands.

Variations:

Snowballs
Shape warm mixture into balls; wrap in plastic wrap. If desired, after shaping, roll warm balls in shredded coconut. Try making a face with raisins, candies, nuts or icing (coconut for hair). This is a great favourite with young children at birthday parties.

Chocolate Frosted Rolls
Shape warm mixture into 2 rolls - each approximately 12 inches long and about 1-1/2 inches in diameter. Allow to set. Melt semisweet chocolate pieces and drizzle rolls. Allow chocolate to set. Slice.

Sandwich Wafers
Press warm mixture very thin in buttered pans. Cool. To serve, cut into 3-inch squares. Slice ice cream in 3-inch squares. Place cereal wafers on either side of ice cream. Serve immediately.

Cereal Tart Shells
Press warm mixture in a thin layer into buttered muffin cups to form a tart shape. Allow to set. Remove tart shells from muffin cups. To serve, fill shells with vanilla ice cream, cream filling or well drained fresh, tinned or frozen (thawed) fruit and dizzle with appropriate flavoured sundae sauce. Top with a swirl of whipped cream and garnish with nuts or glace cherries.

Coconut Lemon Tarts

12 Large tart shells, unbaked
2 eggs
1 cup sugar
juice and rind of 1 lemon
2-1/2 cups coconut
1/4 cup melted butter

Beat eggs until light and fluffy. Fold in sugar. Add lemon juice and rind. Fold in coconut. Stir in butter, combining all ingredients. Fill tart shells 2/3 full. Bake in a 375 degree F. oven for 25 minutes. Chill and serve cold. These tarts freeze well.

Party Squares

1 pkg. chocolate Oreo cookies (42); 1 pint whipping cream; 1 cup pastel mints; 2 cups miniature pastel marshmallows.

Crush cookies; spread 1/2 of mixture on bottom of pan. Whip cream; add in mints and marshmallows. Top with remaining crushed cookie mixture. Place in refrigerator for 2 days.

Rum Balls

2 cups fine graham
  cracker crumbs,
2 tbsp. cocoa,
1 cup sifted icing sugar,
⅛ tsp. salt,

1 cup finely chopped
  walnuts,
1½ tbsp. honey,
¼ cup rum or brandy,
extra icing sugar, sifted.

In large bowl, combine graham cracker crumbs, cocoa, icing sugar, salt and walnuts. Mix until well distributed. In small bowl, combine honey and rum or brandy. Add rum mixture to graham crumb mixture and stir with spoon and knead with hands until well combined.* Coat hands with confectioners sugar and roll into little balls. Roll rum balls in sifted icing sugar. Place in an airtight container such as a tin box and allow to ripen at least 12 hours. Yields approximately 40 rum balls.

*Note: If mixture seems too dry add a little extra rum or brandy until mixture is the desired consistency.

Chocolate Dreams

Bottom layer:
1/3 cup butter; 1/4 cup white sugar; 1/4 cup brown sugar; 1 tsp. baking powder; 1/4 tsp. salt; 3/4 cup flour; 1/2 tsp. vanilla; 1 cup chocolate chips; 2 egg yolks; 1/4 cup chopped walnuts (optional).

Topping:
2 egg whites; 1 cup brown sugar; 1/2 cup coconut (optional).

Cream butter and add both sugars, egg yolks and vanilla. Beat well. Sift flour, salt and baking powder. Mix both mixtures together and spread on bottom of square or round cake pan. Sprinkle chocolate chips and walnuts on top. Beat egg whites until stiff but not dry; fold in brown sugar and coconut. Pour over chips. Bake approximately 30 minutes in a 350 degree F. oven. Meringue should brown slightly.
If a sweeter, more chocolate flavour is desired, add a few more chocolate chips.

Sesame Toffee Bars

1/4 cup sesame seeds; 1 cup margarine or butter; 1 cup packed brown sugar; 1 egg, beaten; 1 tsp vanilla; 2 cups sifted all-purpose flour; 1/4 tsp cinnamon; 1/4 tsp allspice; 1/8 tsp nutmeg; 1/2 cup chopped nuts; 1 (12 oz) pkg. semi-sweet chocolate chips.

Toast sesame seeds in a 350°F oven for 10 to 15 minutes, or until golden brown. Cream butter and sugar; add in egg and vanilla, mixing well. Sift flour, and spices. Add to creamed mixture and blend. Stir in nuts. Spread 1/4-inch thick in a 13x15 inch rectangle on a greased cookie sheet. Bake in a 350°F oven for 20 minutes. Meanwhile, melt chocolate chips in a small pan over boiling water. When cookies are done, remove from oven; spread chocolate over top while still hot. Sprinkle top with sesame seeds; cut into bars while warm. Makes approx. 4 dozen bars.

Jumble Cookies

1 cup butter or margarine, 2 cups white sugar, 1 cup brown sugar, 1 tbsp. vanilla, 2 eggs, 2 cups flour, 2 tsp. baking powder, 1 heaping tsp. baking soda, 1/4 tsp. salt, 1 cup chopped walnuts, 2 cups quick cooking oats, 2 cups coconut, 2 cups corn flakes.

In large bowl, cream well together butter, white sugar, and brown sugar. Add vanilla and eggs. In medium-size bowl sift together flour, baking powder, baking soda and salt. Add flour mixture to butter mixture and combine until well distributed. Add walnuts, oats and coconut. Combine well. Add corn flakes and combine well taking care not to crumble flakes more than necessary. Drop from a teaspoon on to a greased cookie sheet and bake at 350 degrees F. for 12 to 15 minutes or until done. When cookies are cooked allow to sit on sheet 1 minute - no longer and remove to rack. This cookie freezes very well. Yields 9 to 11 dozen.

Graham Wafer Chocolate Squares

1/2 cup butter; 1 cup icing sugar, sifted; 1/2 tsp. vanilla; 1 egg, separated; 1/2 cup coconut; 3/4 cup chopped walnuts; whole graham wafers; 2 crushed double graham wafers; 2 squares semi-sweeet chocolate, melted; chocolate curls, optional.

Butter 8"x8" cake pan. Line pan with whole graham wafers. Cream butter and sifted icing sugar, creaming well. Add well beaten egg yolk. Add vanilla, coconut and chopped walnuts. Add melted chocolate; fold in stiffly beaten egg white and blend well. Spread mixture in pan over whole wafers. Sprinkle crushed graham wafers over top. If desired, chocolate curls may be sprinkled over top for an attractive appearance. Chill and cut into squares.

Mona says . . .

Pastry — *Use a pastry blender for cutting the shortening into the flour. The particles formed will flatten during the rolling out and thus provide the tenderness and flakiness characteristic of good pastry. A fork or spoon should not be used as it "creams" or blends rather than cuts.*

Use cold water — it will keep the shortening from melting.

Add just enough water to moisten flour. If dough is sticky, too much flour has to be added during rolling. This toughens the pastry.

Handle as little as possible. Rerolling and over-handling toughens pastry.

When using oranges for cooking: *grate the peel before cutting them. Store the peel in the freezer. Canned or frozen juice may be used with peel when recipe calls for both juice and rind. No waste!*

When using canned fruit: *drain off the syrup and store in your refrigerator. It can be used with mayonnaise for dressing fruit salad. Another taste change is to use it instead of cold water when making flavoured gelatin desserts (the jelly variety).*

Storing and Using Chocolate — *The best method of storing chocolate is to keep it cool and dry. If chocolate is allowed to get warmer the cocoa butter comes to the surface, melts, and forms a greyish-white film when it cools. This does not affect the flavour but does affect the appearance if the chocolate is meant to be used for garnish. If this happens, the colour can be restored by melting the chocolate. If chocolate is to be kept in your refrigerator — place it in a tightly covered container so it won't absorb odours. Do not store cocoa in your refrigerator but do keep it in a tightly covered container in a cool place.*

There are several methods to melt chocolate. Always be careful not to burn chocolate. Use as little heat as possible. Unsweetened, semi-sweet and sweet chocolate may be melted over hot not boiling water. One easy way to melt chocolate is to place it in a greased pie plate in a warm oven until melted. Watch carefully — don't forget about it! Another popular method that is simple is to place chocolate in a double boiler over water; cover; heat until water bubbles, then turn off the heat. Let stand until chocolate softens; stir until smooth. When possible, cooking steps can be doubled up (such as for brownies) by melting the chocolate with the shortening or butter or margarine; or in the liquid (milk, water or coffee).

To Garnish with Chocolate — *Garnishing with chocolate can give a professional look to many dessert recipes.*

To Grate Chocolate — *Place grater and chocolate in refrigerator to chill thoroughly. Run your hands under cold water to cool them. Dry hands thoroughly. Grate chocolate, using an up and down motion, as quickly as possible and handling chocolate as little as possible.*

To Curl Chocolate — *Have chocolate warmed slightly at room temperature. For little curls, shave thin strips from narrow side of chocolate with a vegetable parer. For large curls, scrape chocolate from the bottom. Use a toothpick to pick up curls (otherwise they shatter) and chill until firm before arranging on food.*

Mona says . . .

Sundae Dessert Ideas — *To brighten ice cream desserts, try one of these toppers:*

Chocolate Chow — *Over low heat, stirring constantly, melt together 1 package (6 oz.) semi-sweet chocolate bits; ¾ cup whipping cream; when completely melted add 1 tsp. vanilla and 2 tbsp. chopped walnuts. Serve warm.*

Flaming Strawberry Sauce — *Melt 1/3 cup red currant jelly. Stir in 1 package (15 oz.) frozen, sliced strawberries, thawed. Heat till mixture comes to a boil. Pour ¼ cup brandy into centre of fruit and heat undisturbed. Light and serve flaming.*

Parfait Sauce — *Combine 1 tbsp. each sugar and cornstarch. Add 1 package (15 oz.) frozen raspberries, thawed. Cook, stirring constantly until thickened and clear and mixture comes to a boil. Serve warm.*

Maple Nut Sauce — *Boil 1 cup maple syrup and 2 tbsp. butter for 5 minutes. Cool, stir in ¼ cup light cream and 3 tbsp slivered almonds.*

Quick Citrus Sauce — *Combine ¾ cup sugar, 4½ tsp. cornstarch, ½ cup water and 1 (6 oz.) can frozen lemonade, limeade or orange juice concentrate, thawed. Cook, stirring constantly till thickened and clear and mixture comes to a boil. Cool.*

PASTRIES AND DESSERTS

Old-Fashioned Apple Pie

Basic Pastry
- 2 cups flour
- 1 tsp. salt
- 2/3 cup chilled shortening
- approx. 6 tbsp. cold water

Sift flour; measure. Add salt and sift again. Using a pastry blender, thoroughly cut in half of shortening until mixture resembles coarse corn meal. Cut in other half of shortening coarsely or until particles are about the size of peas. Sprinkle water, 1 tbsp. at a time, over small portions of mixture; press the flour particles together as they absorb the water (use a fork); do **not** stir. Toss aside pieces of dough as formed; sprinkle remaining water over dry portions use only enough water to bind pastry together. Press together **lightly** with fingers or wrap dough in waxed paper and press together gently. Handle dough as little as possible for the most tender and flaky results. Chill dough. Makes one 9-inch 2-crust pie.

- 3/4 to 1 cup sugar
- 1 to 2 tbsp. flour
- 3/4 tsp. cinnamon or to taste
- 1/8 tsp. salt
- 4 to 5 cups peeled, cored and sliced apples
- 1 tbsp. lemon juice
- 2 tbsp. butter

Prepare pastry; roll out bottom crust; fit into 9-inch pie plate. Trim edge even to fit outside of pie plate rim. Combine sugar, flour, cinnamon, and salt. Spread half of mixture over pastry in pie plate. Place prepared apple slices over this. Sprinkle remainder of sugar mixture over apples. Sprinkle lemon juice over all; dot with butter. Roll, fit, and seal upper crust. Bake on lower rack in 425 degree F. oven for 30 to 40 minutes (place pie plate on cookie sheet to catch any juice spills).

Danish Puff Pastry

1 cup butter
(divided into 1/2 cup portions)
2 cups flour
(divided into 1 cup portions)
2 tbsp. cold water

1 cup water
1 tsp. almond extract
3 eggs
Icing Sugar Glaze (below)

Cut 1/2 cup butter into 1 cup flour. Sprinkle with 2 tbsp. cold water. Mix with fork and gather into ball. Divide into 2 equal parts or portions. Form dough into 2 long 12 inch x 3 inch strips. Place on ungreased baking sheet. Bring 1 cup water to boil; add remaining 1/2 cup butter; stir to melt. Add 1 tsp. almond extract. Remove from heat, stirring vigorously add remaining 1 cup flour. Continue stirring until smooth. Beat in eggs, one at a time. Continue stirring until batter leaves sides of pan. Divide mixture in half and spread evenly over each of dough strips. Bake in 350 degree F. oven for 1 hour or until top is crisp and nicely browned.

Icing Sugar Glaze

2 cups icing sugar, sifted
1/2 tsp. almond extract

3 tbsp. water (approximately)
toasted slivered almonds

In small bowl, stir icing sugar, almond extract and water until smooth. Beat well. Stir in toasted slivered almonds. Drizzle icing over hot, baked puffs. Cut into sections while still warm. Serve Danish Puff warm.

Sour Cream Pastry

1½ cups unsifted flour; 2/3 cup corn oil margarine; 1/2 cup sour cream.

Place flour in medium size mixing bowl; with a pastry blender cut in margarine until particles are fine. Stir in sour cream to form a dough. Wrap in plastic wrap; chill thoroughly - at least 2 hours.

Fresh Berry Pie

pastry for 2-crust pie
4 cups fresh raspberries
[or blueberries]
1 tbsp. lemon juice
1/4 cup all-purpose flour
1 cup sugar
sweetened, whipped
whipping cream [or
vanilla ice-cream],
[optional]

1/4 tsp. cinnamon
1/8 tsp. nutmeg
1 1/2 tbsp butter
1 egg yolk
1 tbsp. water

Prepare pastry. Line 9-inch pie plate with half of pastry. Refrigerate pie shell and remaining half of pastry. Wash berries; drain thoroughly. Place berries in large bowl; sprinkle with lemon juice. In separate bowl, combine flour, sugar, cinnamon and nutmeg. Toss mixture gently with berries until well distributed.

Turn into pastry-lined pie plate, mounding berries in centre. Dot with butter. Roll out remaining half of pastry. Make several slits near centre for steam vents. Place pastry over filling. Fold edge of top crust under the bottom crust; press together to seal; crimp pastry attractively. In small bowl, beat egg yolk with water. Brush mixture over top crust lightly. Place pie on baking sheet to catch any juice. Bake in 400 deg. F oven for 45 to 50 minutes or until done. Cool on wire rack at least 45 minutes before serving. Serve warm with sweetened, whipped whipping cream, if desired. Makes 8 servings.

Pumpkin Preparation

To Freeze Pumpkin
Use a well-matured pumpkin. Peel. Cut into 1 inch cubes and steam until soft. Mash. Cool by placing pumpkin in bowl into bowlful of ice cold water. Stir often to speed cooling. Pack into cartons. Label and freeze.

Canned Pumpkin
Wash firm, fully ripe pumpkin. Cut into large pieces. Discard seeds. Steam or bake until tender. Scoop out pulp. Put through sieve or food mill. Add boiling water to make pulp a little thinner than needed for pies. Pour, hot, into hot jars, leaving 1 inch head space. Add 1 tsp. salt to each quart. Adjust caps. Process pints 1 hour and 5 minutes, quarts 1 hour and 20 minutes at 10 lbs. pressure. **Note:** Squash may be canned this way also.

Pumpkin Pie

1-1/2 cups canned or
cooked and mashed pumpkin
3/4 cup sugar
1 tsp. ground cinnamon
1/2 to 3/4 tsp. ground ginger
1/4 to 1/2 tsp. ground nutmeg
1/4 to 1/2 tsp. ground cloves
1/2 tsp. salt

3 slightly beaten eggs
1-1/4 cups milk
2/3 cup evaporated milk
1 9-inch unbaked pastry shell
(have edges crimped high)
sweetened whipped whipping
cream and walnut halves or
pecans for garnish, if desired

In large bowl, thoroughly combine pumpkin, sugar, cinnamon, ginger, nutmeg, cloves and salt. Blend in eggs, milk and evaporated milk. Pour filling into unbaked pastry shell. Bake in 400 degree F. oven for approximately 50 minutes or until knife inserted halfway between centre & edge, comes out clean. Cool thoroughly before serving. If desired, garnish with sweetened whipped whipping cream and walnut halves or pecans. Makes 1 9-inch pie.

Basic Crumb Crust

1½ cups crushed corn flakes or graham cracker crumbs ; 1/3 cup sugar; 1/3 to 1/2 cup melted butter or margarine.

Combine crumbs and sugar; blend in melted butter. Press firmly in pan. Chill for 1 hour or bake in a 350°F oven for about 8 minutes (the baked crust is firmer).

Rum Cream Pie

6 egg yolks; 1 scant cup sugar; 1 pkg. unflavoured gelatin; 1/2 cup cold water; 1 pt. cream for whipping; 1/2 cup dark rum; chocolate curls; finely chopped pistachio nuts; crumb pie shell.

Make a crumb pie shell in a glass serving dish. Beat 6 egg yolks until light; gradually add sugar. Sprinkle gelatin in cold water in a saucepan. Place over low heat and bring to a boil. Pour gelatin over sugar-egg mixture; stirring briskly. In a bowl, whip cream until stiff; fold into egg mixture. Add rum. Cool until mixture begins to set. Pour into pie shell; chill until firm. Sprinkle top with chocolate curls or finely chopped pistachio nuts. Garnish with whipped cream, if desired. Serve cold.

Apple Cottage Pie

2 cups apples, pared, cored, sliced thin (approx. 3 medium); 1 cup sugar; 1/2 tsp cinnamon; 1/4 tsp nutmeg; 2 eggs; 1/4 tsp salt; 1/2 cup light cream; 3/4 cup milk; 1 cup creamed cottage cheese, sieved; 1 tsp vanilla; 9-inch unbaked pie crust, chilled.

Cook apple slices with 2 tbsp water and a pinch of salt, covered, in a saucepan until tender (apples should be quite dry but still retain shape). Remove from heat and stir in 1/2 cup sugar, cinnamon and nutmeg; set aside. Beat eggs and salt slightly. Heat cream and milk together until a film appears on the surface. Slowly pour into eggs, beating vigorously. Add cottage cheese, remaining sugar and vanilla.

Spoon cooked apple slices into pastry shell. Pour cottage cheese mixture over top. Bake 15 minutes in 450°F oven, then at 325°F for 30 minutes longer; test doneness by inserting a knife in centre, should come out dry. Serve at room temperature.

Boston Cream Pie

2 egg whites; 1/2 cup sugar; 2¼ cups sifted cake flour; 1 cup sugar; 3 tsp. baking powder; 1 tsp. salt; 1/3 cup salad oil; 1 cup milk; 1½ tsp. vanilla; 2 egg yolks.

Beat egg whites until soft peaks form; gradually add in 1/2 cup sugar, beating until very stiff peaks form. Combine and sift together remaining dry ingredients in a separate bowl.

Add salad oil, **half** the milk and vanilla. Beat 1 minute at medium mixer speed, scraping bowl often. Add remaining milk and egg yolks, beat 1 minute, scraping bowl. Gently fold in egg white mixture with down-up motion, turning bowl. Pour batter in 2 greased and lightly floured 9-inch round pans. Bake in 350°F oven for about 25 minutes or until done. Let cool 20 minutes before removing from pans. Cool completely. Fill with Jiffy Vanilla Filling. Frost with Chocolate Glaze.

Jiffy Vanilla Fillings: Prepare one (3 3/8 oz) pkg. regular vanilla pudding mix according to package direction BUT use only 1¾ cups milk.

Chocolate Glaze: Melt 1½ (1 oz) squares unsweetened chocolate and 2 tbsp. butter over low heat, stirring constantly. Remove from heat and stir in 1½ cups sifted icing sugar and 1 tsp. vanilla, until mixture is crumbly. Mix in 3 tbsp. boiling water, adding enough water (about 2 tsp.) at a time to form medium glaze of pouring consistency. Quickly pour over top of cake and spread glaze evenly over top and sides.

Blender Instant Pie

    4 eggs
    1 cup milk
    1 cup buttermilk
1/2 cup sugar
1/2 cup bisquick
1/4 tsp. nutmeg

Place all ingredients in blender. Blend thoroughly. Pour into 9-inch greased pie plate. Bake in 375 degree F. oven for 50 minutes or until done. Bisquick will combine to form crust on bottom.

Sour Cream Cherry Pie

1 1/2 cups fine graham cracker crumbs	3 eggs, well beaten
1/4 cup sifted icing sugar	3/4 cup sugar
6 tbsp. melted butter	3/4 cup sour cream
1/2 tsp. cinnamon	2 cups fresh tart cherries, pitted
	1/2 tsp. vanilla

Combine crumbs, icing sugar, butter, and cinnamon. Pat into 9-inch pie plate, reserving one quarter of the crumbs for topping (an easy way to form the crust is to place crumb mixture in pie plate; distribute crumbs fairly evenly. Press another pie plate of same size into the crumbs; trim any excess which comes to the top edge). Chill pie shell thoroughly. Beat eggs well, add sugar, sour cream, pitted cherries, and vanilla. Combine well. Pour mixture into prepared chilled pie shell. Sprinkle with reserved crumbs. Bake in 325 degree F oven for 1 hour or until cherry custard is firm. Serve pie very hot or very well chilled.

Strawberry Glaze Pie

1 pkt. plain gelatin	1 cup water
1/4 cup cold water	1 cup sugar
4 cups sliced strawberries (or raspberries)	8 inch baked pie shell

Soak gelatin in cold water. Cook 1 cup strawberries in 1 cup water until soft. Strain. Add sugar and gelatin to hot liquid. Stir until dissolved. Let chill until consistency of egg white. Fold in remaining 3 cups of berries. Pour into baked pastry shell. Chill until firm. Serve with whipped cream.

Puddings and Sauces

Sherry Chocolate Sauce

1/2 cup light corn syrup	1/8 tsp. salt
4 squares (1 oz. each)	2 tbsp. butter
semi-sweet chocolate	1/4 cup sherry

Combine corn syrup and chocolate. Heat gently, stirring constantly until chocolate is melted and mixture is blended. Remove from heat and stir in salt, butter and sherry. Cool to lukewarm. Serve over ice cream or pudding. *Makes approximately 1-1/4 cups.*

Steamed Apple Pudding

1 tbsp. butter	1 egg
1 tbsp. sugar	1/4 cup milk
1 cup all-purpose flour	1/4 cup brandy
1 tsp. baking powder	1/4 cup molasses
1/4 tsp. baking soda	1 medium-size apple,
1/2 cup fine bread crumbs	peeled and chopped
1/4 cup butter, softened	1/3 cup raisins
1/2 cup brown sugar	

Grease sides and bottom of a 1 pound coffee can with 1 tbsp. butter. Sprinkle in 1 tbsp. sugar. Put plastic lid on can. Shake until sides and bottom are coated with sugar. Remove lid. Set aside. Sift flour, baking powder and baking soda together. Stir in bread crumbs. Beat remaining 1/4 cup butter, brown sugar and egg until smooth. Mix milk, brandy and molasses together. Add to butter mixture alternately with flour mixture, blending well.

Stir in chopped apple and raisins. Pour batter into prepared can. Cover can with piece of foil, allowing space for pudding to expand. Fasten with string. Place can on a ring of foil in large kettle. Pour 1 inch of boiling water into kettle. Cover kettle and keep water at a simmering temperature. Add more boiling water occasionally so water stays at the 1-inch level. Steam pudding for 2 hours. Remove foil from can. Let pudding stand for 5 minutes. Open bottom end of can with can opener and pudding will easily slide out. Serve pudding with hard sauce. *Makes 8 servings.*

Hard Sauce
3 tbsp. butter
3/4 cup icing sugar
3 tbsp. heated brandy

Melt butter in a small saucepan. Stir in sugar and brandy. Beat until smooth. *Makes 2/3 cup.*

Uncooked Mincemeat

1 c. finely chopped beef suet, ½ c. mixed shredded peel, 4 c. currants, 2 c. sultanas, ¼ c. blanched, chopped almonds or cashews, 1¼ c. brown sugar, 2 lbs. apples, peeled and chopped, 1 tsp. cinnamon, 1 tsp. nutmeg, 1 tsp. allspice, ½ tsp. salt, juice and rind of 1 lemon, juice and rind of 1 orange, ½ c. brandy, sweet cider or syrup from canned fruit, ¼ c. fruit juice.

Combine all ingredients.

Bottle in sterilized jars and seal. Store in a cool place. A little brandy or molasses poured over the top of the mincemeat in each jar helps to preserve the mincemeat.

Apple Dumplings

1 recipe pastry for double crust pie, 6 medium apples, pared and cored, brown sugar, cinnamon, nutmeg, butter.

Roll prepared pastry dough into a 12 x 16 inch rectangle, 1/8 inch thick. Cut into 6 squares. Onto each square place one apple. Fill centre of apples with brown sugar, then sprinkle each with additional brown sugar, cinnamon and nutmeg. Dot with butter.

Gently gather up corners of each square to the centre and pinch edges together. Place dumplings on ungreased baking sheet. Bake in 375 F. oven for 25 to 40 minutes, or until apples are tender and pastry is golden. Serve warm with cream or Brown Sugar Sauce.

Brown Sugar Sauce

½ c. brown sugar, packed, 1 tbsp. cornstarch, 1/8 tsp. salt, 1 c. warm water, 1 tbsp. butter, 1 tsp. vanilla.

In a small saucepan, combine brown sugar, cornstarch and salt. Stir in warm water gradually. Cook over medium heat, stirring constantly, until thickened and and clear, about 3 to 5 minutes. Remove from heat; stir in butter and vanilla. Serve hot, with Apple Dumplings. Makes about 1 cup.

Apple Oat Crisp

4 c. sliced apples, 2 or 3 tsp. lemon juice, 1/3 c. flour, 1 c. rolled oats, ½ c. brown sugar, 1 tsp. cinnamon, 1/3 c. melted butter.

Sprinkle lemon juice over apple in greased baking dish. Combine dry ingredients, add melted butter mixing until crumbly. Sprinkle crumbs over apples.

Bake at 375 F. for about 30 minutes or until apples are tender. Serve warm. If apples are a little tart, add a little sugar to them just before sprinkling with the topping.

Broken Glass Cake

1 (3 oz.) pkg. orange jelly powder; 1 (3 oz.) pkg. cherry jelly powder; 1 (3 oz.) pkg. lime jelly powder; 3 cups boiling water; 2 cups cold water; 1 cup pineapple juice; 1/4 cup sugar; 1 (3 oz.) pkg. lemon jelly powder; 1½ cups graham crumbs OR 16 to 18 ladyfingers, split; 1/3 cup melted butter or margarine; 2 cups whipping cream.

Prepare 3 flavours of jelly separately (use 1 cup boiling water and 1/2 cup cold water for each). Pour each flavour into an 8-inch square pan. Chill until firm. Then mix pineapple juice and sugar, heating until sugar is dissolved. Remove from heat. Dissolve lemon jelly in the hot juice, then mix in 1/2 cup cold water. Chill until slightly thickened. Meanwhile, mix crumbs and butter; press into bottom of 9-inch spring form pan, (and on sides of pan, if desired), or line pan with ladyfingers (omit butter). Cut the firm jellies into 1/2 inch cubes. Prepare whipping cream; then blend with lemon jelly. Fold in jelly cubes and pour into pan. Chill overnight (or at least 5 hours). To remove from pan, run knife or spatula between sides of pan and cake, and remove sides of pan before serving. Whipped cream can be spread on top and sides of dessert, if desired. *Makes 16 servings.*

VARIATIONS: Other jelly flavours can be used, forming any combination of colours desired (for example, using all cubes of black raspberry or lime jelly and using strawberry jelly in place of lemon jelly).

Broken Glass Cheese Dessert

Prepare Broken Glass Cake EXCEPT substitute dessert topping with 2 (3 oz. each) pkgs. cream cheese, beaten with 1/4 cup milk until fluffy and soft.

Broken Glass Pie

Prepare Broken Glass Cake. Pour mixture into two 9-inch graham crumb lined pie pans. If using ladyfingers, use about 18 ladyfingers, split; line the bottoms and then cut remaining fingers in half crosswise and line the sides of pans.

Broken Glass Mold

Prepare Broken Glass Cake, omitting crumb mixture. Pour into a 3-qt. mold or 9-inch spring form pan or loaf pan.

Brownie Pudding

1 cup sifted all-purpose flour	2 tbsp. salad oil
3/4 cup sugar	1 tsp. vanilla
2 tsp. baking powder	1 cup chopped walnuts
2 tbsp. cocoa	3/4 cup brown sugar
1/2 tsp. salt	1/4 cup cocoa
1/2 cup milk	1-3/4 cups hot water

Sift together flour, sugar, baking powder, 2 tbsp. cocoa and salt. Stir in milk, salad oil and vanilla. Mix until smooth. Stir in walnuts. Pour batter into a greased 8-inch square pan. In small bowl, stir together brown sugar and 1/4 cup cocoa. Sprinkle mixture evenly over batter. Pour hot water over entire batter. **Do not Stir.** Bake in 350 degree F. oven for approximately 45 minutes or until done. Serve warm. Delicious with vanilla ice cream or sweetened whipped whipping cream. *Makes 6 to 8 servings.*

Sour Cream Rhubarb Crumble

5 cups raw rhubarb, cut in 1 inch pieces, ¾ to 1 cup granulated sugar, 2 tbsp. quick-cooking tapioca, ½ cup flour, ¼ tsp. salt, 1 tsp. cinnamon, ½ cup rolled oats, ¾ cup lightly packed brown sugar, 1/3 cup soft butter.

1 cup dairy sour cream, 2 tbsp. icing sugar, 1/8 tsp. cinnamon.

Butter a broad, shallow baking dish. Preheat oven to 375 F. Wash and cut up rhubarb. Place fruit in prepared baking dish; sprinkle with granulated sugar and tapioca; mix lightly. Combine flour, salt, the 1 tsp. cinnamon, rolled oats and brown sugar. Add and mix in butter. Sprinkle crumb mixture over fruit. Bake in preheated oven 40 to 50 minutes. Meanwhile combine sour cream, icing sugar and 1/8 tsp. cinnamon, mix well. Chill thoroughly. Serve Crumble warm with sour cream topping.

Berry Buckle

1/2 cup butter
1/2 cup sugar
1 egg, well beaten
2 cups sifted all-purpose flour
1/4 tsp. salt
2 1/2 tsp. baking powder
1/2 cup milk
2 cups fresh blueberries
[or raspberries]

1/2 cup sifted all-purpose flour
1/2 cup sugar
1/8 tsp. nutmeg
1/4 tsp. cinnamon
1/4 cup butter
sweetened, whipped
whipping cream

In bowl cream well 1/2 cup butter and 1/2 cup sugar. Add beaten egg; mix thoroughly. Set aside. On waxed paper, sift together 2 cups flour, salt, and baking powder. Add dry mixture to creamed mixture alternately with milk, beating until smooth after each addition. Pour mixture into well-greased 1 1/2 x 7 1/2 x 1 1/2-inch baking pan; sprinkle blueberries evenly over batter. In bowl, combine 1/2 cup flour, 1/2 cup sugar, nutmeg and cinnamon. Cut in 1/4 cup butter until mixture is crumbly. Sprinkle over blueberries. Bake in 350 deg. F. oven 45 to 50 minutes. Cut into squares. Serve warm with sweetened, whipped whipping cream, if desired. Makes 6 servings.

Mona says . . .

To frost glass rims: dip in lightly beaten egg white, then in extremely fine sugar. Let dry before using. Use to dress up fruit cocktails and drinks.

When filling small, easily tipped over molds, place molds in muffin pans.

To build up a supply of ice cubes for entertaining, freeze cubes in ice cube trays until frozen hard and very dry. Remove to a heavy-weight large plastic bag and place in freezer. Repeat until you have enough ice cubes.

For best results, when serving chilled foods, have plates, serving dish and serving utensils chilled in refrigerator for 15 to 30 minutes before serving.

If your Hollandaise Sauce curdles when being prepared, remove sauce from heat and beat in 1 tsp. hot water a few drops at a time. Do not return to heat. Serve sauce warm or at room temperature.

To aid in keeping sour cream from curdling, when making sauces, etc., bring it to room temperature before adding to hot mixture. Never allow mixture to boil after sour cream has been added.

To prevent food from overbrowning as it bakes, wrap it in aluminium foil with the shiny-side out.

When cooking beets and red cabbage, add 1 tbsp. (approximately) cider vinegar or lemon juice to the cooking water for brighter results.

When flaming a flambe, if the liqueur or brandy refuses to ignite, heat fresh spirit separately in a spoon over chafing dish flame; add to the hot foods and ignite.

Decorative Ice Cubes, Rings and Blocks
It is really very easy to make attractive ice cubes for drinks or ice ring or block for a punch bowl. To make decorative ice cubes, half-fill an ice cube tray, ring mold or a 9 x 5 x 3 inch loaf pan with water, (plain or pastel tinted). Partially freeze. Add maraschino cherries, citrus slices, pineapple chunks in decorative design. Freeze to anchor fruit; fill with ice water and freeze until firm. To use, float cubes, ice block or ice ring in punch bowl or cocktail.

Frosted Fruit
Try frosting fruit, to attractively garnish appetizer trays, decorate fruitcakes or steamed puddings, garnish turkey, ham or game, or as a table centrepiece. It's easy to do and the results are very eyecatching.

Pick a selection of fruits such as lemons, limes, seedless green grapes, concord grapes, tokay grapes or the grapes of your choice. Wash fruit well and pat dry very thoroughly. The number of egg whites and the amount of sugar to be used will vary according to the amount of fruit to be frosted. For 3 lemons, 3 limes, ½ lb. green grapes, and ½ lb. concord grapes, use 2 lightly beaten egg whites. Dip or brush fruit with egg whites, sprinkle with superfine granulated sugar (use your blender). Allow fruit to dry on wire racks until coating is firm.

FESTIVE FARE FOR SPECIAL OCCASIONS

Entertaining at home is easier today than it was at York Factory in 1843. We don't have to go out and shoot our own fowl. We don't even have to dress and draw the bird.

"Our Christmas dinner was a good one . . . True, there was no carpet on the floor, and the chairs were home-made; but then the table was mahogany, and the walls were hung round with several large engravings in bird's-eye maple frames. The stove, too, was brightly polished with black lead . . . the table covered with a snow-white cloth, whereon reposed a platter containing a beautiful, fat, plump wild-goose, which had a sort of come-eat-me-up-quick-else-I'll-melt expression about it that was painfully delicious. Opposite to this smoked a huge roast of beef, to procure which one of our most useless draught oxen had been sacrificed. This, with a dozen white partridges, and a large piece of salt pork, composed our dinner. But the greatest rarities on the board were two large decanters of port wine, and two smaller ones of Madeira." BALLANTYNE, R.M., *Hudson Bay:* An early Christmas at York Factory (1843).

Wine Jellies

5 (6 oz.) glasses *; 1 paraffin stick; 2 cups red wine (claret, burgundy, port); 3 cups sugar; 1/2 bottle liquid pectin; candied cherries.

* Tall parfait, fat brandy snifter, long-stemmed champagne flutes. Make sure glasses are sturdy enough to withstand very hot water. Do not use fragile crystal.

Sterilize glasses in hot, soapy water; rinse. Place on rack in large kettle. Cover with water; bring to a boil. Lower heat and simmer 10 minutes. Turn off heat, leaving glasses in hot water until ready to fill with jelly. Place paraffin stick in an empty can; place in saucepan of boiling water. Keep water at low simmer while preparing jelly so paraffin remains melted.

JELLIES: Mix wine and sugar in top of double boiler over boiling water. Heat, stirring quickly, until sugar dissolves. Remove from heat. *Quickly* stir in liquid pectin. Pour mixture into hot, sterilized glasses, leaving at least 1-1/2-inch space at top. Seal immediately by pouring enough paraffin into each glass to form a 1/4-inch thick layer. Garnish with red and green candied cherries after seal has hardened and cooled.

NOTE: To make green jelly, substitute with a pale wine (sauterne or sherry) for the red wine; add a few drops of green food colouring for desired shade.

Coco-Mint Sandwiches

3/4 cup margarine or butter; 1 cup granulated sugar; 1 egg; 1/2 tsp. vanilla; 2 cups sifted all-purpose flour; 3/4 cup cocoa powder; 1 tsp. baking powder; 1/2 tsp. baking soda; 1/4 cup milk; Mint filling.

Cream butter and sugar until fluffy in mixing bowl. Add egg and vanilla; beat well. Sift together flour, cocoa, baking powder, soda and 1/2 tsp. salt. Add to creamed mixture alternately with milk, mixing well. Shape dough into two 10 x 1½-inch rolls. Wrap each roll in waxed paper; chill several hours or overnight. Cut chilled rolls in 1/8-inch slices. Bake slices on ungreased cookie sheet in 325°F oven for 10 minutes. Remove from cookie sheet at once. When cookies are cool, sandwich together with Mint Filling. *Makes 3½ dozen.*

MINT FILLING: Combine 3 tbsp. margarine or butter, 1½ cups sifted icing sugar, 1 tbsp. milk, 2 or 3 drops green food colouring, and 1 or 2 drops oil of peppermint (or 1/2 tsp. peppermint extract) until smooth and creamy.

Vegetable Lime Ring

1 (3 oz) pkg. lime-jelly powder; 3/4 cup boiling water; 3/4 cup shredded unpared cucumber; 1/4 cup finely sliced green onion; 1 (8 oz) ctn. cream-style cottage cheese; 1 cup mayonnaise or salad dressing; 1 tsp. prepared horseradish; 1/4 tsp. salt.

Dissolve jelly powder in boiling water; chill until partially set. Combine remaining ingredients and fold into jelly mixture. Pour into 3½-cup ring mold. Chill until jelly mixture is firm. *Makes 5 or 6 servings.*

Brandied Cranberries

4 cups fresh cranberries   1/4 cup brandy
1-1/2 cups sugar

Place cranberries in a shallow baking dish. Sprinkle sugar over. Cover and bake at 300 degrees F. for 1 hour. Remove from oven. Gently stir in brandy. Store in covered container in refrigerator. *Makes 3 cups (approximately).*

Cranberry-Orange-Lemon Relish

4 cups fresh or frozen   1 medium lemon,
  cranberries (thawed and well   quartered (remove seeds)
  drained if using frozen)   1-1/2 cups sugar
1 large orange,   1 tsp. ground cinnamon
  quartered (remove seeds)   1/2 tsp. ground cloves

Wash cranberries; drain thoroughly. Remove any stems. Put cranberries, orange and lemon quarters through coarse blade of food chopper. Place prepared fruits in large bowl. Add sugar, cinnamon and cloves; mix thoroughly. Cover. Refrigerate several hours or overnight, to allow flavours to blend. *Yields about 4 cups.*

This is a delicately spiced, refreshing accompaniment to a holiday meal.

Sherry Jelly

1 package (3 oz.)   juice of 1 lemon
  lemon flavour jelly powder   1 cup sherry
2/3 cup boiling water   sweetened whipped whipping
juice of 1 orange   cream for garnish, if desired

Dissolve jelly powder in 2/3 cup boiling water. Add fruit juices and sherry. Pour into 4 individual molds and chill until firm. To serve - Unmold. Top with sweetened whipped whipping cream if desired. *Makes 4 servings.*

Note: For a special treat, top with sliced fruits in season, such as raspberries, strawberries or peaches.

Minted Pineapple

1 (3 oz.) pkg. lime or lemon-lime jelly powder; pinch of salt; 3/4 cup boiling water; 1 (20 oz.) can crushed or cubed pineapple; 6 drops mint extract; 1/2 tsp. vinegar.

Dissolve jelly powder and salt in boiling water. Stir in remaining ingredients, saving can to use as mold. Chill until thickened slightly. Pour mixture into can and 1 individual mold or a serving bowl. Chill until firm; unmold. (To unmold from can, puncture bottom before dipping in warm water.) *Makes 6 side salads or 3¼ cups.*

Marshmallow Fudge Squares

3 squares unsweetened   1/2 tsp. vanilla
  cooking chocolate, melted   dash salt
1 tin (14 oz.) sweetened   18 large unflavoured
  condensed milk   marshmallows, halved
2 cups fine graham   1 square semisweet chocolate
  cracker crumbs   1 tsp. butter or margarine
1/2 cup chopped walnuts

In top of double boiler, melt 3 squares unsweetened chocolate. Add condensed milk, graham cracker crumbs, walnuts, vanilla and salt. Stir to combine thoroughly. Spread mixture into a greased 8-inch square pan. Bake in 325 degree F. oven for 25 minutes. Immediately after removing square from oven, cover with halved marshmallows, cut side down. Cool. In top of double boiler, melt 1 square semi-sweet chocolate and butter. Drizzle chocolate over marshmallows. Cool. When completely cold, cut into small squares. *Yields approximately 30 small squares.*

Chocolate Truffles

6 (6 oz) squares semi-sweet chocolate; 1/4 cup sifted icing sugar; 3 tbsp. butter or margarine; 3 slightly beaten egg yolks; 1 tbsp. rum or brandy; finely grated semi-sweet chocolate; finely chopped nuts; coconut.

In top of double boiler, melt 6 squares semi-sweet chocolate over hot, but not boiling water; add icing sugar and butter. Remove from heat. Stir in a small amount of hot mixture into beaten egg yolks; return to hot mixture, stirring well. Blend in rum. Chill, without stirring for 1 to 2 hours. Shape into 1-inch balls. Divide balls into 3 parts.

Roll 1/3 into finely grated chocolate; another 1/3 in finely chopped nuts; add the last 1/3 coat with coconut. *Makes about 2 dozen.*

Oatmeal Truffles

1 cup quick-cooking oats   *1 to 3 tsp. water,
3 tbsp. cocoa   if necessary to bind
1 egg, well beaten   extra sifted icing sugar
2-1/2 cups sifted icing sugar   and extra cocoa
1 tsp. instant coffee   corn syrup
1/4 tsp. vanilla extract   coconut

In large bowl, combine quick-cooking oats, 3 tbsp. cocoa, egg, 2-1/2 cups icing sugar, instant coffee and vanilla. Work all ingredients together until mixture is a stiff smooth paste. Add water as necessary to bind. In small bowl, combine a small amount of extra sifted icing sugar and cocoa to taste. Roll oatmeal mixture with hands, dusting palms with sugar and cocoa mixture. Set truffles aside and allow to set for 2 hours; then brush with corn syrup and sprinkle or roll with coconut. (If desired tinted coconut can be used for an attractive effect.)

*The amount of water required, depends on the size of egg used. Mixture should be a stiff smooth consistency (not sticky). Omit water if desired consistency is obtained without it.

Pomeroy's Shortbread

2 cups butter; 1 cup brown sugar; yolk of 1 egg; 5 cups all-purpose flour.

Cream together butter and sugar; add in egg yolk and stir well. Add flour, a small amount at a time, until the consistency of putty. Roll dough out to 1/2 to 3/4 inches thick. Prick with fork and cut into shapes. Bake in 325°F oven until firm or golden brown, about 30 minutes.

Whipped Shortbread

1 lb. butter
1 cup icing sugar
3 cups sifted cake flour

1/2 cup corn starch
1 tsp. vanilla

Using electric mixer, cream butter until very light and fluffy. Continue beating while adding sugar, flour, and cornstarch. Beat until all ingredients are well combined. Add vanilla. Beat again. Drop short bread by spoonful on cookie sheet. Bake in 350 degree F. oven for approximately 12 minutes or until done.

Chocolate Cherry Souffle

1 cup (6-ounce) package semisweet chocolate pieces; 3/4 cup firmly packed light brown sugar; 1 envelope unflavoured gelatin; 1/4 cup maraschino cherry juice (syrup); 4 eggs, separated; 1/2 cup water; 1 teaspoon vanilla; 1¼ cups cream for whipping (1/2 pint); 6 to eight maraschino cherries; 1 square semi-sweet chocolate.

Combine chocolate pieces, 1/4 cup brown sugar, gelatin and cherry syrup in top of a double boiler. Heat over simmering water, stirring often, 10 minutes, or until gelatin dissolves. Beat egg yolks slightly with a fork; stir in water. Blend in a few spoonfuls of hot chocolate mixture, then quickly stir into chocolate mixture left in double boiler. Cook stirring constantly, 3 minutes; remove from heat; stir in vanilla.

Chill just until mixture is thick enough to mound slightly on a spoon. Beat egg whites until foamy-white and double in volume. Beat in remaining 1/2 cup brown sugar, 1 tablespoon at a time, until meringue forms soft peaks. Beat cream until stiff. Beat gelatin mixture until fluffy-light; gently fold into meringue, then fold in whipped cream (save a little whipped cream for decorating) until no streaks of white remain. Prepare a mold by folding a piece of foil or, wax paper 12 inches wide and long enough to go around a 4 cup baking dish (with straight sides) or souffle dish and overlap slightly in half lengthwise. Wrap strip around dish to make a 2-inch stand-up collar; hold in place with a rubber band or paper clip. Spoon mixture into dish. Chill several hours or until firm. Melt square of chocolate over double boiler (if you wish to have a glossy chocolate coating, melt just a shaving of paraffin wax along with the chocolate). Coat drained maraschino cherries in chocolate so that they are entirely covered. Top chilled souffle with dots of whipped cream crowned with chocolate coated cherries.

Scottish Shortbread

2 cups flour,
1 cup butter or margarine,
½ cup (generous) white sugar,
pinch salt.

Put all ingredients in a bowl. Mix and then knead very well. Shape as desired and bake on ungreased brown paper 20-25 minutes in a 350 degree F. oven. This dough may be rolled out for cut cookies. The more the dough is worked the better it is.

Steamed Walnut Potato Pudding

1 cup sugar; 1 cup ground suet; 1 cup sifted all-purpose flour; 1 tsp. salt; 1 tsp. baking powder; 1 tsp. nutmeg; 1 tsp. allspice; 1 cup raw apple, finely chopped; 1 cup grated carrots; 1 cup grated long white potatoes; 1 cup walnuts, coarsely chopped.

Combine sugar with suet. Sift flour, salt, baking powder, nutmeg and allspice together. Add to suet–sugar mixture. Add apple, carrot, potato and walnuts; blend thoroughly. Pour into a well-greased and floured 1½ quart mold. Cover tightly with lid or aluminum foil. Steam 2 hrs. in tightly covered container. Let stand 5 minutes before unmolding. Serve with lemon, brandy or hard sauce. *6 to 8 servings.*

Hard Sauce with Variations

1/3 cup butter; 1 cup icing, brown or granulated sugar; few grains of salt; 1 tsp. vanilla (or other flavouring.)

Cream butter thoroughly. Sift sugar and gradually add to butter until mixture is very smooth; add salt and flavouring.

Brandy or Wine Sauce: Add 1 tsp. brandy or 1 to 3 tbsp. sherry.

Lemon Sauce: Add 1 tsp. lemon juice and 1 tbsp. grated lemon rind.

Orange Sauce: Add 2 tbsp. orange juice and 2 tbsp. grated orange rind.

Rich Hard Sauce: Beat in 1 egg or 1/4 cup cream.

Spicy Hard Sauce: Add 1/2 tsp. cinnamon, 1/4 tsp. cloves and 1/2 tsp. lemon juice.

Almond Butter Coffee-Cake

1/4 cup sugar; 1/4 tsp. salt; 1/4 cup shortening; 1 cup milk, scalded; 1/2 cake yeast; 1 egg; 3-1/2 cups sifted flour; 1/16 tsp. cardamom.

Add sugar, salt and shortening to milk and cool to lukewarm. Add crumbled yeast and let stand 5 minutes. Add egg and 1-3/4 cups flour; beat well. Add remaining flour sifted with spices; then knead well. Let rise until doubled in bulk, about 1-1/2 hours. Knead down and let rise again. Shape into 2 coffee cakes and place in greased pans. Let rise 15 minutes. Spread almond mixture on top and let rise until doubled in bulk. Bake in moderate oven (375 degrees F.) 45 minutes to one hour. *Makes two cakes.*

Almond Mixture

2 tbsp. sugar; 1 tbsp. honey or syrup; 1 tbsp. butter; 1 tbsp. chopped almonds.

Cook sugar, syrup and butter until it spins a thread. Add almonds and spread on cake.

LIQUID REFRESHMENTS YOU'VE ALWAYS WANTED TO MAKE

Hot Tomato Punch

2 cups tomato juice   1/2 tsp. Lawry's Seasoned Salt
1 tbsp. Lawry's Garlic Spread

Pour tomato juice into a 1-quart saucepan. Add Garlic Spread and Seasoned Salt. Simmer for 10 minutes. *Makes 4 servings.*

Quick Eggnog Punch

1 quart eggnog
1 pint softened vanilla
  ice cream

2 cups lemon-lime carbonated
  beverage, chilled
dash cinnamon and/or nutmeg,
  if desired

In punch bowl, combine eggnog and ice cream. Stir to combine. Slowly add lemon-lime beverage. If desired sprinkle top **lightly** with a dash of cinnamon and/or nutmeg. *Makes about 16 (4oz.) servings.*

Happy Lemon Punch   (Base)

2 cups strong hot tea, 1½ to 2 cups sugar, ½ cup grenadine, 2 cups freshly squeezed lemon juice, chilled, 2 cups unsweetened pineapple juice, chilled.

Combine tea and sugar, stirring until sugar has dissolved. Chill thoroughly. Add grenadine and chilled juices. Pour over block of ice in punch bowl. Makes 24 punch cup servings. Add lemon and orange cartwheels for garnish.

Sparkling Punch

(Non-alcoholic)

Add 1 (28 oz.) bottle lemon-lime soft drink, chilled, to Happy Lemon Punch Base. Stir gently. Makes 2¾ quarts.

Champagne Punch

Add 1 (4/5 quart) bottle champagne, chilled and ½ pint vodka, chilled to Happy Lemon Punch Base. Stir gently. Makes 3 quarts.

Cafe Brulot

½ cup instant
  quality coffee,
4 cups boiling water,
3 sticks cinnamon,
1 tbsp. whole cloves,

¼ to ⅓ cup sugar
½ cup brandy,
peel from 1 orange and
  1 lemon, cut in strips.

Dissolve coffee in boiling water. Add cinnamon sticks and cloves; cover and let stand 15 minutes. Strain and reheat. Meanwhile, combine sugar, brandy and fruit peel in chafing dish. Heat; then flame the brandy mixture. Slowly add coffee. When flame is extinguished ladle into demitasse cups. *Makes 4½ cups or 9 servings 4 oz. each.*

Coffee Carioca

2 oranges, peeled,
½ cup instant
  quality coffee,
¼ cup sugar,

4 cups boiling water,
¼ cup rum,
sweetened whipped
  whipping cream.

Remove all white membrane from oranges, slice into ¼ inch thick slices and remove seeds. Place in large heat proof bowl with the coffee and sugar. Stir in boiling water; let stand 30 minutes. Strain coffee into saucepan. Heat almost to boiling. Remove from heat and stir in rum. Serve in demitasse cups topped with sweetened, whipped whipping cream. If desired, garnish with grated orange rind, shaved chocolate or cinnamon. *Makes 4½ cups or 9 servings of 4 oz. each.*

Hot Spiced Wassail

This is a great recipe for holiday open house entertaining.

6 inches stick cinnamon,
  broken into pieces,
16 whole cloves,
1 tsp. whole allspice,
3 medium oranges,
whole cloves to stud
  oranges,
6 cups apple juice or cider,

2 cups cranberry juice
  cocktail,
¼ cup sugar,
1 tsp. aromatic bitters,
1 cup rum, or to taste,
extra orange slices for
  garnish, if desired.

In piece of cheesecloth, wrap broken cinnamon pieces, 16 cloves and allspice. Tie; Set aside. Stud oranges with cloves. In large saucepan, combine juice or cider, cranberry juice cocktail, sugar and aromatic bitters. Add spice bag and studded oranges; simmer, covered, 10 minutes. Add rum and heat through. Remove spices and oranges. Pour into warm serving bowl and float studded oranges and fresh orange slices on top. *Makes 9 cups.*

Mexicali Hot Chocolate

1 quart milk; 3 squares semisweet chocolate; 1 tsp ground cinnamon; 2 eggs.

In a large saucepan, heat milk just to scalding. Blend in chocolate and cinnamon, stirring until chocolate melts, then beat with a rotary beater until smooth. In a small bowl, beat eggs; slowly beat in about 1 cup of the chocolate mixture, then beat back into remaining chocolate mixture in pan. Heat slowly, stirring constantly, 1 minute. Beat again until frothy. Ladle into heated glasses or mugs. Add a cinnamon stick to each glass for a stirrer. Serve warm. *Makes 6 servings.*

Spiced Snowball Drink

A great favourite with children.

1 cup water,	¼ tsp. cinnamon or
1 package (6 oz.)	to taste,
semisweet chocolate	⅛ tsp. nutmeg or to taste,
pieces,	1 tsp. vanilla extract,
¼ cup sugar,	sweetened, whipped
dash salt,	whipping cream and
2 cups milk,	chocolate curls for
1 cup light cream,	garnish, if desired.

In large heavy saucepan, bring water to boil. Add chocolate, sugar and salt; stir constantly, just until chocolate has melted and the mixture is smooth. Add milk, cream, cinnamon and nutmeg. Stir constantly and bring just to the boil. Remove from heat. Add vanilla. Just before serving, beat with rotary beater until foamy. Serve warm. Top with whipping cream "snowball" and garnish with chocolate curls. *Makes 6 servings.*

Fruit Punch Wreath

Orange-Lemon Ice Wreath
Prepare Orange-Lemon Ice Wreath by pouring 3 cups water into a 5-1/2 to 6 cup ring mold. Freeze for approximately 1 hour or until top is solid. Slice 1 medium orange and lemon (remove seeds); cut slices in half. Arrange in attractive petal fashion in 2 layers on ice around ring. Pour 1 cup water over fruits and freeze until solid.

Fruit Punch

1 tin (48 oz.) red fruit punch	2 to 2-1/4 cups water
(Hawaiian - Tropical punch etc.)	maraschino cherries
2 tins (6 oz. each) frozen orange	with stems for garnish,
juice concentrate (just thawed)	if desired

To make up punch, pour red fruit punch, orange juice concentrate and water into punch bowl. Stir to combine thoroughly. Unmold ice wreath by placing quickly in a dish of warm water - just long enough to loosen. Add ice mold to punch, fruit side up. Garnish with maraschino cherries if desired. *Yields approximately 18 (4 oz.) servings.*

Note' 1 to 2 cups of vodka can be added to punch, if desired.

Orange Cooler

1/2 of (6 oz.) can frozen orange juice concentrate (1/3 cup); 1/2 cup milk; 1/2 cup water; 1/4 cup sugar; 1/2 tsp. vanilla; 5 or 6 ice cubes.

Add all ingredients into blender. Cover and blend until smooth, about 30 seconds. Serve immediately. *Makes about 3 cups.*

Refreshing Coolers

Cranberry Fizz

1 tin ('14 oz.) jellied	ice cubes
cranberry sauce	3-1/2 cups well chilled ginger ale
1/4 cup lemon juice	orange slices and maraschino
3/4 cup orange juice	cherries, for garnish

In large bowl, beat cranberry sauce until smooth; stir in lemon juice and orange juice. Place ice cubes in 2-quart punch bowl or juice pitcher. Pour cranberry mixture over ice cubes. Carefully, pour ginger ale down side of bowl, mix with up and down motion. Float orange slices and maraschino cherries on top. *Makes 12 to 15 servings.*

Melon Punch Bowl
Try this idea for a stunning "punch bowl" at your next patio party. Select 1 large watermelon; stand it on end; cut a very thin slice off bottom to make it level and stand upright easily and securely. Cut top third off watermelon. Use a cup as a guide to trace scallops around top outside edge of melon. Carve scalloped edge, following pattern. Scoop out fruit for later use. Chill melon "punch bowl". If desired, use a sawtooth pattern for top of watermelon rather than scallop pattern.

Double Strawberry Soda
For each serving, place 2 scoops strawberry ice cream in bottom of large glass. Drizzle 2 tsp. strawberry jam over ice cream. Fill to top with lemon-lime carbonated drink; stir well with a long spoon.

Minty Chocolate Soda
For each serving, combine 2/3 cup milk, 1 tbsp. chocolate syrup and a dash of peppermint extract; stir well. Add 2 scoops vanilla ice cream. Fill to top with ginger ale or lemon-lime carbonated drink; stir well. Top with swirl of whipped whipping cream; drizzle 1 tsp. chocolate syrup over top.

Berry Milk

2 cups fresh straw-	1/4 cup sugar
berries or raspberries	1 1/2 cups milk
[or sliced fresh fruit	
of your choice]	

Combine all ingredients in blender container; blend for 30 seconds. Serves two.
Shake variation: Add 2 large cups vanilla ice cream to above ingredients, proceed as directed.

Mona says . . .

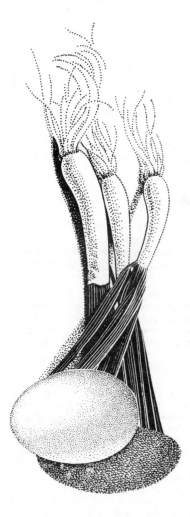

In quantity sandwich making, always prepare filling first. Refrigerate prepared fillings until bread is sliced and ready for spreading. The only exceptions to this rule are process and cream cheese, butter and margarine, which should be at room temperature or well creamed. Use edible garnishes — they not only look attractive but also can taste delicious. Pick a selection from the following ideas:

Cucumber Twists

Wash cucumber but do not peel; slice thinly; make a cut from edge to centre. Twist into a bow shape. For added looks, sprinkle with paprika and/or chopped parsley.

Green Onion Ruffles

Wash green onions, trim off root ends and all but 2 to 3 inches of tops. Beginning at root end, make crisscross cuts deep into stalk up to where green begins to show. Quick-chill in ice water; drain well.

Pickle Fans

Choose the small to medium-sized pickles. Make several thin lengthwise cuts from top to approximately ¼″ from bottom. Spread slices to form a fan.

Egg Cups

Hard-cook eggs; chill; shell and halve crosswise. Scoop out yolks. Serrate edges of the whites with paring knife. Fill with devilled-egg mixture, sharp cheese spread or meat spread, pate or with meat, poultry or seafood salad.

Tomato Twists

Prepare as for cucumber twists.

Carrot Curls

Pare carrot; cut long thin, shavings with vegetable parer; roll up, fasten with toothpicks; chill in ice water. Drain; remove toothpicks.

Freezing Sandwiches

1. Spread a thin layer of butter or margarine on both slices of bread, being careful to cover from crust to crust. DO NOT USE mayonnaise, salad dressing or jelly as a spread, they will make the sandwiches soggy.

2. Moisten filling with as little mayonnaise as possible — cheddar, cream cheese, sliced and ground meat, canned tuna, salmon, cooked egg yolks, peanut butter are suitable fillings.

3. Do not use salad greens, green pepper or carrots as they lose their crispness when frozen.

4. Wrap each sandwich individually in freezer paper, foil, saran wrap or plastic material designed for freezing.

5. Frozen sandwiches will thaw in three hours.

Fillings That Freeze

Cooked egg yolk; cooked or canned turkey, chicken or fish; cooked or canned meats. Sandwich binders which freeze well are fruit juices such as lemon, orange or pineapple; applesauce; dairy sour cream. Hard cooked egg white will toughen when frozen; raw vegetables lose their crispness; mayonnaise or salad dressing will soak the bread.

SANDWICHES FOR ALL OCCASIONS

Monte Cristo au Gratin Sandwich

6 slices bread, lightly buttered on one side of each slice
9 slices turkey or ham or a combination of both
1 large tomato, cut into 6 slices
salt and pepper to taste
3 tbsp. chopped green onions
3 eggs, slightly beaten

3 tbsp. water
2 tbsp. salad oil (or as needed)
1 1/2 cups shredded Swiss cheese
1/2 cup milk
1/2 cup mayonnaise
1/8 tsp. garlic salt
1/8 tsp. dry mustard
1/8 tsp. nutmeg

Prepare bread slices. Place 3 slices of turkey or ham or combination of both on 3 slices buttered bread. Top each sandwich with 2 slices of tomato. Season with salt and pepper to taste. Sprinkle 1 tbsp. chopped green onions over each. Place remaining 3 slices bread on sandwich, buttered side down. Beat eggs with water. Dip sandwiches in egg mixture (skewer with toothpicks for handling ease if desired). Fry both sides in oil until golden. Place in baking dish. Mix remaining ingredients in saucepan. Heat, stirring constantly, until mixture thickens and cheese melts. Pour over sandwiches and broil 3 to 5 minutes, 6 inches from heat until bubbly. *Makes 3 hearty sandwiches.* A delicious way to use up leftover turkey or ham.

Bread Spreads

Try making up one of these hefty sandwich fillings. Great for variety in the lunch box or midnight snacks.

Cheese-Pimiento-Olive Filling

2 cups coarsely shredded sharp cheddar cheese
1/2 cup mayonnaise
1 tbsp. minced onion

1 tsp. Worcestershire sauce
3 tbsp. chopped pimiento
1/2 cup chopped black olives

Allow shredded cheese to stand at room temperature 20 minutes; add mayonnaise and beat until smooth. Add onion, Worcestershire sauce, pimiento and olives. Mix well. Store, covered, in refrigerator. Yields approximately 2 cups and will keep 2 weeks.

Spicy Corned Beef Filling

1 tin (12 oz.) corned beef
1/4 cup sweet-pickle relish
3/4 cup chopped celery
1 tbsp. chopped parsley

1 tsp. onion powder
1/8 tsp. garlic salt
pepper to taste
1/3 cup mayonnaise

In medium bowl, break up corned beef with a fork. Add remaining ingredients and mix well. Store, covered, in refrigerator. Yields approximately 2 1/2 cups and will keep 1 week.

Savoury Ham Filling

1 tin (7 1/2 oz.) tomato sauce
1 tin (2 1/4 oz.) devilled ham
1 package (8 oz.) cream cheese

1/4 cup finely chopped celery
1 tbsp. chopped parsley
1/4 cup chopped pimiento stuffed olives
pepper to taste

In bowl, mix all ingredients well. Store, covered, in refrigerator. Yields approximately 2 cups and will keep 5 to 6 days.

Frosted Sandwich Loaf

With sharp knife, trim all crusts from unsliced day-old sandwich loaf. Cut 4 lengthwise slices and butter each. Spread first slice with filling; top with second slice buttered side down. Spread filling over bread; top with third bread slice, buttered side down. Repeat, placing fourth slice, buttered side down. Do not press layers together too firmly, as filling may ooze. When all slices are together gently arrange loaf with hands to ensure all sides are even. Wrap loaf tightly with aluminium foil and chill 1 hour. A few suggestions for fillings are: egg salad; chicken salad; ham salad; sharp cheddar cheese spread and tomato slices; tuna salad; crab or shrimp moistened with mayonnaise; liverwurst mixed with dried thyme, snipped chives and mayonnaise; pimiento cheese mixed with chopped ripe olives; and cream cheese mixed with pineapple. To make the Cream Cheese Frosting for the sandwich loaf beat 3 to 4 (4 oz.) packages softened cream cheese with rotary or electric beaters until light and fluffy. To obtain desired spreading consistency a little mayonnaise or cream may be added to cream cheese. Frost top and sides of sandwich loaf.

Refrigerate until serving time. Garnish with any of the following: radish slices, radish roses, onion rings, snipped parsley, sliced olives, pimiento strips, sliced or fanned gherkins, chopped chives, watercress, lemon twists, egg slices or nuts. When serving your Frosted Sandwich Loaf it is best to slice loaf with a very sharp knife. It should be served on individual plates and eaten with a fork.

Salmon Salad Sandwich Filling

1 tin (15 1/2 oz.)
  OR 2 tins (7 3/4 oz.) salmon, drained and flaked
2 tsp. lemon juice
1/2 cup mayonnaise
1 tsp. prepared mustard

1/4 tsp. dill weed
1/8 tsp. nutmeg
1/2 cup finely chopped celery
2 hard cooked eggs peeled and chopped
freshly ground black pepper

In medium bowl, combine all ingredients and blend well. Cover. Chill thoroughly.

Yields 2 1/2 cups - enough filling for 10 to 12 sandwiches.

Cream Cheese Varieties - divide 1 package (8 oz.) cream cheese into thirds. To 1/3 add 3 or 4 small gherkins, finely chopped. To second third, add 2 ripe olives, chopped and 1 tbsp. chopped pimiento. To remaining 1/3 cream cheese, add 2 tbsp. grated carrot and 1 tbsp. chopped walnuts.

Devilled Ham Spread - mash 1 tin (2 1/4 oz.) devilled ham; add 2 tsp. mayonnaise and a dash of dry mustard. If desired add 1 tsp. chopped parsley and combine well.

Try also your favourite recipe for egg salad, salmon salad, tuna salad or chicken salad filling. Give them added variety and crunchiness with the addition of celery, green pepper, green onion or chopped nuts.

Crispy Onion-Egg Bunwich

4 split hamburger buns, sandwich spread, 1 (4 oz.) can French Fried onions, 4 hard-cooked eggs, shelled and sliced lengthwise, 6 stuffed green olives, sliced.

Spread buns with sandwich spread. Place onions onto bottom halves, then arrange egg slices, flower fashion, over onions; top with olive slices; cover with top halves of buns. Makes 4 bunwiches.

Mini Subs

Split French Bread Minis in half lengthwise, but don't cut quite through. (To make room for plenty of filling, scoop out some of the centers.) Spread with mustard, garlic butter, and/or mayonnaise with curry powder. (Or sprinkle bread with clear French or Italian dressing and dash with oregano, basil, or other herb.) On bottom halves, place a layer of lettuce; then a choice of boiled ham, bologna, corned beef, pickled tongue, tuna, herring, chicken — or all.

Add slices of Canadian and Swiss cheese, onion rings, green and ripe olive slices, sweet pickles (or whatever you prefer). Place another layer of lettuce. Secure sandwiches with cocktail or tooth picks. Each loaf makes 1 sandwich.

Zippy Sardine Sandwiches

8 slices white bread, tartar sauce, 1 medium size cucumber, scored and sliced thin, 2 (4 oz. each) cans tiny sardines in oil, drained, 1/4 cup dairy sour cream, 2 tbsp. catsup.

Spread bread with tartar sauce. On 4 slices arrange a layer of cucumbers, double layer of sardines and another layer of cucumbers. Blend together sour cream and catsup. Spread a generous tablespoonful over filling for each sandwich. Cover with remaining bread slices. Makes 4 sandwiches.

Roly Poly Sandwiches

8 slices white bread, 1 cup sandwich spread, 1 (8 oz.) pkg. sliced process Canadian cheese, lettuce, 3 medium size tomatoes, sliced thin, 1 (4 oz.) pkg. sliced chicken white meat, 1 (14 oz.) jar sliced sweet pickles, drained, 1 (5 oz.) pkg. sliced bacon, 1 (4 oz.) pkg. sliced tongue, cauliflowerets, green pepper squares, small tomatoes.

Spread bread with sandwich spread. Arrange a layer of each of the following on 4 slices: cheese, lettuce, tomato slices, chicken, pickles, bacon, cheese, tongue, lettuce. Top with remaining bread. Cut sandwich in half. Makes 4 sandwiches. As an additional treat, thread 2 cauliflowerets, 2 green pepper squares and a small tomato onto each of 4 skewers. Wrap separately from sandwich and tuck into lunch bag or box.

Swiss-Wiches

8 slices bread; 1½ cups diced cooked chicken; 1/3 cup mayonnaise; 1/4 cup diced celery; 1/4 cup diced process Swiss cheese; 1 (12 oz.) can asparagus spears, drained; 1/2 cup butter or margarine; 1 (2½ oz.) pkg. seasoned coating mix for chicken (Shake 'n' Bake).

Blend together chicken, mayonnaise, celery and cheese. Spread filling on 4 slices bread. Arrange asparagus spears, drained, on top of filling. Top with 4 more slices bread.

Melt butter on griddle or in skillet; use to brush on outside of sandwich. Coat sandwiches with coating mix. Brown sandwiches on both sides in remaining butter. *Makes 4 sandwiches.*

Chicken Dinner Sandwiches

1 pound chicken breasts, boiling, salted water, 4 slices bacon, 2 English muffins, split, toasted and buttered, 1 medium onion, cut into 4 thin slices, 1 large tomato, cut into 4 thick slices, 1/2 cup shredded cheddar cheese.

Simmer chicken in small amount of salted water until meat is no longer pink throughout; about 15 minutes - discard skin and bones and slice meat. Meanwhile cut bacon slices in half crosswise and partially fry bacon to remove most of the fat; bacon should still be limp. Set aside. Distribute the chicken evenly over the 4 toasted muffin halves; top each with 1 onion slice and 1 tomato slice. Distribute cheese evenly over each and top each with 2 pieces of bacon. Broil about 4 inches from heat until cheese is bubbly and bacon is crisp - about 3 to 5 minutes. *Makes 2 servings of 2 open sandwiches each for dinner or 4 savories. This recipe can easily be doubled.*

Serve with a fresh raw vegetable salad tray such as carrot and celery sticks, red or green pepper strips, and condiments such as pickles and olives.

Grilled Crab Sandwiches

1 tin (6-1/2 or 7-1/2 oz.) crabmeat well drained and flaked
1 tsp. lemon juice
1/2 cup shredded sharp process cheese
1/4 cup chopped celery
2 tbsp. drained sweet-pickle relish
2 tbsp. chopped green onions

1 hard cooked egg, chopped
3 tbsp. salad dressing or mayonnaise (approximately - to gain desired consistency)
1/2 tsp. prepared horseradish
10 slices bread, each buttered generously on one side
5 tomato slices
salt and pepper

In bowl, sprinkle crabmeat with lemon juice. Add cheese, celery, relish, green onions and egg. Add mayonnaise and horseradish. Stir to combine well. Spread mixture on unbuttered sides of 5 slices of bread. Top with tomato slices; season to taste with salt and pepper. Top with bread slice, buttered side up. Grill in griddle, sandwich grill or in skillet until sandwiches are golden brown and filling is piping hot. To serve, cut sandwiches in half

Fancy Sandwiches

To keep party sandwiches fresh and moist until serving time, arrange them in shallow pan lined with damp paper towelling; then cover with a clean towel or plastic wrap and refrigerate.

Shrimp Filling

Use 1 small can shrimp; save several whole shrimps for garnish; drain and mash the remainder, adding a dash of lemon juice, salt, pepper and mayonnaise to moisten.

Corned Beef on Pumpernickel

1 (16 oz.) carton coleslaw, 2 tsp. caraway seeds, 1 (12 oz.) can corned beef, chilled, 2 small tomatoes, 12 slices light pumpernickel, 6 tbsp. butter or margarine.

Drain coleslaw well; then blend with caraway seeds in a small bowl. Cut corned beef into 12 slices. Cut each tomato into 6 thin slices. Spread pumpernickel with butter or margarine.

On each of 6 slices, arrange a layer of corned beef, tomato slices and coleslaw, in equal portions; top with remaining bread. Cut each sandwich diagonally in half. Makes 6 sandwiches.

Turkey Dagwood Sandwiches

8 slices rye bread softened butter	1 avocado, peeled, pitted; cut into 8 rings or wedges
1 cup shredded lettuce	1/4 cup sour cream
4 large slices cooked turkey [more slices if pieces are small] salt and pepper [to taste]	1/3 cup crumbled blue cheese
	1 large tomato, cut in 8 wedges
12 slices crisp-cooked drained bacon	2 hard-cooked eggs, quartered finely chopped green onion [garnish]
1/4 cup mayonnaise	

Cut four slices of bread in half. For each sandwich, arrange on plate, one whole slice bread with 1/2 slice on either side. Lightly spread softened butter over bread. Cover bread with shredded lettuce; top with turkey slice (or slices). Season to taste with salt and pepper. Top each with three slices bacon and two avocado rings or wedges. In bowl combine mayonnaise, sour cream and blue cheese. Drizzle mixture over prepared sandwiches. Top each with two tomato wedges and two hard-cooked egg quarters. Garnish with finely chopped green onions. Serve with fork and knife. Makes 4 hearty open-faced sandwiches.

Checkerboards

Use 4 bread slices of 2 contrasting colours (light and dark) for each stack. Alternating colour of bread slices, fill and press gently but firmly together. With sharp knife, using sawing motion, cut crusts from bread. Wrap and refrigerate until filling is firm. Slice stacks into thirds; spread slices with filling and put stack back together, reversing centre slice so contrasting colour breads alternate in checkerboard fashion. Press together; wrap and refrigerate. To serve cut each stack into slices about 1/2-inch thick.

Pinwheels

Cut off all crusts except bottom from unsliced loaf white bread, with a long sharp knife. Turn loaf on its side; cut lengthwise into slices about 1/2-inch thick (retaining bottom crust makes cutting easier). To keep slices of bread from cracking as they are rolled, flatten first with a rolling pin. Work with only a few slices at a time to keep them from drying out. Spread bread edges with filling. Across one narrow end, place 2 or 3 stuffed olives, or 1 slivered dill pickle or 2 small gherkins or 2 Vienna sausages, if desired. Starting at that end, roll bread tightly but carefully in jelly-roll fashion. Wrap rolls separately and refrigerate. To serve, cut rolls into 1/2-inch thick slices. If desired, broil slices to serve hot.

Ribbon Sandwiches

Use 5 bread slices for each stack; fill with variety of any easily spread filling and press gently but firmly together. Dark and light slices of bread can be alternated but they must be the same size. With sharp knife, using sawing motion, cut crusts from bread. Wrap and refrigerate until filling is firm. To serve, cut each stack into slices about 1/2-inch thick, then cut each slice into thirds, halves or 2 or 3 triangles.

Ham-Celery Triangles

2 cups finely diced cooked ham, ½ cup finely diced celery, 1 tsp. grated onion, 1/3 cup mayonnaise or salad dressing, 1 tsp. prepared mustard, 12 thin slices white bread, buttered.

Mix together ham, celery, onion, mayonnaise or salad dressing, mustard. Spread bread with mixture to make 6 sandwiches. Cut each sandwich diagonally into quarters. Makes 6 sandwiches.

Notes

Woodward's Delivery Wagon
1913 Style ★★★★★★★★★★★★★★